THE
SOCIAL
IMPERATIVE

by
Gregory Baum

PAULIST PRESS
New York/Ramsey/Toronto

ACKNOWLEDGEMENTS

"The Christian Left at Detroit," "Theology After Auschwitz," "Political Theology in Canada," "The French Bishops and Euro-Communism," and "Multiculturalism and Ethnicity" all originally appeared in *The Ecumenist* and are reprinted with permission.

"The Impact of Sociology on Catholic Theology" originally appeared in *Catholic Theological Society of America: Proceedings* 30 (1975) 1-29 and is reprinted with permission.

"Spirituality and Society" originally appeared in *Religious Education* 73 (1978) 266-283 and is reprinted with permission.

"Science and Commitment: Historical Truth According to Ernst Troeltsch" originally appeared in *Philosophy of the Social Sciences* 1 (1971) 259-277 and is reprinted with permission.

"Religion and Socialism" originally appeared in *Catholic Dimension* (1979) and is reprinted with permission.

Two articles were given originally as public lectures: "Nationalism and Social Justice" at McGill University, Montreal, May 1977, and "Sociology as Critical Humanism" at King's College, London, Ontario, November 1976.

BT
738
.B322

Library of Congress
Catalog Card Number: 78-70824

ISBN: 0-8091-2187-5

Published by Paulist Press
Editorial Office: 1865 Broadway, New York, N.Y. 10023
Business Office: 545 Island Road, Ramsey, N.J. 07446

Printed and bound in the
United States of America

Contents

Preface

Christians have gone crazy, I have been told many times, to think that God's will shall be done on earth. It is this strong conviction against all cultural pessimism that has produced, over the last decade or so, a growing emphasis on social justice and a shift to the political left in the official teachings of the Catholic Church and the World Council of Churches. The expanding gulf between the industrialized world and the underdeveloped nations has introduced a new seriousness among all thinking people concerned with justice. Many Christian theologians have come to regard it as their primary task to clarify the social imperative implicit in the Gospel of Jesus Christ. They call this "political theology," and their starting point is the same crazy idea that God's will shall be done on earth as it is in heaven. The clarification of the social meaning of the Gospel has made them into critics of the present world order and proponents of an alternative society based on sharing and cooperation. Church groups have become involved in new types of social action. When, some years ago, I wrote reports on theological conferences dealing with political theology and published them in *The Ecumenist,* requests continued to come in—so many, in fact, that Paulist Press decided to make these reports the core of a book, a collection of articles, written by me on political theology and the impact of sociology on Christian thinking.

Since Catholic social teaching has moved through what Robert McAfee Brown has recently described as "the Catholic journey" from Leo XIII's repudiation of socialism to Paul VI's acknowledgement of socialism as a Christian option, I was tempted to call this collection "The Socialist Imperative," but since North Americans tend to think of socialism in monolithic terms, such a title might have been confusing. It is this monolithic think-

1

ing about socialism that Paul VI sought to overcome in his 1971 letter, *Octogesima adveniens,* where he distinguished between various forms of socialism, some of which are in keeping and others at odds with Christian social principles.

One of the central concepts in political theology is "social sin," a term used in the Church's official teaching for the first time in the 1971 synod of bishops. In order to spell out the social meaning of the Gospel, Christians must analyze the structures of evil operative in their society. Here the turn to sociology is inevitable. Since this field of study has become my special interest, I am often asked to give lectures on the contribution that sociology must make to the theological task of understanding God's will for the world. Included in this collection are several essays, written for different audiences, some popular, others more learned, which apply sociology to theological reflection, while keeping intact the integrity of each discipline.

My thanks go to Paulist Press which has been the generous supporter of *The Ecumenist* for sixteen years and which has always encouraged my research and writing by putting into print the results of my studies. Father Kevin Lynch has been a very good friend.

The Christian Left at Detroit, 1975

A week-long conference, "Theology in the Americas: 1975," was held in Detroit in August 1975. It brought together Christians from South and North America to study theology by taking as their starting point their respective historical experiences. The first idea of the conference, entertained by the Chilean priest Sergio Torres and a group of friends, was to invite the well-known Latin American representatives of liberation theology and bring them into conversation with theologians of the U.S.A. Such a dialogue, Torres hoped, would prompt U.S. theologians to rethink their relationship to the dominant culture of their country and engage in critical reflection on the American experience from the viewpoint of the poor. The conference was to be prepared by study groups all over the country, who would discuss what this new approach to theology meant to them. As soon as this process was set up and the various study groups reacted to the suggestions sent by the organizers, the nature and purposes of the intended conference began to change. The planning and holding of the conference, I should add, remained a process open to feedback and modification.

The first critical remark made by the study groups was that there was no single American experience. A theological reflection on American history cannot be complete unless one invited Christian speakers for the black community, for Mexican Americans, for Puerto Ricans, for Asian Americans. And since the experiences of men and women have been so different, Christian women should be invited to reflect on their struggle for emancipation in Church and society. The second critical recommendation made to the organizers was that a conference of this kind should not simply be a gathering of scholars. Intellectuals, by their specialized knowledge and, possibly, a certain professional deformation, easily create an elitist climate in which less educated people are condemned to silence. At the conference Christian activists should be invited to

3

speak for their struggling communities. The conference should give voice to the voiceless people. Moreover, should not members of the workers' movement be invited?

Following these suggestions, the nature of the Detroit conference significantly changed. The Latin American theologians were there in good number; the U.S. experience was represented by white academics and social organizers willing to engage in theological reflection, by black Christians and their theologians, and by other Christian representatives of marginalized peoples and groups in the U.S.A. The conference became a more complex undertaking and its purpose was no longer clearly defined. It brought together people and groups that had never talked to one another before. It intended to focus on various forms of oppression—economic, racial, sexual—which are usually considered separately, but which are interrelated in ways that remain largely hidden. The change in the purpose of the conference accounts for the extraordinary richness of the experience, but as we shall see it also produced some of the difficulties that were to emerge.

Since I regard the conference as an important theological event and since it challenged ordinary academic theology in significant ways, I wish here to describe and analyze the Detroit meeting. This is not an easy undertaking. The papers that were sent to the study groups prior to the conference were simply drafts. For this reason, I shall not quote from them. Secondly, the speakers at the conference often spoke as representatives of a community—we shall analyze what this means further on—and hence mentioning their names may not do justice to them nor to the concern they represented. Since the conference was prepared by, and tried to deal with, a wealth of material, a single article must of necessity be a selection. Finally, this account reflects my own interpretation of the conference.

The Common Faith

Since the participants belonged to different groups struggling for freedom in their particular historical situations, and since it was not easy to perceive how these various movements were historically interrelated, it was too soon for the participants to speak of mutual solidarity. In a summary report made at the end of the conference, it clearly said: "At the present time our solidarity is tenuous. It is preferable to suffer for some time with our present consciousness of the difference which we have just begun to explore and not try to contrive solidarity." At the same time, a common faith did pervade the entire conference and created the taken-for-granted atmosphere of all the discussions. What was this faith? Since it provided the accepted starting point, no one paid much attention to it. Still, I wish to analyze this common faith as the theological dimension underlying the entire conference.

The participants shared a common unwillingness or even inability to accept the world as it is because they believe that it was meant to be different. They believed, moreover, that this world could be changed. This faith was present with such a density that one could touch it with the hands. It was a faith one could breathe. This common faith is of course a form of traditional Christian faith. According to Christian teaching, the world is indeed under the judgment of God; it is sinful yet meant to be different. Despite its sinfulness it is still divinely destined to salvation, and because of God's redemptive work in Jesus Christ, Christians hold that fulfillment of the divine promises is becoming a reality, however provisionally, in human history. I call this "the common faith" not only because it was the shared conviction of the participants at the conference (a few exceptions I shall mention further on), but also because it combines in an important way doctrinal trends taken from the Catholic and Protestant traditions.

The biblical faith understood in the Catholic tradition has always included the conviction that the grace of God *truly transforms* human life. God's redemption brings creation marred by sin to the fulfillment of its own inclination. In traditional Scholastic language, "grace perfects nature." Against the Reformers' emphasis on the abiding sinfulness of life, the Council of Trent insisted that the sanctification produced by divine grace was an actual transformation of the human being. In the Catholic tradition, God has always been understood as a divine mystery, operative from within people's lives as the source from which they reach out for truth and justice. The metaphysical system of the Scholastics provided a framework in which the divine causality in human life (as *causa prima*) enabled people to become the causes of their own historical destiny (a *causae secundae*). Admittedly, the weight of this theological tradition in the Middle Ages and in modern times was applied to the transformation of *personal* life. It is applied by contemporary Christians also to that of the *social* reality constituted by persons and their interrelationships.

The Protestant traditon has some difficulties here. Can human life be significantly changed? This is a great problem for Lutherans, and it is not always clear whether sanctification as understood in the Calvinist tradition implies a constitutive transformation of human life. These difficulties have to do, I think, with a peculiarly Protestant view of divine transcendence. (We shall return to this topic later.) Yet the common faith I have described embodies a critical dimension characteristic of the Protestant tradition. Protestants have always been greatly impressed by the sinfulness of the world. Protestants were more ready than Catholics in the sixteenth century to submit intellectual systems, ecclesiastical institutions, and all cultural expresstions to an evangelical critique. They were unwilling to make positive affirmations in regard to human life unless they first measured it by the Gospel norm. The radical inability to accept the world as it is because it is meant to be different and the trust that it can be changed—"the common faith" in our terminology—combine Catholic and Protestant trends in a perception of the Gospel. I have called this the common faith, moreover, because it is sometimes shared with people who do not call themselves Christians.

This common faith deserves further attention. It made the Detroit conference a theological conference even when traditional theological subjects were not at the center of people's attention. It is interesting to contrast this common faith with the shared convictions present at other kinds of meetings. What is the common spirit, for instance, at ordinary, academically-oriented theological conferences? At such meetings there is the personal faith of the theologians; each theologian in his or her own way lives and explores his or her understanding of the Gospel. But there is usually no shared explicitation of what this faith implies in regard to society, its sinfulness, and its future. I suppose that the sociohistorical dimension of divine revelation only emerges in people's consciousness when they are profoundly disturbed by the injustices in the world, when they find themselves struggling against the destructive trends in their society, and when out of this socio-political engagement they begin to perceive the message and the promise of Jesus in a new way.

At the Detroit conference this common faith was also shared by sociologists and economists. They, too, read and analyzed the society to which they belonged out of the convictions that it was unacceptable, that it was meant to be different, and that it could be changed. This differs strikingly from the presuppositions that dominate at professional meetings of social scientists and most university departments of sociology and economics. The majority of social scientists still defend the value-free nature of their research and their scientific conclusions. But is not the perception of reality in some way linked to our place in history? Should not scientists clarify for themselves the values and images out of which they perceive society? At Detroit, at least, they shared a common conviction.

The common faith was shared by some people at the conference who did not think of themselves as believers. But since they were involved in struggling against the oppression inflicted on their historical communities, they not only refused to accept the world as it is but also hoped that it could be significantly changed, even if they felt no need to ask questions about the hope that was within them.

The Latin American Theologians

The first group to address the conference was composed of the Latin American theologians who had been invited. Many of them were known to the participants through the English translations of their books and articles. Present among them were Juan Segundo, Hugo Assmann, Beatriz Couch, Enrique Dussel, José Miranda, and José Míguez Bonino. (Gustavo Gutiérrez arrived later during the conference.) The group decided to speak as a community on the subject of liberation theology. They wanted to present the analysis of their historical situation and their theological reflections as the product of a common struggle and a shared intellectual process. Instead of arguing out the differences between them, they wanted to give witness to theology as a collective enterprise. What emerged very clearly was how their approach differed from customary academic theology. Theology, understood in terms of personal scholarship and achievement, tends to become the possession of the individual thinker. At universities and divinity schools theologians argue out the right and wrong of their positions. Academic theology usually presents itself as individualistic and competitive. The Latin American thinkers, as well as the other Christian groups who addressed the conference on subsequent days, sought a different approach to theology. While the Latin Americans differed among themselves, especially when it came to deciding with what struggling political group in their countries the Christian communities should ally themselves, they still regarded themselves as a community of thinkers reaching out for the truth in solidarity.

The Latin American theologians acknowledge their total inability to accept the world as it is because they believe that it is destined to be different. Because of this, their epistemology differs from that of traditional philosophy and theology. They refuse to regard truth as the conformity of the mind to a given object. Such a concept of truth only confirms and legitimates the world as it now exists. The world, for these theologians, is not a static object which the human mind confronts and attempts to understand; the world is, rather, an unfinished project which is being built by the people who make it up, and its reality tomorrow and in the future depends in part on what these people think and do. Knowledge is not the conformity of the mind to the given, but a dimension of this world-building process. Our perception of society affects our action and hence inevitably enters into the making of the future. Truth then cannot be measured by conformity to the given. The norm of truth must be taken from the kind of world that knowledge helps to create. If concepts legitimate an evil world and help it to endure, they cannot be called true even if they could be verified by the application of scientific method. But if concepts enable people to perceive the oppressive structures in the present and discover the trends in history that seek to transform and overcome these structures—this, too, is a scientific task—then they contribute to the process by which the world becomes more truly human. The true and the good are inseparable.

The Latin American theologians applied this epistemology to the revealed truth of Christianity. What is revealed to us is God's judgment on an evil world and God's gracious presence to the world as source of transformation and new life. This revelation took place at particular moments in time, in particular historical situations; it dealt with the concrete circumstances of an historical people. To understand what this revelation means today—and this is the task of theology—Christians must listen to God's word addressing them from within their concrete historical situation, with ears shaped by their own collective struggle. Truth, divine truth, then is not the conformity of the mind to a divine message uttered ages ago, but the discernment of present evil judged by this message and the discovery of the redemptive movement in history promised by this message. The norm of theological truth, then, is not drawn from an analogy with classical philosophy; it is drawn rather from its role in the on-going process of world-building. Divine truth is redemptive. The norm of theology is taken from its weight and power in history. God's truth, mediated through Christian faith, enters into the transformation of the sinful world in accordance with the divine promises. In the vocabulary of the Latin American theologians, the norm of truth in theology is "liberating praxis." Christian truth is the perception of the world mediated by Jesus Christ that leads to the divinely promised transformation.

The Latin American theologians explained this viewpoint as if it were foreign to the North American intellectual tradition. But since American pragmatism is a left-wing Hegelianism of sorts, since contemporary process thought regards knowledge as part of the process of world-building ,and since the critical sociology of our day evaluates the perception of society in terms of its legitimating or transforming effects, the Latin American epistemology was not strange to North American ears. Catholic theology, it is true, has been in contact with left-wing Hegelian thought only in recent years through its dialogue with Marxism and post-Marxist criticism.

To understand the meaning of the Christian faith, the Christian community must come to a correct understanding of its concrete historical situtation. Conversion to God implies self-knowlecge. This principle also applies to communities. They too must come to a correct collective self-understanding. The assessment of evil powers which oppress people in their concrete situtations is, therefore, an essential part of theology, for without it the meaning of divine revelation cannot be grasped. The Latin American theologians called this part of theology "social analysis." What they meant by this was mainly an economic analysis of their people's oppression.

In presenting this analysis to the conference Latin American theologians and social scientists worked together. They explained in some detail how the economic dependence of the Latin American countries on the system of corporate capitalism, with its center in the North Atlantic community and more especially in the U.S.A., has not only led to the impoverishment of the mass of the population in city and country but also affected the cultural and educational institutions and through them the consciousness of the people in general. With the help of their national bourgeoisies, the Latin American countries supply raw material and cheap labor to the international economic system. Yet the major part of the profit goes to the owning classes in the developed countries. The economic system, in search of cheaper production costs and wider markets, has generated a new imperialism, the heir of the old political colonialism. According to this analysis, the further industrial development in Latin America, based on capital controlled from the North and following the "Western model" of production for profit, contributes some wealth to the national bourgeoisies and vastly enriches the economic life of the northern countries. The center of the system inevitably enriches itself at the expense of the periphery. The Latin American thinkers insisted that the success and prosperity of the Northern democracies were dependent on the on-going exploitation of third world countries.

Yet the exploitative dynamics between center and periphery

operates even within the developed countries. The industrialized areas enrich themselves at the expense of the outlying regions. Even in these countries, the exploited classes afflicted with poverty and insecurity will grow while the class of those who derive enormous benefits from the economic system will shrink in size. A point in history has been reached, according to this social analysis, when South America and North America have become a single interconnected economic unit. The multinational corporation transcend national boundaries, they make decisions without loyalty to any national community, and they acquire power that exceeds that of many national governments. The fate of all countries has been conjoined. Who protects this corporate capitalism? Since the owning classes in the northern nations, especially in the U.S.A., derive most of the benefits from the present system, their governments are willing to protect and use various forms of power in the world, especially in Latin America, to crush the movements of people who seek to sever their destiny from capitalist economy. The speakers stressed as a point of important theological significance that the Latin American peoples cannot escape their oppression and have access to food and the necessities of life unless the whole world is changed. Change at the periphery today demands the dismantling of the center. What follows from this is that when North American thinkers analyze the ills and injustices in their own countries, they should not confine their view to the conditions at home but take into consideration the total picture, the economically interconnected world. Any analysis of the oppressive trends in society must be "holistic."

To make this point before a North American theological audience was, in a sense, the main reason why the Detroit conference had originally been planned. I already mentioned that this original intention had been significantly modified by subsequent developments. But even when the perspective shifted from economic to other forms of oppression and it seemed almost impossible to arrive at a holistic approach, the struggling groups agreed that the meaning of Christian faith and theology emerges in a community only as a reflection on their struggle and only through a clear analysis of the structure of their oppression. Engagement precedes reflection. In the words of Gustavo Gutiérrez, theology is never *actus primus*; it is always *actus secundus*. It is the reflection on the struggle for emancipation. Theology cannot be produced from any historical position whatever. It can be done only by Christians identified with a movement dedicated to the emancipation of oppressed people. This viewpoint distinguishes liberation theology from customary academic theology.

The key word in this connection is "praxis." What does this strange word mean anyway? The English word "practice" refers to any action that applies a particular theory. Praxis, on the other hand, is practice associated with a total dynamics of historical vision and social transformation. Through praxis, people enter their historical destiny. Since praxis changes the world as well as the actors, it becomes the starting point for a clearer vision and a more correct understanding of history. Praxis is the pre-condition of knowledge, even though in turn this knowledge issues forth into a new praxis. The dialectics of truth begins with praxis. The Latin American theologians explained that for the Christian communities involved in a common struggle the dialectics of praxis and truth is guided by the vision of God's promised reign and the forward movement of history guaranteed by God's revelation in the passover of Israel and the resurrection of the marginalized and crucified Jesus. Even the Latin American theologians who regarded themselves as Marxists understood the logic that moves human history through the class struggle to universal emancipation as guided and assured by the redemptive presence of God to the world.

Let me say a word about what the Latin American thinkers called "social analysis." Why did they use this word in the singular? When we turn to the social sciences, we actually find many different analyses of society and its ills. The Latin Americans used the word in the singular because they define their approach in opposition to the dominant social science (functionalist or positivistic) which presents itself as value-neutral but which, in their eyes, legitimates the existing order and contributes to its stability. The Latin American theologians have opted for a conflictual sociological model, making use of a Marxist-style class analysis, which brings to light not the stability but the contradictions present in the social order and orients the imagination toward the transformation of the present system. In this perspective, social science and emancipatory commitment cannot be separated. There are obviously different ways of making a class analysis, just as there are diverse schools of Marxist and post-Marxist social thought, and in fact when the Latin American theologians decide on the practical course of action to be adopted in their countries, they differ considerably in their analysis of the situation. But in the face of the dominant social science approach, they feel united in the use of a critical method and the emancipatory commitment and hence use the word "social analysis" in the singular. The differences between them do not shatter their solidarity. Since the left under political pressure tends to splinter into small, competing, and often sectarian groups and thus weaken its impact on society, the Christian left in Latin America wants to avoid this splintering. They believe that the Christian symbols out of which they define their identity contain resources that enable them to wrestle against the divisive tendency.

The Black Theologians

The struggle of the black community in the U.S.A. was represented by a group of speakers including well-known theologians such as James Cone, Herbert Edwards, Major Jones, Deotis Roberts, and Preston Williams. Their ideas were familiar to many participants from their publications. The typical U.S. American liberation theology is black theology. Black theological thinkers, participating in and reflecting on their people's struggle for freedom, have developed (without the epistemological preoccupation of the Latins) a critical analysis of the oppression in which they live in the U.S.A. and of the legitimation of this oppression mediated by the culture and religion of the nation. They have repudiated traditional theology as white theology, that is to say, as being vitiated by a largely unconscious ideology which makes the black people invisible, which marginalizes their problems, which sacralizes the white man's history in America, and which serves as a defense of white racial supremacy. The god of white

America is not the true God, nor is the lord of the white churches the Jesus in whose name alone there is salvation. Black theology affirms God's victory in the exodus from slavery and God's ultimate triumph in Jesus as the repudiation of the gods of the dominant cultures, whatever their theological names may be. Black theology has developed its own original language of negation, not derived from Hegel and Marx but from the Scriptures themselves. We must negate the world before we can find the true God. The model for the inversion of history is not class conflict but the divine promises that the first shall be last and the last shall be first.

The black theologians were confident that their religious tradition provided power and vision for their people's struggle for freedom. In this regard their experience differed considerably from that of other Christian groups struggling for emancipation. Most of these saw the oppressive trends right in their own religious traditions and therefore had to subject them to a radical critique. This was certainly true for the Latin Americans. Since the Catholic Church had been largely identified with the seigneurial system, and finally with the national bourgeoisies, Catholics had to submit their religion to an ideological critique before they found access to its liberating core. The blacks insisted that theirs was a different experience. Their faith had always been in the God of the black, in the true Lord over the white masters who subjugated them, who promised them freedom and empowered them to persevere in the struggle. While there were traces in black preaching that promised the people "pie in the sky," pacified their angers, and fostered their passivity, these did not constitute the dominant trend. The lived religion and its most authentic expression in the spirituals expressed the soul of the black movement for freedom in America. The black theologians were therefore content with the traditional evangelical images of divine transcendence.

On this issue an important controversy broke out later at the conference. The Latin American theologians in particular preferred to think of God as transcendent mystery *present in history* as ground and dynamics of the forward movement toward the promised liberation. For the blacks, the divine Lord *over and above history* was reassuring even in the perspective of liberation. For if this Lord is higher and stronger than the pharaohs of oppression, there is hope for the people's freedom.

It is worth noting that the black theologians also presented themselves as a community. They differed in many ways among themselves, but to demonstrate their solidarity in a common struggle and to illustrate how their theological approach differed from current academic theology, they adopted a common stance. Why should they allow the highly rational conceptualization characteristic of the Western tradition to dominate their thinking? Blacks, they said, prefer to think in terms of stories and metaphors, and since the Bible itself was written in this style, they preferred to keep their theology more specifically black. The competitive model of truth, found in the Western academy, makes the effort to clarify various positions an argument between many thinkers, each wanting to be right; but if truth is uttered in metaphors and stories, it may be more helpful to adopt a cooperative model of truth which allows different perceptions to be clarified by understanding them as perspectival contributions to a collective self-understanding. A similar critique of Western intellectuality was made by the Christian women on the subsequent day.

Yet the black theologians had to formulate their disagreement with the Latin Americans who had spoken to the conference on the first day and whose critical economic analysis had dominated the subsequent discussions. The blacks felt that a class analysis is not enough. The name of the oppression under which they suffer is racism, and while racism is related to economic exploitation and class identification, it cannot be reduced to economic oppression. The blacks complained that the holistic approach recommended by the Latin Americans subordinated and underplayed the problem of racism. It was no accident that in their talks the Latin American theologians had not paid much attention to the racial inequalities in their own countries. The blacks feared, moreover, that arguments over the economic system might divide the black community and weaken them in the face of the white majority. For the blacks the primary enemy is racism, and since the Latin Americans defined as principal enemy the economic imperialism of the northern nations, especially the U.S., the blacks could not declare themselves in solidarity with them.

What emerged was a conflict of different views, grounded in different concrete historical struggles, which the conference had to confront again and again. The common faith that the world in which we live is meant to be different and destined to be changed was unable to create perfect solidarity, but it did keep the differing groups in an on-going conversation, first in public and later in small groups. Their historical struggles were different, but as Christians they were unable to let go of one another. They belonged together, even if their common faith could not at this time be translated into solidary action. In the words of a Latin theologian, the blacks suspect Latin theology of being too white, and the Latins suspect black theology of being too American. What does the black community want? Freedom and power to participate in the American empire? Or freedom and power to make the world the home for all peoples? There was no need, however, to read the statement of the black theologians as a defense of American power. What they wanted to affirm in the strongest language was simply that any separation of a class analysis from the analysis of race makes them suspicious. For if this separation takes place, then they, the blacks, shall be bypassed in terms of the more universal problem and hence remain where they have always been—at the lowest rung.

At the same time it would be unrealistic for the black community to look away from the link between racial and economic oppression and for the sake of supposed unity omit to analyze their own community in terms of class identification. Since the black community is in fact divided according to class, an unwillingness to see this would only make the community more vulnerable. It was pointed out in the discussion that black Americans successful in education, commerce, and organization are easily lured away from their communities to white institutions where they learn to identify with the interests of their colleagues of equal status and income. This institutional trend often leaves the black community without leadership. Such issues of class may prevent a black neighborhood from becoming a strong and vital community producing its own leaders.

The Voice of the Chicanos

After the presentation of black liberation theology on the third day, the important shortcoming of the conference came to the fore, a shortcoming related to the shift that had taken place in its essential purpose. As I explained at the beginning of this article, at first the conference intended to introduce a team of Latin American theologians to groups of U.S.A. theologians, and it was only after the critical recommendations of the preparatory study groups that the Christians invited to the conference became more representative. Present at Detroit were the Latin American theologians in good number; present were theologians and representatives of the black community and Christian thinkers involved in the women's movement. The blacks and the women could rely, as much as the Latin Americans, on a fully developed liberation theology. Invited to the conference were also active Chicano groups, Puerto Ricans, representatives of the native peoples, and Asian Americans. But upon arrival, these groups found that they had no opportunity to address the full assembly. This omission was due to the change in the nature of the conference, which had been inadequately assimilated by the orginizers. Since originally the accent had been on theology and since the last-mentioned groups are only beginning to reflect on the Christian meaning of their struggle and have not worked out a full-blown liberation theology, they were not assigned adequate space. The organizers saw the mistake and regretted it. Fortunately the Spanish-speaking U.S. Americans got hold of the microphones and made their presence heard, and thanks to their active participation in the full assembly and the discussion groups, they communicated their message well and made an important contribution to the conference. Even the silence of the native peoples gave eloquent witness to the ambiguity of the American enterprise.

Let me add at this point that the organizers of the conference tended to identify North America and the U.S.A. so that they forgot—Americans often do—that there was a country in the north called Canada. When Canadian Christians were invited it was too late to organize study groups in preparation and formulate a Canadian contribution to the topic. Several Canadians attended the conference as sympathetic observers. It would have been worthwhile to introduce the conference to the complexity of the Canadian historical experience, so different from the U.S. American one, and to report on the Christian reflection on the struggle for justice in Canada, especially as found in Protestant theologians of the 1930's and in Catholic thinkers of Quebec over the last fifteen years. But to have insisted on a Canadian presentation at the conference would have silenced even more the less affluent peoples. The Canadian Christians who attended the conference as sympathetic observers resolved to create a network of theologically-concerned persons to reflect on the struggles for freedom and justice in Canada, including the Quebec people, the heirs of the British tradition, the more recent immigrants, now English-speaking, from Europe, Asia and the Caribbean Islands, and of course the cruelly humiliated native peoples.

Let us return to the Chicanos. The Chicanos do not regard themselves as an ethnic minority in the U.S.A.; they think of themselves as a conquered people whose land, language, and culture came under the control of the U.S.A. in 1848 with the Treaty of Guadalupe Hidalgo and who have come to live as exiles in their own territories. They regard themselves as metizos, Spanish and Indian, and when they speak of themselves as a race, *la raza*, they refer to the synthesis of two distinct anthropological races produced by a common history. While the Chicanos have clung to their cultural heritage, their poverty kept them from developing themselves; many even lost the hope of ever rising from the lowest level. Among the small groups, guided by courageous leaders, the struggle for self-possession has always continued. Over the last decade, largely inspired by the blacks' determination to change their situation in America, Chicano activists have begun a movement to bring together the people dispersed among several states of the Union and organize them in a common cause. In this emancipatory struggle the Chicanos have discovered that their Church had largely identified itself with the dominant culture and the ideals of white Anglo-America. While they constitute a large minority in the Catholic Church, in some areas even a majority, they have practically no hierarchical representation. The Chicanos regard their Hispanic-Indian form of

Catholicism as their authentic religious heritage which they have defended against the Anglo spirit demanding efficiency and mastery even in religious matters. These men and women refuse to abandon their own form of the Catholic religion, which to outsiders often appears superstitious but to them signifies their closeness to nature—the earth and their bodies. This nature is the place where God is present to them. This closeness to nature they contrast with an Anglo-Christianity, even in its (Irish) Catholic form, that is principally concerned with the domination of nature—the earth and the body. The Chicanos feel that the ecological wisdom of ancient Indian religion survives in their Catholic faith.

The firm but gentle protest of the Chicanos brought out more than any other event the radical impossibility to generalize about movements of liberation and the theology which may accompany them. Even the black theologians found themselves accused that, by dividing the United States into two groups, the white oppressor and the black oppressed, they made invisible other oppressed groups in the country, such as the Chicanos. Could it be that out of this inadequate perception of reality the blacks were unable to find ways of cooperating with Chicanos in the parts of the country where they share a common position of oppression? But, then, should these two disadvantaged peoples argue in front of a white audience? Is not disunity among the disadvantaged, bred by the psychology of oppression, an element that strengthens the power of the oppressive system? The suggestion was made that the two peoples, the black and the brown, enter into conversation by themselves, without white listeners. It is to be hoped that such a network of conversations between black and Chicano groups will be created as a result of this conference.

The Chicanos had messages for various participating groups. They expressed their disappointment with the Catholic theological community which, instead of being a voice reminding America of the forgotten Catholic people, tends to overlook their existence altogether. Catholic theologians carry on their theological reflections as if all Catholics in the U.S.A. were identified with a specifically European tradition. Could not a greater awareness of the Chicanos on the part of theologians lead to a more pluralistic and hence more authentic vision of the Catholic Church and become a lever for wrestling for a more decentralized Church organization? At this early point of their struggle, the Chicanos are still looking for visibility in the country. The symbols and structures of their own Church tend to disguise them rather than proclaim their presence.

Of importance was also the Chicanos' reaction to the leadership offered by the Latin American theologians. These latter theologians appeared as sons of successful people, well educated and well spoken, possessing an articulate intelligence associated with university life. We are different, the Chicanos said; we are just beginning to acquire a greater number of educated leaders; we are more simple people; we are still closer to the level on which we were held by the oppressor. If we permit you to be our leaders, they said to the Latins, we shall be in the situation in which we have been for so long, unable to find our own words to express our situation and incapable of devising modes of action that correspond to our present needs and our past experience. Even the confident, holistic economic analysis proposed by the Latin Americans posed a problem for the Chicanos. The analysis may be correct in principle, the Chicanos said, but if we receive from you the key for understanding our own subjugation before we reach the maturity to argue with you from a basis of equal education and equal confidence, we will not move toward a liberated form of self-possession. Our struggle is our own. Other people can help us by being in solidarity with us, but the leadership and direction of the movement must come from ourselves, however tentative these may be at the beginning.

These conflicts were important; they were painful to the participants, but they were also deceptive. They allowed members of the conference, especially those belonging to the dominant culture, to let these disagreements relativize unduly the plight of the oppressed peoples and make one critique to take off the edge from the other. We often tend to balance contrasting positions in the creation of a single, complex picture and thus permit our mind to reconcile—and thus falsify—what remains as yet objectively unreconcilable in history.

The conference listened to other voices. What do academic

theologians know of the Puerto Ricans' struggle to find themselves as a people and of the Catholic participation in this movement? At best we think of Puerto Ricans as the underprivileged poor in New York City for whom the Church must provide pastoral care. But of centers where Catholic activists carry on theological reflection we know very little. And what do we know of the Christians among the native peoples who participate in their emancipatory struggle and who discover the complicity of the Christian churches in the subjugation of their brothers and sisters? How can these Christians relate themselves to the ancient Indian wisdom? Who listens to their theological reflections? Who lends an ear to Asian Americans who try to understand their struggle for emancipation out of their Christian faith?

The Emancipation of Women

On the fourth day of the conference, Christian women presented their theological reflections on the struggle for emancipation. Again they presented themselves as a community. Their very mode of dealing with their subject provided a critique of traditional academic theology. Several women, including well-known scholars such as Sheila Collins, Alice Hageman, Beverly Harrison, and Rosemary Ruether, sat on the chairs that had been put on the platform in front of the auditorium. Each of them contributed to the presentation from her own perspective. The experienced scholars among them had the self-discipline to give equal space to others. The women in the audience who wanted to add their own reflections were asked to take a chair on the platform. To make room for a new speaker, a woman who had already spoken would empty her chair and move back into the audience. This style of critical reflection tried to replace the highly competitive understanding of truth, proper to academia, with a more cooperative understanding that makes room for contributions from various perspectives as long as they are born of the emancipatory struggle. Why should it always be necessary to cut the flesh of living reflection with the knife of scientific reason? A more contemplative reason may be able to gather the insights based on a variety of experiences and discern in them, despite possible conceptual discrepancies, a shared movement toward truth. The highly individualistic context of research and reflection in the male world of academia often persuades the thinker that the truth is his. Actually the entry into truth is a communal process.

The women insisted that sexism—that is, the subjugation of women as women—is a distinct form of oppression. It is historically interrelated with economic and racial oppressions and hence can never be found in pure form; still, it is an oppression *sui generis*. Sexism is very ancient. It is part of the patriarchal culture we have inherited; it is woven into the very consciousness of our civilization. Unless the historical struggles against economic exploitation and racial injustice become conscious of the ancient sexist heritage, they will not greatly change the lot of women. The speakers remarked that the published works on Latin American liberation theology and U.S. American black theology do not mention the subjugation of women at all. In Latin America this should be an important issue since an oppressive *machismo* dominates the entire culture. At the same time, in presenting the elements of their liberation theology, the women made it clear that they did not identify themselves with the middle-class women's movement, especially as it appears in the mass media, where women often seek new freedoms for themselves in terms of the individualistic and competitive nature of contemporary culture. Only too often do successful women seek new opportunities by asking other women, often black women, to assume a servant role for them. The feminist theologians at Detroit did not want to separate their liberation struggle from the struggle against other forms of oppression.

Contrary to the popular view, modern industrial capitalism did not improve the situation of women in society. Beverly Harrison briefly summarized her research in this field. The new dominant class, the bourgeoisie, created the ideal of "true womanhood," that is, the image of the spiritual, passive, nonproductive woman who defines herself wholly in terms of her husband and children. Since the new industrialization had destroyed the family home as a unit of production and made men work in offices and factories away from their dwelling places, what took place was strict separation between the public and the private spheres. The public sphere of industry, commerce, politics, and education belonged to men, and the private sphere of home and religion belonged to women. Women were excluded from public responsibility and participation in the productive process. The nineteenth century women's movement in the Anglo-Saxon world was the reaction of spirited women against this form of genteel but paralyzing subjugation. At the same time, while society upheld the ideal of true womanhood for the successful classes, working class women were condemned to live in conditions of oppression: hard work, insecurity, utter poverty, and often humiliation. To this day, the poor women in our society are torn apart by the actual conditions of their lives as workers and the image of "true woman" which the mass media and the instruments of culture communicate to her.

Sexism is ancient in our culture. It is woven into the very consciousness we have inherited. The split between spirit and body in human self-understanding and the subsequent quest to achieve the mastery of the spirit over an unruly body created a consciousness which allowed men to identify themselves with the spirit while projecting the body image on women. Since in patriarchal society the negative side of any dualism is projected on women, the women's movement must wrestle against every kind of dualism in the perception of reality. Women must therefore be critical of the place of rationality in Western culture. Here reason rises above and triumphs over the web of life; here reason is aggressive, competitive, and vindictive; it is "the trump card against matter." In a less alienated world, reason might actually emerge out of life, promote its unity, direct the forward passage of this life toward maturity, and be "the very lifeblood of matter."

Women's liberation theology must eventually question the dualistic theism which seems to dominate biblical religion. Dualistic consciousness expresses itself in perceiving God as the master over the earth and thus in making God the supreme image protecting the mastery of men over women and legitimating other forms of domination in society. The women at Detroit were at one in rejecting the view of divine transcendence that has prevailed in Christian thinking, especially in popular religion, Catholic and

Protestant, and found a particuarly strong expression in Protestant evangelical and neo-orthodox piety. Dualistic theism may not be universal in the Christian tradition. In the ancient Church some thinkers spoke of God as the ground and matrix of existence. Thomas Aquinas thought of God as *ipsum esse subsistens*, and in modern times Paul Tillich understood God as the ground of being. The women were not certain whether these traditional attempts to understand divine transcendence as the mode of God's presence (or immanence) in life and cosmos were helpful at this time. They wanted to wait for a while, experience the transformation of society, and then see whether a more adequate way of speaking of divine transcendence will emerge.

Divine Transcendence

The question of divine transcendence became important at the conference at a later point, after the lecture given by a Protestant theologian. While this lecture acknowledged the oppressions in society, saw God's judgment on the sinful world, and recognized the need to struggle against economic, racial, and sexist exploitation, it was delivered in a tone of evangelical piety that annoyed many members of the conference. The theologian had expressed his sympathy for black theology, especially—it was felt—because of its emphasis on the lordship of God. People vehemently criticized the tenor of his lecture. They felt that he had spoken of liberation so easily and so globally that he escaped concreteness and thus bypassed people's actual struggles. They felt, moreover, that he clung to the story of Jesus as if the manner in which this story is communicated to us and understood by us could not be subject to ideological distortions and hence was not in need of being critically examined. Finally, it was the view of divine transcendence that offended many participants. The lecture gave the impression, though the text did not specifically say so, that God and Jesus were available to Christians wherever they were situated, just by turning inward in their hearts. According to the theologies of liberation proposed by Latin Americans, blacks, women, and other struggling groups, God is not available to people in any position whatever, but only as they identify themselves with the historical struggle against evil and injustice.

What took place at the conference was a clash between two views of divine transcendence. In the course of this argument the theologian who had given the lecture was misunderstood and treated, I think, unjustly, but the clash brought to light a significant difference between two kinds of Christian spirituality, an issue crucial in the development of contemporary theology. Traditional piety in the Protestant and Catholic Churches visualized God as the supreme Lord over and above human history. This God was available to believers as they reached out to him, inwardly or upwardly, beyond the actual, historical situation in which they lived. God's transcendence was here unrelated to history. It was, as it were, at right angles to history. Contrary to this, the spirituality associated with many forms of contemporary theology holds that God's transcendence is mediated in and through history. Believers encounter the divine by involving themselves in the struggle for humanization. Since the transcendent mystery is operative in the promised transformation of human life, personal and social, it is here, in *active* engagement and *contemplative* presence to this engagement, that believers encounter the living God. The "non-historical" understanding of divine transcendence, so the Latin American theologians insisted, makes God the eternal protector of an existing order and religion and guardian of the status quo; the "historical" understanding of divine transcendence, on the other hand, reveals God's presence in history as the source of its redemptive transformation. God is present in people's struggles for their emancipation. The idea that the transcendent divine mystery is immanent in human life and the cosmos is in keeping with the major trends in Catholicism; the idea is more difficult to assimilate in the Protestant tradition, except in the trends influenced by Hegel. The idea is clearly opposed to the view of divine transcendence entertained by neo-orthodoxy, which still exercises a strong influence on American Protestantism, even when preachers have consciously repudiated it.

Black theologians, as I mentioned above, unashamedly affirm God as the Lord of lords. They do not fear that such a view of God will legitimate the existing order. Why not? The meaning of religious language depends in part on the socio-political situation of the people who utter it. When oppressed people invoke God as the Lord of lords, they mean that God is more powerful than the pharaohs of the world. But when the king's men who lord it over their subjects invoke God as the King of kings, they legitimate their king's rule as the one who governs in the name of God. What follows from this is that when a theme of black theology is taken over into white theology, it changes in meaning. If in the dominant culture God's self-communication is understood as taking place in the sacred space, apart from and superior to human history, then the historical struggle for justice and social change is only of secondary and derived importance. The really real is then quite independent from the political order. This is a common view in white America. But if religion is used to trivialize history in this way, it becomes an ideology for the successful classes. In the biblical perspective it is clear, however, that the Holy One of Israel reveals himself in the liberation of his people. Any attempt to separate divine transcendence and human liberation, as we find it for instance in the Hartford Appeal, is against the authentic understanding of Christian teaching.

No Doctrine of Total Depravity

Where did the theologies of the struggling peoples leave the white male participants of the conference? It is a temptation for Christians, especially if they are heirs of a doctrine of total depravity or the utter sinfulness of the human being, to fall into masochistic self-accusations and indulge in protracted convulsions of guilt. Some participants occasionally fell into this trap. They were willing to identify themselves remorsefully as enemy and oppressor. A few men even wanted to get together to develop a theological theory appropriate to their own situation. This was strange, for the important point made at the conference was that traditional theology (and social science) was precisely the theory appropriate to the white man's situation. The wish of the few to sit together meant that they had not yet fully grasped the message of the conference that this is exactly what the American world is: the few white males sitting together and planning society. The more common response of the white participants was the determination to be in solidarity with the struggling peoples, to act in new and untried ways, to enter upon new experiences, and eventually to produce religious reflection from this perspective.

Certainly, to the extent that we are sociologically identified with exploitative institutions, we participate in the social sins of our communities. We even continue to derive advantages from our privileged position. The injustices in the world and our social participation in them produce a painful realization. This makes us sad; sometimes it burdens us with great sadness. But this does not send us on "a guilt trip." It should be clear that we do not find ourselves where we are through personal guilt. The last thing the struggling communities want is to see us indulge in masochistic self-denunciations. While we are sociologically identified with our class and country, we have the freedom personally to identify ourselves with the poor, to find actions that give body to this identification, to perceive the world in a changed manner, and eventually to think thoughts and develop theology that actually promote the transformation and liberation of God's world.

Gustavo Gutiérrez tried to clarify the task of Christian theology, wherever it may be developed, as the systematic effort to reread history from the viewpoint of the rejected and humiliated. This effort defines the Christian left, in the sense I have used the term in the title of this chapter. Normally history is written by the victors. The successful classes mediate their self-understanding to the entire nation through lore, culture, and the telling of history. But what would happen, for instance, if Canadians were willing to reread their history from the viewpoint of the native peoples? They would discover dark sides of their own culture, related to their material interests, which normally remain unacknowledged and unrecognized. It is the task of Christians in Canada to integrate these repressed elements into the Canadian self-understanding and to seek modification of the material interests which produced the oppression of the native peoples in the first place. One does not have to be a Christian to reconsider one's cultural self-understanding in terms of the oppressed communities. But Christians ought to do this. Gutiérrez specifically demanded that the Christian churches, in fidelity to the humiliated and crucified Jesus, identify themselves with the poor of the world and thus, by relying on the divine promises, come to a proper theological perception of world history. Such a rereading of history is not a purely intellectual task. One cannot identify with the world's poor abstractly and in general. The poor are concrete, historical classes, peoples, and sections of humanity, and hence identification implies solidarity with their struggles. Here too, then, theology must be reflection on praxis. We learn from the story of Jesus that history is changed not by the powerful but by the weak. The current that transforms history comes from below, from the underclasses, and moves society toward greater freedom by subversion. "God has put down the mighty from their thrones, and exalted those of low degree; God has filled the hungry with good things, and sent the rich away empty."

In a recent pastoral letter, the Canadian Catholic bishops, seconded by the other Christian churches in Canada, were willing to look at the development of the Canadian north from the viewpoint of the native peoples and gave voice to the voiceless by demanding that any plans of government and industry to exploit the natural resources of the north must be worked out in consultation with the native peoples. These peoples must at all costs be allowed to protest the land which is the matrix of their survival.

Since the foundations of the white settlements in North America were commercial and expansionist, since the new colonies, whether French or British, were extensions of European empires for the benefit of the rich, and since even the American Revolution did not challenge the inherited system but only shifted the center of profit-making, it is possible to read American history purely and simply in terms of conquest and exploitation. A document, "The American Journey," distributed to the participants prior to the conference, did this brilliantly. Economics was the driving force for the creation and development of the American republic. The author had been willing to reread American history in terms of the humiliated communities. Many participants, however, felt that this was not the whole story. The spiritual and cultural aspirations of the early settlers and their descendants were not simply ideologies legitimating the exploitative and expansionist nature of the American enterprise. They were also the endeavor of a people in a new historical situation to create a civilization for themselves, reflecting the values of their religion and their vision of a new humanity. In other words, a rereading of history in the light of the humiliated communities should not—this, at least, is my position—make one overlook the cultural symbols of the past that at this time could produce a new imagination and provide impetus and direction for radical social change. The Latin Americans, to give an example, may be fully justified in looking at the North American journey simply in terms of their dependency and exploitation, for it is in their own Latin American history that they hope to discover positive cultural symbols to strangthen their solidarity and inspire their common struggle. But U.S. Americans of the dominant culture, while acknowledging the repressed side of their people's past, must search for more in American history than for the sources and patterns of exploitation. They must try to discern in the American experience symbols of new life which can become at this time the sources of a new national self-understanding and an impetus to costly social change.

Do we know that symbols of reconstruction are present in a people's history? One theologian at the conference felt that our present trouble is linked to the demonic nature of the entire Western enterprise. By linking the quest for understanding to the quest for mastery, the progress of Western civilization inevitably leads to the domination of weaker peoples and the destruction of the earth's surface, whether this be through capitalist or communist empires. Most members of the conference, I think, rejected such a doctrine of total depravity. It went against the "common faith." But are there persuasive arguments to show that present in any people's history are cultural elements that provide strength and direction for a movement of social reconstruction? At this point some participants turned from Marx to Durkheim. According to the sociology of Emile Durkheim, the social insititutions with which people are identified generate cultural symbols, values, ideals, and ultimately even religion, which reflect not so much what society actually is—this would be the Marxist view—but what society wants and aspires to be. The collective self-understanding of a people, generated by reflection on the great moments of their history and by experienced closeness at the time of crisis, contains symbols that transcend ethnocentric ideology, judge the actual situation of the society, and provide images for possible social change. There is no national history without hope. This is the context in which a discussion of Robert Bellah's contribution to the U.S. self-understanding would have been useful.

Let me also present a theological argument against the doctrine of total depravity, applied to a culture or a nation. According to the Catholic tradition at least, wherever people struggle for their self-understanding and cooperate in the creation of a representative culture, the mystery of God is present to them. God's victory in Jesus Christ assured the universality of divine grace. There is no culture from which God is wholly absent. A purely demonic enterprise can not endure for long. The Nazi reign only lasted twelve years. Present in the culture of any people are the dream of the promised land and the yearning for the peaceful community. There are hints of sacramentality in the experience of any nation. In my view, it is the task of critical theology to discover these hints. For if the pressure for social change comes upon a people, in this case the American people, purely from without, without connection with their own historical experience, they must reject it as a foreign influence. If an entire nation is to reconstruct its social life, the driving force must be fidelity to its own history.

Marxism

At the Detroit conference the term "Marxism" was constantly used. It is not easy to know what people mean when they use this word. Marxism could refer, for instance, to the system of ideas found in the writings of Karl Marx. Marxism, I suppose, could also refer to the various political institutions that call themselves Marxist, be they Communist empires and Communist countries or be they the Communist parties in the West, e.g., those of France and Italy. But Marxism could also refer to the development of Marx's ideas by subsequent thinkers who adopted Marx's perspective but carried forward his thought. From this point of view, Marxism is a complex and often divergent intellectual tradition, constituted by the systematic attempts of various scholars or even schools to use principles derived from Marx to come to a better understanding of society and its history. It was in this latter sense that the word Marxism was used at the conference.

I should remind the reader that a certain Cold War rhetoric has created the image of Marxism as a uniform and fixed system of ideas, institutionalized in identical ways in Communist countries and Communist parties. Catholic thinkers, in particular, tended to speak of Marxism in a reified way—very much as we used to speak of "Protestantism" as a single reality, defined by a few principles, thereby dispensing ourselves from studying the actual currents of the historical phenomenon. In the Catholic Church, a new approach to the study of Marxism has been generally accepted only after Pope John's recommendation in *Pacem in Terris*.

In order to clarify the use of the word "Marxism" at the Detroit conference, let me introduce a distinction made by Yves Vaillancourt during one of the discussions. Marxism can be understood (1) as a philosophy, (2) as a plan of political action, and (3) as an instrument of social analysis. The Christians gathered at Detroit did not speak of Marxism as a philosophy. For them the dynamics of history was ultimately revealed by God in the history of Israel and the person of Jesus Christ—even if they should hold that this dynamics moves through class conflict and dialectical reconciliation. Nor did the participants generally speak of Marxism as a plan of action, except for few members from Latin America who were discussing the strategies of liberation in their countries and the search for suitable political allies. The constant references to Marxism at the Detroit conference understood it almost exclusively as an instrument of social analysis.

The Latin American theologians, as I mentioned earlier, showed that Christian theology, in an attempt to come to an understanding of its historical situation, must engage in a social analysis that brings to light the sins of the world, that is, the contradictions within the inherited system and the oppression which they produce. While there are a variety of Marxist social theories, it is possible to define a social analysis as "Marxist" if it forcuses on the economic system as the key factor of oppression, if it makes class analysis the central and indispensable element for understanding the social situation, and if it tries to account for political and cultural developments mainly, even if not exclusively, in terms of the interests of the class that owns and controls the major industries. Marxist social analysis at Detroit did not refer to any kind of Marxist "orthodoxy." Who is still interested in Marx's analysis of early industrial capitalism or his theory of surplus value? What contemporary Marxist analysis deals with are the contradictions of modern, corporate capitalism and their link to the recurring economic crises, to the expansionist policies of the capitalist world, to the creation of dependent territories with impoverished masses, and to the spread of poverty and unemployment even in the industrialized capitalist countries. Are the disturbing events we read in the newspaper accidents of history, or are they related to the economic system that we have inherited?

If Marxism is understood as an instrument of social analysis, it is easy to see that Christians can learn from it, and that if they make it an essential element of their theology of liberation, they may even be willing, in this sense, to call themselves Christian Marxists. In similar fashion Christians have called themselves Christian Platonists and Aristotelians without endorsing the elements of these philosophical traditions irreconcilable with the Christian faith. Yet how useful the Marxist analysis is for understanding the whole of United States society is a matter of dispute. Since the racial and ethnic identities are so strong in the United States that they form cohesive patterns which mediate, and in some cases impede, the formation of economic classes, a Marxist social analysis must be highly qualified and nuanced if it is to shed light on the oppressive structures in such a non-homogeneous society.

Nevertheless the kind of critical social analysis, called Marxist in the sense defined above, has been used by Christians in many parts of the world to formulate their social positions. It is my contention that with Pope Paul VI's *Populorum Progressio* this kind of analysis has entered Catholic social teachings. Let me give an example of Marxist social analysis (as defined above) drawn not from papal documents but from a recent pastoral letter, "Powerlessness in Appalachia," written by the Catholic bishops of the region.

Why are the people of Appalachia always oppressed, the Catholic bishops ask? When the mines were working and the people had jobs, they were exploited; when the mines closed, the people were unemployed; and now that many mines are open again, the people's exploitation has not really changed. What is the reason for this? The bishops insist that it does not lie in a lack of generosity on the part of the more successful people in the area, nor is it due to any bad will on the part of the men who run the large corporations. What is involved here is a systemic evil. The principles operative in the large corporation which determine the fate of Appalachia—and the rest of the world—are at odds with the well-being of people. The letter mentions two such principles. The first is called "technological rationalization." This means that in the planning of the operation by the decision-making board all factors of production are considered in terms of their contribution to the total process. Each factor is technologically perfected to make it more efficient in the operation of the whole. These factors include the laborers. The policies made by the board of directors in regard to the workers are produced by the same logic that determines the decisions in regard to all other factors of production. Decisions regarding people are made as if they were things. This is the principle of technological rationalization. The second principle mentioned in the pastoral letter is called "the maximization of profit." This is not a reference to personal greed or lack of charity. It refers, rather, to a principle of planning and decision-making. It simply states that when the board of directors is confronted with various plans of action and development, they will study them carefully, compare them one with the other, and eventually choose the plan that promises to maximize the profit of the company. It is fidelity to this principle and not lack of personal virtue that causes these corporations to make decisions regarding people and their environment that have such devastating effects on Appalachia. The Catholic bishops go so far as to say that Appalachia is here a symbol of the country and the world. The analysis applied to understand powerlessness in Appalachia provides the key for understanding the exploitation in other parts of the United States and in the third world. The theology of captivity, movingly developed in the bishops' pastoral letter, is based on what at the Detroit conference was called "Marxist" social analysis.

Let me add that the pastoral letter makes it clear that it does not recommend Marxism as a plan of political action. It does not advocate the public ownership of the giant corporations. It insists, rather, that these corporations are not the only power in the land. There is political power, and its task is to restrict and restrain the activity of these corporations. What is needed, therefore, is that the people dedicated to justice organize, reach out for political influence, and demand that the government protect the well-being of the poor and the integrity of the environment. The letter adopts a reformist position. Still, the radical analysis of the ills of society will make people dream of an alternative economic system where production is determined by the realistic needs of people in society and not by technological rationalization and the maximization of profit.

Theologies of Liberation

Throughout the conference it became clear that one should speak of liberation theologies in the plural. Each such theology is based on a community struggling for freedom in a concrete historical society, and while they share in a common faith (as I described it at the beginning of this article) they do not wrestle against the same enemy and hence for the time being remain somewhat distinct in their efforts. The participants agreed that there were several forms of oppression, especially those of class, race, and sex, and that these are always interstructured in ways that are historically different in different societies. This point was most clearly expressed by Rosemary Ruether. It could well be that for some peoples the economic oppression is the central, overriding element, to which all other oppressions are subordinated. These people could not be faulted if other groups, struggling out of their situation, regard racist or sexist oppression as the principal enemy. What each group should do in their own place, however, is to examine the forms of oppression which appear secondary and come to a clearer understanding of how these are interstructured with the principal oppression. In some incipient way, then, all liberation theologies reach out for what the Latin Americans called the holistic view.

The participants also agreed that there is no overarching theology of liberation, of which each particular theology is just a special case. Some members even asked the theologians of the dominant culture not to elaborate a general theory of liberation. It would be idealistic (in the bad sense of the word) to suppose that theology could reconcile social movements and mediate between various forms of self-understanding which are grounded on conflicting material conditions and interests. At the same time, since the participants wanted to remain in conversation and discover the historical relationship between their various emancipatory struggles, they actually strained to find a universal language for their respective conditions, a language which would not neutralize or suppress but rather protect and strengthen that particularity of their struggles. For the time being, however, if I understood the drift of the conference correctly, the participants wanted to speak of liberation theology only in the plural.

Theologians of the dominant culture in America are unable to produce a liberation theology. The Latin American theologians even asked them not to use liberation theology as a new toy to make their classes more interesting. Liberation theology is born out of a concrete struggle, and hence when it is presented outside of this context, its very meaning is transformed. This does not mean, of course, that there is no liberating, intellectual task for the theologians of the dominant culture. By opting for solidarity with the marginalized sections of society, especially in their own country, they are able to develop a critical theology, that is, they are able to discern in the inherited religion the ideological trends and liberate the customary theology from its identification with the structures of domination. These theologians are able to come to a more Christian understanding of their society by rereading its history from the viewpoint of the oppressed peoples and develop what Rubem Alves has called "a theology of captivity." The above-mentioned pastoral letter on Appalachia and several pastoral letters on social issues written by the Canadian Catholic bishops have produced important elements of such a theology of captivity. Difficulties in theology, Gutiérrez said at the Detroit conference, used to be only difficulties in theology. We have come to realize today that many difficulties in theology cannot be resolved prior to significant social change.

Since American theology, which here means white, male American theology, did not make a very impressive showing at the Detroit conference, some participants were overly dejected and spoke of the bankruptcy of our theological resources. But is it surprising that we do not have a theology that can deal successfully with the contradictions of our society? Theology cannot perform miracles, Yves Vaillancourt said at one discussion: Since theology can only move a little ahead of the actual historical situation, how can we expect theology to be an instrument of reconciliation when we are in fact divided by objective factors of history? Had American theologians of the dominant culture presented themselves as the self-confident interpreters of the struggles of their country, that would have been the great deception.

Before closing this essay, I wish briefly to mention three more related points. First there is the ecclesiological implication of liberation theology. The Latin American theologians insisted that their reflections, though well researched and hence academic, were based on the reflections of the struggling Christian communities in their own countries. The blacks too spoke of the meaning of the Gospel as it emerges in living congregations. The women admitted that when they first discovered the weight of anti-feminism in their religious tradition, they were estranged from Christianity. It was only later, in consciousness-raising groups, that they discovered the meaning of *Ecclesia*. It was this experience of struggling community, of shared insights, shared burdens, shared confidence, that gave them access again to the meaning of the Gospel. There was common agreement that liberation theologies are not the product of single thinkers. They are reflections of communities involved in struggle.

But why should struggling people be concerned with theology at all? What does religion have to do with the quest for emancipation? This question was asked several times by participants who did not regard themselves as Christians even though they shared what I have called the common faith. One sociologist, Michele Russell, said that she could understand why middle-class people who involved themselves in the struggle of the poor were in need of relating themselves to a transcendent. This was for them the source of motivation. But she could not understand why the poor or the oppressed themselves were in need of such a reference. She thought that the struggle itself would provide community, vision, direction, and inner strength. This question presupposes, of course, that religious experience is in the long run dispensable. But is this true? Most of the participants had not asked themselves this question at all. They thought of religion as a dimension of life that would participate in all the significant events of their existence, and hence also in their struggle for emancipation. But when asked the question, they were willing to attempt a tentative answer. Some said that their faith provided them with a vision beyond the concrete aim of their emancipation and critique of the means used in the collective struggle. Others stressed that the Christian call to love prevented the collective aims of the struggle from overshadowing the meaning of personal destiny. Christians who experience their religion as a constant obstacle to their social engagement will soon abandon it, yet such a decision in no way solves the question out of what symbols they want to define their lives and with what faith they will move into the future.

I wish to make a final remark on the ubiquity of sociology at the Detroit conference. Many of the arguments that emerged among the participants were in fact classical arguments in the history of sociology, even if the participants were not aware of this. Karl Marx and Max Weber were both present at the conference. The unwillingness to understand society purely in terms of an economic analysis were expressed in terms that recalled Weber's criticism of Marx. Class and status, not just class, must be analyzed to understand the power structure in society. The marginalization of blacks and women, for instance, is the low status assigned to them, which then affects their economic life and acquires class significance. I mentioned earlier that Durkheim was not absent from the conference, especially among the participants interested in the cultural factors through which people define their identity. Curiously enough, Max Weber's analysis of alienation and powerlessness through expanding bureaucratization was hardly dealt with. It was mentioned once by a few workers, present at the conference, involved in wrestling against the bureaucratization of their unions. The absence of the Weberian analysis was regrettable, for it supplies a critique applicable to capitalist as well as socialist societies. Incidentally, I might add that present at the conference were a group of workers as well as representatives from Appalachia.

All in all the conference was an important theological event. Inevitably it bore the mark of the confusion characteristic of our time. A tidy conference in a broken world is possible only if the real problems are forcibly kept outside. What the conference did was to help the groups present to see the viewpoints of other struggling communities and to reach out for a commitment to their own position that *in some way includes* the concern of these others. Such an inclusion, however partial, anticipates what the Latin theologians called the holistic view. While the historical conditions for achieving a holistic view are not present at this time, the conference helped the various groups to stretch their self-understanding and initiate some action toward a more total vision of humanity, free and reconciled. The conference facilitated the creation of many networks of research and cooperation among various groups as the *praxis* dimension of the week-long conversation.

Theology After Auschwitz

Under the theme of "Auschwitz: Beginning of a New Era," a theological symposium involving Christians and Jews met from June 3 to 6, 1974, at the Cathedral of St. John the Divine, New York City. A group of Christian and Jewish scholars, under the chairmanship of James Morton, dean of St. John the Divine Cathedral, had planned this Conference to examine the changes in the self-understanding of Christians and Jews produced by the extermination of six million Jews in the death camps of Nazi-dominated Europe.

Auschwitz was a manifestation of evil with proportions transcending the human imagination; it does not fit into any accepted categories. Auschwitz differs from other genocides and other forms of extermination practiced in wars and political struggles. The extermination of the Jews in central Europe was a carefully planned and technically complex operation, involving the collaboration of thousands of people over a long period of time, in the death camps themselves as well as in the vast network of transportation that collected and shipped the Jews from various parts of Europe to the death camps in the East. Auschwitz was unique in the sense that the executioners, the Nazis, did not hope to derive any benefit or advantage from this genocide that would help them in waging a world war and in winning world domination. The extermination of the Jews continued even at a time when the Germans were fighting a losing battle, and the staff and equipment used in the death camps might have helped in the war effort to defend Germany from the invading armies. While the great crimes of history—including those connected with World War II, such as the exploitation and extermination inflicted by the Germans on the Polish and Russian peoples—were meant to serve some sort of purpose in the achievement of final victory, the Jewish Holocaust seems to have been a totally irrational event, born out of passionate and pathological hatred, the sources of which were largely hidden from the executioners themselves. Auschwitz does not fit any categories.

At the same time, Auschwitz is rooted and situated in Western history and hence not unconnected to the culture and the cruelty of preceding centuries and millennia.

How do Jews and Christians respond to this demonic event? To Jews Auschwitz has become a significant moment of a new self-understanding. Many of them find it impossible to define their role and mission in history without taking account of the Holocaust. Very few Christians, on the other hand, have reflected on what this genocide means for the self-understanding of Western culture and in particular for the Christian tradition. One purpose of the Conference was to foster Christian reflection on the Holocaust and to create a response in faith to the violent death of six million Jews. There was the hope that the Conference would move away from the ordinary form of Jewish-Christian dialogue—which in any case seems to have dwindled away—and bring into conversation representatives of various Jewish trends among themselves and representatives of various Christian trends among themselves, and then, as an unplannable consequence, create conditions where some Jews and some Christians, finding themselves united in a common conversation, would talk to one another about their own self-understanding. The Conference, I think, achieved something of what is set out to do.

Since the encounter with the Holocaust affects the future of theology, I wish to report some of the significant ideas and important discussions. This article is not a summary of the Conference. It simply records some topics that I, as a participant in the Conference, regarded as crucial for the religious self-understanding of the modern world. Many important papers, including Elie Wiesel's beautiful lecture, will not be dealt with. The Proceedings of the Conference, including the lectures and prepared responses, have since been published.

I
JEWISH REFLECTION ON THE HOLOCAUST

The most important lecture from the Jewish theological perspective was "Theological Reflections on the Holocaust" by Dr. Irving Greenberg, Professor at the City University of New York. This lecture tried to summarize and in a sense synthesize various Jewish religious reactions to the insane tragedy of Auschwitz. Greenberg's brilliant lecture in fact raised the significant theological issues for Jews as well as Christians and defined the theological coordinates in which the discussion of the entire Conference took place. Before entering upon his reflections, he spent some time describing the organized extermination of European Jewry. To enable the participants of the Conference to respond to the Holocaust in a genuine way, he tried to lift it out of the abstract, make it concrete, present some actual accounts, and permit the voices of the victims to be heard. He made the audience get a glimpse of the evil and be confounded.

"Judaism and Christianity," Greenberg said, "do not merely tell God's love for man as the central key to life and history. They stand and fall on their fundamental claim that, therefore, the human being is of ultimate and absolute value." Can Jews after Auschwitz still believe in a heavenly Father who cares for them and loves all human life? And can Christians still believe, especially when they discover that their own reprobation of the Jews is related to the social negation of Jewish existence? Greenberg quoted a German Protestant Conference held at Darmstadt in 1949, four years after the end of World War II, which interpreted the Jewish Holocaust executed by their own nation as a divine visitation upon the Jews and a call addressed to the survivors to stop rejecting Jesus and crucifying him by their unbelief. Is it still moral to be Christian after this? Yet Greenberg insisted that there is no group without guilt, not even the Western democratic nations, not even the Jews in these countries. For all groups shared some responsibility in the Holocaust by their silence, by their unwillingness to act—an unwillingness that is deeply rooted in the symbols of Western history. While American bombs were dropped over many German cities, none were dropped on the railway lines that carried the Jews to the extermination camps. No group was interested. Even the Jews in the Western nations did not react to Nazi anti-Semitism with courage and determination. The Holocaust implicates the whole of Western history.

This universal Western responsibility does not relativize the guilt of the criminals and groups of criminals who conceived, planned, and executed the systematic extermination of European Jews in an operation they themselves called the Final Solution. The Nazis bear their guilt. But some responsibility lies with all the groups in Western history. Even the Jews, Irving Greenberg said, cannot make use of the Holocaust triumphalistically and affirm their superiority over other religious groups. The Jews who use the Holocaust as a polemical tool against all groups except their own are tempted, Greenberg said, to slide into indifference in regard to the holocausts of others. As examples of such temptations he mentioned the general policy of the American Orthodox Rabbinate on U.S. involvement in Vietnam and the use of Israeli strength on the weak without moderation. After the events of Auschwitz, no one in the West, to whatever religion or whatever culture he may belong, remains untroubled.

Different Reactions Synthesized

Irving Greenberg recalls three different reactions of Jewish religious thinkers to the Holocaust. There is, first of all, the position of Emil Fackenheim who regards Auschwitz as a unique event in Jewish history that has entered into the self-definition of the Jewish people. Fackenheim, who participated in the Conference and gave a lecture on the theological meaning of the State of Israel, has presented his theology in his book *God's Presence in History*. Jews have always defined themselves in terms of special revelatory events in history—the exodus from Egypt, the covenant at Sinai, the conquest of the land, the exile in Babylon, the return to the land, etc. Fackenheim holds that the Holocaust of Auschwitz is so crucial that it is impossible for Jews today to define their existence without reference to it. The Holocaust as such has no message or meaning and no one should try to invest this abomination with any significance. But in its meaningless-ness, in its emptiness, it is revelatory. God utters a sacred com-mand at Auschwitz calling upon Jews to act in such a way that Hitler's intention of destroying them will never be realized. Hitler must not be granted posthumous victories. After Auschwitz, Fackenheim holds, Jewish survival itself assumes religious mean-ing. Jewish survival is no longer a purely secular event, for after the Holocaust the Jewish struggle for survival is a response to God's commanding voice and has a religious meaning even when carried out by nonreligious Jews. After Auschwitz the distinction between religious and secular is somehow transcended, for by defining himself in relation to the Holocaust and responding to it with courage and determination, any Jew, however secular, is related to the divine voice.

The second position is that of Eliezer Berkovits (cf. his book *Faith after the Holocaust*). Berkovits refuses to regard Au-schwitz as a moment of revelation and an event that enters into the self-definition of the Jewish people. For him divine revelation is closed: Israel has received the significant commandments of God in the past. The task of the Jews is to be faithful to the saving events that took place at the beginning of their history. The Holocaust may be a unique manifestation of human malice, but looked upon theologically it is just an evil moment in a long series of human crimes and raises no religious question that is not posed by any sinful act. How can God allow unjust treatment inflicted on a single innocent person? How can we believe in the Lord of the universe after the suffering of a single child? The answer to the Holocaust is the traditional Jewish reply to the presence of evil: We cannot understand God's rule of the world and hence we should not try to fathom it; at the same time God's victory over evil is always sufficiently present to us to give strength to our wavering faith. Even at Auschwitz, Berkovits holds, the signs of God's victory were not absent: they were found in the patience, the gentleness, and the unshakable faith of so many Jews. After Auschwitz it is Jewish survival and especially the State of Israel that strengthen the faith of Jews in the Lord of history. No pro-longed reflection on the Holocaust is needful.

Finally, there is the theological response of Richard Ruben-

stein who holds that after Auschwitz it is impossible to go on believing in the God of Israel (cf. his book *After Auschwitz*). The
most religious response to the extermination of the Jews is to
deny that there exists a divine Lord of history. For if such a Lord
existed, he would surely be a monster. Compassion and spiritual
sensitivity demand that Jews denounce the existence of God. At
the same time Rubenstein remains a religious person and a theologian. Basing himself on the psychology and sociology of religion, he regards religious language and religious ceremonies as
playing a significant part in the building up, the healing and the
transformation of the human community. Religion has human-
izing power and need not be understood with reference to a
supreme divinity: it has meaning and power as the celebration of
the deepest dimension of human life and the social identity of the
worshiping community.

The Christian reader of Rubenstein tends to regard him as an
atheist. However, this is not the only way of interpreting him. For
there exists in the Jewish tradition a recognized language for arguing with God, for protesting against him, for refusing to accept his
government. Many believing Jews have told God, because of the
suffering present in history, that they refuse to acknowledge him.
Hence, Rubenstein's theology can be read as a form of rhetorical
atheism that formulates the negation of God as a protest against
him, based on a faith in God's message that justice and love are to
prevail.

In his brilliant lecture, Irving Greenberg takes these three
reactions seriously and despite their apparent contradiction affirms them as dynamic moments of a responsible reply to the
Holocaust. Greenberg recognizes with Fackenheim that Auschwitz, though utterly meaningless and in itself not worthy to be
remembered, summons forth a response that enters the self-
understanding of contemporary Jews. Jews are called upon to
survive. Responding to Auschwitz, Jews faithfully confess the
Lord of history who summons them to remain his witnesses in the
world by surviving in the face of the evil powers that seek to
destroy them. At the same time, Greenberg admits that it may not
always be possible to affirm the divine Lord after Auschwitz.
This is the side of the dialectic stressed by Rubenstein. If Jews

take seriously the values and ideals their tradition has nourished in them, they must abandon as incompatible with their faith the belief in a divine Lord who permitted the Holocaust. Such a negation seems an authentic religious response. This side of the dialectic makes impossible any expression of untroubled theism.

Greenberg wants to keep both sides of the dialectic. The total, complex response of faith is made up of moments that logically contradict one another. There is fidelity to God's voice despite the awful reality of the Holocaust, and at the same time there is the total inability to recognize the existence of such a divinity. Because of this dialectic, Greenberg holds, the positive affirmation of faith is generated by an honest confrontation with evil in the world and the Holocaust in particular, and hence contains within itself compassion and care for all people. The positive response is not just dedication to survival but to survival as Jews, as witnesses to compassion and humaneness. Greenberg shares with Fackenheim the position that after the Holocaust the easy distinction between religious and secular Jews has disappeared— but while for Fackenheim this is so mainly because by surviving both the religious and the secular Jew are obedient to God's voice, for Greenberg this is so because on the one hand the religious affirmation may be the expression of untroubled theism and, on the other, the religious negation may in fact be an expression of fidelity. While Fackenheim is able to show the moral context of Jewish survival, Greenberg's stress on compassion and humaneness is more direct since it emerges from the very structure of the dialectical faith.

In a certain sense, then, Greenberg is able to integrate Berkovits' position that the Holocaust inflicted on European Jewry is just the ancient story of sin and evil, retold in a new and more horrible way, and that the Jews' response to it is part of their religious response to evil in general. Greenberg insists that after the Holocaust, Jews are summoned as Jews to be angered by all injustices and take sides against the oppression of any people. Greenberg's dialectical method, which includes the moment of unbelief in the dialectics of faith, commits Jews to an unmitigated humanism and makes them sensitive, precisely because of the Holocaust, to the misery inflicted on people anywhere. The shout

"Never again!" which Jews address to the forces that seek to crush their existence reveals their attitude to the crushing of all other peoples: Never again!

Humaneness and Compassion

Greenberg affirmed the State of Israel as the sign and symbol of Jewish survival. Yet the dialectical structure of faith after the Holocaust allowed him to combine in his language about Israel both unwavering affirmation and critical principles. The State of Israel is linked to Jewish existence today, but it is to be a special kind of State, a Jewish State. He realizes, of course, that as soon as Jews acquire national sovereignty and accept the reality of power organization, it becomes impossible to apply purely prophetic norms to the new political body: to do this—and some Jews and many Christians engage in this—would be to impose a double standard on the evaluation of politics that would inevitably be to the detriment of the Jewish State. Once there is political identity, the moral norms must be drawn from the realm of distributive justice, equity, and compromise solutions that reconcile conflicting but justified demands. At this level Greenberg insisted on the Jewish fidelity to humaneness and compassion. Later in the Conference, as we shall see, the topic of the State of Israel was discussed from various viewpoints.

In the history of the West, Greenberg reminded his listeners, the Jews have had a curious mission. They have very often been the first victims of a plague that would eventually come upon the entire population. As canaries and parakeets carried into the depths of the old mines would reveal by their sudden death the presence of poisonous gases and warn the miners of the invading danger, so the Jews have often been the first victims of a more universal threat to human society. Could the Holocaust have been a dress rehearsal for the final destruction of human life on this globe? Here Greenberg took up a theme that was repeatedly discussed at the Conference, namely, the threat to the sense of humanity and even to human survival created by the manipulative technology that has come to dominate Western culture. Extermination as the final solution may be built more deeply than we think into the quantified, technological, efficient world.

Beyond Untroubled Theism

Irving Greenberg raised many questions that are important for the Christian self-understanding after the Holocaust. Most of the Christian participants of the Conference were convinced that Auschwitz *ought* to constitute a turning point in the Church's self-understanding. Crucial for Christians was the fact that the persecution and extermination of the Jews by anti-Christian Nazis were related to the ancient teaching of contempt and the vilification of the Jews contained in Christian teaching and liturgy and that, for this reason, the confrontation with Auschwitz demanded of Christians the submission of their entire tradition to an ideological critique. This was the theme of the lectures by Rosemary Ruether, Gregory Baum and John Pawlikowski which I shall examine further on.

At this point, I wish to discuss another Christian response to the Holocaust, very similar to the one described by Irving Greenberg, which questions the existence of God. Is it possible after Auschwitz to believe in God? The Protestant theologian, Alan Davies, from the University of Toronto, who replied to Greenberg's paper, suggested that the idea of God's providence in Judaism is more closely linked to history than it is in Christianity. In the Christian religion, according to Davies, the cross stands at the center of history, making the entire enterprise fragmentary and thus even the resurrection has a meaning that is ultimately trans-historical. Other Christians disagreed. They felt that Christians confronting the Holocaust had just as much trouble believing in God as did Jews. For according to traditional teaching, God as the ruler of history, while never the author of evil, still gives permission for it and hence traditional Christian theologians find themselves in a position where they have to say that God permitted Auschwitz and that there is room in divine providence for the realm of the Holocaust. Can one believe in such a God?

When Irving Greenberg spoke of the need to overcome untroubled theism, he opened a subject that has become important for many contemporary Christian theologians even if they do not follow the language of the death-of-God thinkers of the 1960's. Christian theologians have come to see that an untroubled affirmation of God as Lord of history, as if present misery did not exist, may not be an expression of fidelity to God's Word. Such an untroubled theism could prevent us from looking reality in the face and drawing the consequences from our own historical experience. Untroubled theism could lead to unenlightened and dangerous social consequences. Untroubled theism could be due to the resistance to God's Word that seeks to make us sensitive to the demonic forces in the world. At the same time, Christians who open themselves to the misery in life, especially the enormous crimes such as Auschwitz that symbolize all the victories of evil over good, may well feel that belief in the God of their religion has become impossible. If a Christian's outrage is based on the commitment to love and justice and his denial of God on the idea that if he existed he must have granted permission for Auschwitz, then this unbelief is—paradoxically theologically grounded. Even the Catholic bishops assembled at Vatican II taught that the denial of God's existence did not by itself exclude a person from salvation, for what ultimately counts is whether such a person is reaching out for truth and love (cf. *Lumen Gentium*, n. 16). For in such a person, according to Catholic theological understanding, the transforming grace of God is operative, unbeknownst to him or her.

Karl Rahner in particular has tried to show in his theology that God creates in us the question long before he offers us an answer and that by making this question central in our lives we are already on the way of salvation. Living out of true questions save us from superficial questions and false perspectives. Living out of the profound question redeems us, even if we never find the answer or lose the answer that made sense to us at one time. Christian theologians, therefore, in keeping with their own theological tradition, are able to affirm the dialectical understanding of faith proposed by Irving Greenberg. In the minds and hearts of believers who are confronted with gigantic social evil and especially the Holocaust, faith is a back-and-forth between the affirmation of God who shall triumph over evil and the total inability to believe in such a God precisely because of their commitment to truth and love. Yet, this back-and-forth does not sever believers from the sources of grace. From the answer they are pushed back into the question. From acknowledging the God of love, they are pushed back into the restless quest for the love that they have been promised. Their unbelief is, paradoxically, theological. Even for Christians, then, the confrontation with Auschwitz leads to the overcoming of untroubled theism. Christians are willing to be confused, experience uncertainty and live without answers because it is their very faith that makes it impossible for them to believe. The Christian message itself has created the sensitivity that makes a simple and untroubled affirmation of God problematic. Some Christians feel more at home with the Gospel in this agnostic stance than in an unquestioning commitment to their creeds.

Let me add before leaving the subject that the Christian theologians who thus seek to overcome untroubled theism have developed a theology of God's redemptive immanence in human life. They therefore find it increasingly difficult to speak of God as Lord of history unless they qualify that this lordship is exercised not from an all powerful throne in heaven but from within history itself as the divine enabling of people, making them builders of a truly human world. The question that could be raised is whether it is easier for a Christian than for a Jewish theologian to develop a doctrine of God as divine presence and to think of God as the heart of the world rather than as the lord of the universe.

II
CHRISTIAN REFLECTION ON THE HOLOCAUST

Let us now turn to the main lecture given by a Christian theologian. Rosemary Ruether's paper, "The History of Christian Theology and the Demonization of the Jews," was the summary of a biblical and historical theme fully developed in her book *Faith and Fratricide* which has since been published by Seabury Press. This is how she formulated the conclusion of her vast study at the beginning of her lecture: "At its roots, anti-Semitism in Christian civilization springs directly from Christian theological anti-Judaism." She said: "The anti-Semitic legacy of Christian civilization cannot be dealt with as an accidental or peripheral element or as a product of purely sociological conflicts between the Church and the Synagogue. Neither can it be dismissed as a mere continuation of pagan anti-Jewishness or a transfer of ethno-centric attitudes from Judaism itself. Although elements of these two traditions feed into Christian anti-Judaic traditions, neither of these sources provides the main data or formative motivation for Christian anti-Judaism." The efforts of Christian apologists to explain anti-Semitism in terms of these sources constitute a refusal to examine the Christian theological roots of anti-Semitism in Christianity. It is this history that Dr. Ruether surveys in her lecture.

Christian Theological Anti-Judaism

With her customary precision she summarized at the outset of her lecture the historical development that has taken place: "It was Christian theology which developed the thesis of the eternal reprobate status of the Jew in history and laid the foundation for the demonic view of the Jews which fanned the flames of popular hatred. This hatred was not only inculcated by Christian preaching and biblical exegesis, but it became incorporated into the structure of Christian canon law and the civil law formed under Christendom and expressed as early as the Code of Theodosius (438 A.D.) and Justinian (6th century). The anti-Judaic laws of the Church and the Christian State laid the basis for the inferiorization of the civic and personal status of the Jews in Christian society from the time of Constantine until the emancipation of the Jews in the nineteenth century. Modern racial anti-Semitism is a continuation and a transformation of the medieval tradition of theological and economic scapegoating of the Jews."

How did Christian preaching generate the ever repeated negation of Jewish existence? Christians read the ancient Scriptures in a Christological perspective. Since for them Jesus Christ was the key for the understanding of the history of Israel, they argued against and repudiated the Jewish reading of the same Scriptures. As "the left hand of Christology"—the term is Dr. Ruether's—the Christian preachers supplied arguments why the Jewish reading of the Scriptures was unreliable and false, arguments that eventually turned into accusations against the Jews. From the acknowledgment that God was present in Israel and that salvation was derived from the Jews, Christian preaching passed on to stress that the Jews were a blind, carnal and stiff-necked people, that they had never heard God's message, that their history was an endless series of infidelities which climaxed in the rejection of Jesus and provoked the dissolution of the covenant.

Eventually the Jews became the symbol of all that is unredeemed, the enemies of God and humanity. This preaching, produced as the left hand of Christology, was continued in the age of the Church Fathers where it created a weighty *Adversus Judaeos* literature and was vastly expanded in the Middle Ages where a regular demonization of the Jews and of Judaism took place. The Jews were to remain forever exiles and reprobates in human history. They would never be allowed to return to their homeland in Palestine. Only at the end of time, at the return of Christ, would they get a second chance, be converted to their Messiah, and thus disappear as a distinct Jewish people. The final solution of the Jewish question would take place only at the end.

With the creation of the modern, secular society and the emergence of new social problems and tensions, we witness the rise of a racial anti-Semitism that has no direct religious roots. However, even this modern racial anti-Semitism takes much of its mythological imagery from the theological tradition. The politics of paranoia and displacement of judgment, carried out within secular conflicts of interest, followed the patterns set by the age-old symbolic tradition within Christianity. The projection of one's own doubts, failures and inner confusion upon a strange people, the Jews, has proven to be a potent instrument for social movements of various kinds, under ever new guises. Rosemary Ruether's important paper, if not her entire *Faith and Fratricide,* must be studied in detail, for there she documents her conclusions with references to history and the Christian tradition.

The Holocaust summons the Church, Ruether holds, to submit its theological tradition to an ideological critique. Is it possible to affirm the Christian message without accompanying it with the negation of Jewish existence? A Christology which makes Jesus the one in whom all things have been fulfilled and all promises have been realized seems to undermine the foundations of other religions, especially Judaism with its longing for the messianic age in the future. Can the Church find a Christology in keeping with its tradition that leaves room for Judaism and other religions? The same question was later posed by Pawlikowski and Baum. As a solution Rosemary Ruether proposed a radical turning to eschatology and the development of proleptic Christology. In our understanding of Christianity we must turn from a messianic triumphalism to a theology of hope. The fulfillment of the divine promises is not simply behind us as an event completed in the past but ahead of us as a horizon of redemption that judges our present shortcomings and calls us toward the renewal of life. Here the longing of Christians joins the longing of Jews for God's ultimate victory in the pacification of mankind.

Reinterpreting the Creed

Important points were raised by the respondents to Rosemary Ruether. Father Walter Burkhardt, a patristics scholar, had reservations in regard to some of the generalization in Ruether's paper. He felt that she had classified as evidence of the same value texts taken from very different literary documents—from weighty theological treatises to edifying or polemical sermons. But in his critical remarks—if I heard him correctly—Burkhardt did not disagree with Dr. Ruether's fundamental thesis that "at its roots anti-Semitism in Christian civilization springs directly from Christian theological anti-Judaism." Since his critical remarks did not touch the concern of the Conference, Burkhardt felt the need to propose his own personal creed in regard to Christians and Jews. In keeping with Vatican Council II, the Catholic theologian first acknowledged that the Jews are God's chosen people, that their religion is holy and a means of salvation, and that they have a mission and meaning in history; he then moved over, in an untroubled way, to the traditional Christological and ecclesiological affirmations that are part of the Christian creed. He did not seem to think that the acknowledgment of Judaism (and other religions) posed difficult problems to the Church's traditional teaching. But if we recognize as valid, meaningful and salvational the Jewish waiting for the messianic age, can we then simply repeat the Christological position according to which all things have been completed in Jesus? Can we place the *new* acknowledgment cheerfully and confidently side by side with the traditional teaching? Or must we admit that the new acknowledgment demands a rethinking of the Church's Christological position and that we are not quite certain how this can be done? Even here, in response to the Holocaust as the final historical outcome of the negation of Judaism, we must be willing to be troubled. Walter Burkhardt had been detained from attending Irving Greenberg's lecture and hence had not been initiated to the theme of troubledness in religious affirmations. If we are able to add the new and untraditional acknowledgment of Jewish religion to the inherited Christian creed without hesitation and without feeling the need to interpret it in a new light, then this new acknowledgment will be marginalized by the power of the traditional affirmations and have next to no effect on the life of the Church. If Christians hold that the Jewish religion is authentic, that it is not destined to disappear if Jews were more enlightened, that Jews are honored not as potential Christians but for what they are, then they must present their Christology in a new light. The serene recitation of the creed is then replaced by a more troubled reaching out for a formulation of the Gospel that leaves room for others.

Modern Racial Anti-Semitism

Yosef Yerushalmi, professor at Harvard University, replied to Rosemary Ruether's paper by raising a point that occupied the Conference throughout. He too approved of Ruether's basic thesis. What he wanted to stress, however, was the significant difference between the anti-Semitic tradition in the Church that allowed the Jewish people to survive and the racial anti-Semitism of modern times that led to their extermination. Rosemary Ruether had mentioned the transformation of anti-Semitism in the modern period, but to demonstrate her thesis she had put more weight on the continuity between religious and racial anti-Semitism.

Why did the Church protect the Jews even while placing

them in a situation of social inferiority? Why did the Church not eliminate the Jews as it had done with the Albigenses and Cathari? The answer is not clear. Yerushalmi thought that the Church's memory of its own Jewish religious matrix had something to do with it. It is remarkable that the medieval papacy and many bishops, while approving the subdued status of the Jews, protected the Jews against popular outbursts of hatred and persecution. The ecclesiastical hierarchy demanded justice for the Jews, at least the protection of life and property, within the discriminating legislation. Professor Yerushalmi thought that, considering the role of the popes in the Middle Ages in condemning popular and organized outbursts of hatred against the Jews, the silence of Pope Pius XII during the period of the Holocaust was quite untypical of the papal tradition. In Rome the Jews had always been safe. While they were excluded and marginalized, they were never expelled, they were free to worship, and they were left at peace to build their own community. Yet on October 25, 1943, over a thousand Jews, more than two-thirds of them women and children, were deported from Rome to Auschwitz. On October 28, the German ambassador, Ernst von Weizsacker, reported to Berlin that "although under pressure from all sides, the Pope (Pius XII) has not let himself be drawn into any demonstrative censure of the deportation of the Jews from Rome." Yerushalmi asked, "Are we confronted here by a medieval or a modern phenomenon?" In modern times alone has anti-Semitism led to extermination and holocaust.

What is the new element that modernity has added to traditional anti-Semitism? This theme kept recurring at the Conference. Irving Greenberg had already spoken of modern, technological society where problems are solved in terms of efficiency without attention to values. Yosef Yerushalmi alluded to the same manipulative, impersonal, utilitarian spirit of the modern age. The Lutheran theologian, Aarne Siirala, from Waterloo, Canada, analyzed the spirit of Western culture as the source of unprecedented achievement and unparalleled destruction. The Canadian philosopher, Lionel Rubinoff, in another context, accused what he called "the functional rationality" of the modern age, which uses reason as an instrument for the measurement and manipula-

tion of reality. Here all quality is translated into quantity. Here the
human being is dissolved into needs and wants. Here people tend
to become objects, appear as items in an inventory, and serve the
needs and efficiency of the system. The solution of functional
problems dominates over the fate of individuals. It is this spirit,
deeply inscribed in modern institutions, that accounts for the difference between traditional religious anti-Semitism and the dread-
ful political forces of the twentieth century which manipulated,
subjugated, and even eliminated altogether tens of millions of
people, including the Jews. What we see in the Holocaust, then, is
the underside of our own society, the visible, grotesque outbreak
of a monstrous illness that in a more hidden form exists in all our
institutions. Yesterday the Jews were destroyed, tomorrow possibly all of humanity.

The Church's Mission

Closely related to Rosemary Ruether's critical reflection on
the Church's life and teaching were the lectures of Baum and
Pawlikowski. The topic of Baum's lecture was "Christian Mission
in Crisis." He began by pointing out that after Auschwitz the
major Christian Churches no longer want to convert the Jews;
they have come to acknowledge Judaism as an authentic religion.
This is true for Christian groups associated with the World Council of Churches as well as for Catholic groups following the Vatican II documents. But this new attitude raises questions regarding the mission and the universality of the Christian Church. Auschwitz, however, is not the only event that demands the rethinking of ecclesiology. The protest of the Third World has made
Christians conscious of the facts that traditional Church teaching
at one time legitimated the colonial invasion of America, Africa
and Asia on the part of the European nations. According to the
Church's self-understanding then, the Christian people were
situated at the center of world history; they were the carriers of
truth and salvation, while the rest of the world was significant
only to the extent that it was related to the Christian society. The
white man's conquest of the continents was regarded as God's
providential design to prepare the spread of the Christian Gospel.

Today Christian theologians ask themselves whether it is possible to formulate the Church's mission without any trace of triumphalism and without the intention of converting people away from the great world religions.

Contemporary theologians tend to define the Church's mission in terms of God's kingdom, that is, in terms of God's approaching victory over the powers of darkness. The Church's mission is to serve this kingdom. This is done by service and cooperation with others in the humanization of life; this is done through conflict and struggle with others against the forces of evil and oppression; and this is done in honest and open dialogue with other religions. Here each partner learns to discern more clearly the ambiguity of his own religious tradition, to distinguish between the authentic and inauthentic trends in his religion, and finally to renew his religious heritage in the light of the contemporary demands of love and justice. Religious dialogue serves the renewal of the religions involved. The specifically Christian witness to the coming of God's kingdom, Baum thought, was such that it could be followed by people wherever they are; they can serve this kingdom in the religion to which they belong.

This approach enabled Baum to define the Church's universality in a way that left room for religious pluralism. The Church is universal not in the sense that it is destined to replace all religions and embrace the whole of humanity, but in the sense that its witness to God's coming kingdom has universal meaning and power and can be followed by people everywhere. It is possible for the Church, therefore, to accept religious pluralism not as a concession forced on it by the circumstances of history but joyfully and freely as a manifestation of God's inexhaustible grace. This new approach does not undermine the missionary endeavor of the Church nor its consciousness of having received a universal message, but it does remove from its language the triumphalism that had such devastating consequences in Western history.

Baum also insisted, following Ruether, that this new approach demands a reinterpretation of the Church's Christological doctrine. Ruether had already spoken of a proleptic Christology. By recovering the eschatological perspective, we link Jesus with the messianic age and refuse to separate his earthly life from his victory over the powers of darkness and his final manifestation at the end of time. What happened in his personal history symbolized and anticipated what is to take place at the horizon of history. Jesus Christ is God's word orienting Christians toward the future and grounding their hope in the coming of the kingdom.

Most of the Christians participating in the Conference were very conscious of the unfinished character of present redemption and therefore welcomed a Christology that refuses to separate Jesus from the final Coming. A few had difficulties here. I have mentioned Walter Burkhardt who felt no need for a new perspective on the Christian creed. Johannes Hoekendijk of Union Theological Seminary, who replied to Baum's lecture, also expressed his hesitations. He agreed, of course, that Auschwitz has revealed a malice hidden deep in the Western tradition and that Christian theology has made its contribution to this. But he thought that the world had always been sinful, that awful things had always happened and that nothing new had taken place in the twentieth century. The whole of Church history is a series of mistakes; the truth was only at the beginning in Jesus Christ. But by denying that something new had taken place in history, something that made previously unheard of demands on us, Hoekendijk was able to hold out against the re-examination of the Church's foundation. The Church's history should be criticized, but not the biblical books on which it is based. Most of the Christian participants, however, believed that God's word addressing the Church through the Holocaust demands an ideological critique even of the Bible and the Church's foundation.

Reinterpreting Christian Teaching

Baum's lecture on the Church's mission in crisis was paralleled by Pawlikowski's lecture on the reform of catechetics and liturgics. Both Baum and Pawlikowski accepted the thesis, developed by Ruether, that the roots of modern anti-Semitism, despite its peculiarly modern character, lie in the Church's theological tradition and that for this reason the confrontation with Auschwitz summons the Churches to re-examine their teaching.

Father Pawlikowski gave an analysis of what has taken place in Catholic and Protestant religious education since World War II as a result of the new appreciation of Judaism. First he listed the studies from various parts of the world that have examined the traditional Christian educational material and established that the distortion of Judaism belongs to the common patrimony of Catholics and Protestants. There was, first of all, the usual silence about post-biblical and contemporary Judaism. In much of the older educational material we find the ancient myths: the myth of the dispersion of the Jews as punishment (even though the diaspora began centuries before Christ), the myth of a degenerate Judaism at the time of Jesus, accompanied by a false picture of the Pharisees, and the myth of deicide which inflicted on an entire people the blame for the crucifixion. Pawlikowski then mentioned the various ecclesiastical efforts to refute these myths and produce catechetical literature that expresses the new and more truthful approach to Judaism.

He then presented the same sort of analysis for the Christian liturgies; he described the anti-Jewish myths contained in Christian worship and recorded the reforms that have been introduced in the liturgy as a result of the new spirit. While much has changed among theological specialists and ecclesiastical policy makers, Pawlikowski thought that the impact of the new spirit on the people has been quite limited.

Why is this so? Pawlikowski proposed that the various anti-Jewish myths are rooted in the theological perspective in which Christians understand themselves—he called this "fulfillment theology"—and that as long as the Church promotes this self-understanding, Christian teaching and Christian worship will continue to generate anti-Jewish symbols. Christians regard themselves as the people in whom have been fulfilled the promises made to Israel and the yearnings of the cosmos. It is this fulfillment theology that makes Christians link Jews, even contemporary Jews, to the period of the Old Testament and disregard their religious development since that time; that leads Christians to think of their Church as having been substituted for the chosen people of the old covenant; that prompts Christians to look upon Judaism as a fossil, a retardation, a religion that got stuck in the past. Can this "fulfillment theology" be overcome, Pawlikowski asked, or is it an authentic statement of the Christian message?

John Pawlikowski arrived at the same question as Ruether and Baum, and like them he sought an answer in the direction of a renewed eschatology. Only if we retain a sense of unfulfillment, Pawlikowski thinks, only if we preserve an awareness of present unredemption and misery and a yearning for the ultimate fulfillment, will we cease to think of ourselves as the people in whom all the divine promises have been fulfilled. Only if we see ourselves with Jesus as servants of God's approaching kingdom, will we be able to leave room for other religions and in particular for Jewish existence. But how can Christians be made to reinterpret their teaching and acquire a new self-understanding as a pilgrim people reaching out for the future? Pawlikowski thought that it was precisely the confrontation with the Holocaust that could produce such a *metanoia* in the Christian people. At the same time, he admitted that Auschwitz is not mentioned at all in the religious educational material of the Christian Churches. Auschwitz is kept a secret.

Claire Huchet-Bishop responded to John Pawlikowski. She strongly underlined the various points he had made. However the second respondent, Father Thomas Hopka, an Eastern Orthodox theologian, registered his difficulties. While he welcomed the removal from Christian teaching and worship of whatever nourishes contempt for the Jewish people, he objected to Father Pawlikowski's criticism of fulfillment theology and his proposal for a more eschatological, proleptic understanding of the Gospel. Father Hopka held that the Church was committed irrevocably to believe in Jesus Christ as the One who fulfilled the promises made to Israel and the hopes of all the world and thus as the ultimate and definitive self-manifestation of God in history. This faith, Hopka said, need not lead to the contempt of people who do not share this belief: Christians respect the freedom of others, they are called to love even those who see life from a different perspective, and they have the duty to collaborate with all citizens in the building of a just society. But in no way must this new readiness to honor Judaism and the world religions be used to undermine the nature of the Christian faith. Father Hopka spoke here in a dignified and forceful way not only for the misgivings of Burk-hardt and Hoekendijk but more especially for a great number of Christian theologians who did not attend the Conference.

Are Christian theologians, then, confronted with a dramatic either/or? I do not think so. If Christians respect Judaism as an authentic religion and live honestly out of this new acknowledgment, they will eventually, through a change of awareness rather than intellectual effort, interpret the traditional Christian creed in a new perspective as affirming rather than negating religious pluralism. Once we change our attitude and action, we often come to look upon the world and the meaning of the Gospel in a new light; this may not be consciously chosen but this happens to us according to the inner logic of involvement. There is no reason to think that this new perspective will falsify the traditional creed. The shift to eschatology is in keeping with the Scriptures and the credal tradition. The giving of ultimate and definitive titles to Jesus remains valid in the new perspective as long as we remember that these titles include and anticipate his return at the end of time and express the total redemption which he came to initiate and complete at the horizon of history. I do not see how the consistent refusal to separate Jesus from his final coming can undermine the orthodox Christian tradition.

III
THEOLOGICAL REFLECTION ON ISRAEL

A Conference on theology after the Holocaust had to assign a special place to reflection on the State of Israel. Emil Fackenheim from the University of Toronto was the main speaker on the topic. The planners of the Conference had tried to invite representative Eastern Christians to participate in the discussion but received only regrets. Gabriel Habib, a consultant to the World Council of Churches on the Middle East, explained his inability to attend in a message addressed to the Conference. He felt that the Conference involved solely the Western conscience in its Judaeo-Christian element as it has developed in Europe and North America since World War II. From his point of view, Auschwitz should not be separated from the other crimes of the twentieth century such as Hiroshima and Vietnam, which all manifest the same madness of the industrialized nations. The Jews should not be singled out in this great tragedy. If Gabriel Habib had been present at the Conference, he would have been able to discover that, whatever the truth of his contemporary analysis, the Christian negation of the Jewish people is not a recent, Western issue but is part and parcel of the ancient Christian tradition of East and West and has found particularly vehement expression in the sermons and liturgies of the Christian East. At the same time, Habib's recommendations that the dialogue between Christians and Jews be extended to include Muslims and that Christians of East and West should get together among themselves to examine the various ideological deformations of their separate traditions, demand attention.

The State of Israel

Emil Fackenheim began his lecture with the quotation from a prayer by the Israeli Chief Rabbinate: "Our Father in Heaven, Rock of Israel and her Redeemer, bless the State of Israel, the beginning of the dawn of our redemption." This is a new accent in Jewish liturgy. Here the messianic ingathering is linked to an event already present; here the divine promises no longer refer purely and simply to the future. Whether God's final victory is understood as a gradual unfolding of history or as a miraculous triumph over catastrophe—the Scriptures entertain both possibilities—it is possible to discern messianic birth-pangs in the present, however ambiguous, that are signs of the eventual victory. Fackenheim did not fail to stress the ambiguity and contingency of the present; "The link between the forever precarious historical present and the messianic future is itself forever precarious." At the same time this must not discourage us from looking for the messianic signs: "Unless the messianic future is ever elusive and irrelevant, its linking with a *possible* present, however precarious, is indispensable." Without dissolving the tension between precarious anticipation and transcendent messianic future, Jews have come to look upon the State of Israel as a visible sign of the age to come, as "the beginning of the dawn of our redemption."

Why is the State of Israel not a purely political or secular reality for Jews? Fackenheim admitted that at first most Zionists desired the normalization of the Jewish people, that it become "a nation like any other nation." The religious "more" of the State of Israel was not so much expressed in Zionist thought as in Zionist life and dedication from the days of the early settlers through the Yom Kippur War. The Zionist reality has overcome the clear distinction between the religious and the secular, and for this reason it is not surprising that it is opposed today only by extreme religious Jews and extreme secular Jews. Fackenheim's theology of the Holocaust—the reader remembers our earlier discussion —insisted that this vast crime beyond imagination was histori- cally unique and unaccountable in terms of historical causalities. He now made the same claim for the creation of the State of Israel: it also was unique and unaccountable. For while it was historically likely that the nations, out of their guilt over the Holocaust, would favor the foundation of a Jewish State, it was equally or even more likely that the Jews, after suffering under the Holocaust, would wish to flee from their Jewishness and refuse to struggle for a Jewish State. The political sovereignty of the Jews in Palestine is a marvelous, unexpected and yet longed for event which anticipates the messianic promises of the return to the land and God's victory over evil.

Faithful to his own theology, Fackenheim refuses to invest the Holocaust with any sense or meaning. The Holocaust is *not* theologically linked to the creation of the State of Israel in a redemptive mystery of death and resurrection: before the Holocaust all theological theories collapse. At the same time, a response to the Holocaust is necessary, and this response has profound implications for the State of Israel. Fackenheim said: "The heart of every authentic response to the Holocaust— religious and secularist, Jewish and non-Jewish—is a commit- ment to the autonomy and security of the State of Israel." The reader recalls that Irving Greenberg had also regarded the affir- mation of the State of Israel, sign and symbol of Jewish survival, as an authentic response to Auschwitz, but he had added that the response to Auschwitz included a "Never again!" in regard to the oppression of any people and hence provided principles of political critique. Fackenheim did not deny this, but he did not make it central to his thesis; he only mentioned the commitment to autonomy and security.

Shlomo Avineri, professor at the Hebrew University in Jerusalem and a well-known Israeli socialist author, developed the implications of the Jewish commitment to justice even further, albeit from a purely secular perspective. He felt that the Jews everywhere should not only be committed to the State of Israel as the outcome of the Zionist movement of Jewish liberation but at the same time should be in favor of the Palestinian liberation movement. As a citizen of Israel and a resident of Jerusalem, he was able to speak with great freedom (and none of the guilt feelings of Jews living in the diaspora) of the two just, though tragically conflicting claims of Jews and Palestinians to the same earth. He insisted that the Jews who love justice should favor a compromise between the two peoples and the co-existence of two nation states as it had first been proposed by the United Nations. Avineri, in a lecture on Israel and socialism, showed that the New Left and some radical Christian theologians apply the model of oppressor and oppressed to the analysis of every political situation, including the Middle East, and thus place Israel in the role of the oppressor. Among others, he mentioned Daniel Berrigan's position that follows this type of reasoning and links it to traditional Christian symbols. In reality, Avineri explained, the Arab-Israeli conflict is a complex conflict between two just but contradictory claims, for the analysis of which the oppressor/oppressed model inevitably leads to falsification. The solution of the conflict must be sought not in the prophetic order of total right and total wrong but in the order of recognition and concession and the willingness to cooperate. He mentioned that it would be a mistake to make the Palestinian terrorists the symbol of the Palestinian people, for the great number of them aspire to a political solution not in terms of victor and vanquished but a compromise and co-existence. In this connection Avineri recalled his own opposition twenty-five years ago to the Israelis who in their struggle against the British had adopted terrorist methods. He then felt, as great numbers of Palestinians feel now, that there must be another way.

Birth Pangs of Messiah

From another point of view, however, Emil Fackenheim had gone further than Irving Greenberg in dealing with the reality of the State of Israel. For Fackenheim, as we saw above, the ingathering of the Jewish people in the land was sign and anticipation, however precarious, of the messianic age promised for the future. Greenberg had not gone that far. Emil Fackenheim involved himself in a reflection on the redemptive present and the messianic future that sounded strangely familiar to Christian ears; he discussed, from a Jewish perspective, the possibility of a betweentime, a time defined by the tension between the joy in the precarious anticipation and the yearning for the total redemption of the future. Eva Fleischner, professor at Montclair State College, New Jersey, in her interesting response to Fackenheim, brought out this parallel very clearly. Fackenheim's wrestling with how a precarious event in history can be said to be the dawn of the final redemption is similar to the Christian wrestling with how, in a world marked by misery and injustice, it is possible to affirm Jesus and his community as the first-fruit, the anticipation, and the pledge of ultimate reconciliation at the parousia. Eva Fleischner explained that this has become a problem especially in contemporary Christian theology. For by taking seriously the pressure of history, theologians have tried to overcome the spiritualization and de-politicization of the Gospel that began to set in so early in the Christian tradition. Theologians today try to understand the social meaning of the tension between the "already" and the "not yet." Eva Fleischner as a Christian theologian had no intention of joining the Jewish conversation, but she did remark that Fackenheim's theology of Israel created a new link between Jewish and Christian self-understanding. For her, Fackenheim's position explained how a rabbi who had been invited to address a Christian assembly was able to say, "Israel is our Jesus."

This messianic theme was taken up by Arthur Waskow of the Institute for Policy Study, Washington, D.C. Waskow was willing, with Fackenheim to do what Jews have often hesitated to do, namely to scan history for possible birth pangs of messiah. "The messianic tradition," he said, "has been buried and repressed in Jewish history out of the sense of a small people that messiah is dangerous—out of the memory of the different kinds of disastrous results that were visited upon Jewry by Christianity, Bar Kochba, and Shabtai Tzvi." In the Christian tradition, Waskow felt, the messianic expectations were buried out of a sense of bigness. The success of Christianity made Christians feel that messiah had come and forget that the redemption from the powers and principalities had been promised for the future. Today, some Jews are recovering a sense of messianic expectation and willingly scan history for the birth pangs of messiah, i.e., for crucial events that translate into reality a measure of the messianic fulfillment and also create a new vulnerability to great destruction. Waskow shared, with Fackenheim, the sense of the precarious nature of the anticipatory events. But while Fackenheim saw the messianic birth pangs only in the return of the Jewish people to the land, Waskow did not want to separate this sign from the other messianic birth pangs such as the overcoming of the subjugation of women, the overcoming of people's exploitation of nature, the overcoming of exploitative and alienating labor, and the overcoming of war and violence. In theological reflections on the Genesis account of God's creation, Waskow tried to show that the expectation of the messianic age includes the redemption from the various wounds inflicted upon humanity by sin: the subjugation of Eve, the enmity between man and nature, the labor in the sweat of one's brow, and the rivalry between Cain and Abel. Waskow accepted with Fackenheim the birth of the State of Israel as a messianic sign, but he thought it was quite impossible to separate this sign from the others. If Jews perform this separation, Waskow feared, they are in danger of destroying Israel as the dawn of the final redemption.

In reply to this wider messianic theology, Fackenheim would say, I suppose, that the radical position adopted by Waskow speaks of Israel's well-being at a moment when its very being is so insecure and threatened. Fackenheim and Waskow had different perceptions of the present historical situation. For Fackenheim, central is the menaced situation of Israel and, with it, that of Jewish life everywhere. For Waskow, ours is an age of great turning when societies are in labor and the birth pangs of messiah are felt everywhere, including Israel. He recalled that the Marxists are also wrestling for human liberation, but since they reject any form of social analysis other than the class conflict, they see no possibility of infusing the struggle for liberation with love, nor of recognizing the divine Comrade as partner in the remaking of human society. Without God, Waskow said, the grain of narcissism in human efforts and human success, especially in the political order, too easily becomes idolatry.

The Christian participants did not join in the Jewish conversation on the theological meaning of the State of Israel. In her response to Fackenheim from a Christian point of view, Eva Fleischner recalled Karl Barth's position that the State of Israel is an eschatological sign, a second entrance into the promised land, a miracle, a new sign of electing and providentially ruling grace—which goes much further than Fackenheim's modest claims. But she did not commit herself to Barth's position. Confronted with the Holocaust, she said, Christians must be determined to speak out whenever Jews are endangered. The Christian commitment, after Auschwitz and after the Six Day War, implies a refusal to remain silent when Israel is in danger. In this sense, then, and out of a special sense of religious sisterhood with Jews, she strongly affirmed the autonomy and security of Israel as a symbol of Jewish survival and freedom, and she did so, I think, in the name of all the Christian participants of the Conference. But she did not engage in theological reflection. What is necessary above all, she said, is that Christians listen more to Jews discussing Israel.

Fleischner did not hide from the audience that while she prayed for the autonomy and security of Israel, she often worried not only about its possible destruction but also about the possiblity that its determination to survive through military struggle could give rise to a new and un-Jewish triumphalism. A few years ago, Fleischner reported, a young correspondent of Elie Wiesel was worried that Israel might develop a conqueror's mentality. Wiesel replied to him in a letter, since published, that his fears were groundless: "Victory in the Jewish tradition does not depend on defeat inflicted on an adversary. Each victory is first of all a victory over oneself." The Christian commitment to Israel—this is how I heard Eva Fleischner's response—is a commitment to an autonomous and secure Israel that is the bearer of the great Jewish tradition.

Socialism and Zionism

The Conference's discussion of the State of Israel remained on the whole in the theological perspective. This had been intended. One political question was raised, however. Why were the socialist movements, from the establishment communism of Russia to the so-called New Left otherwise so critical of Russian policies, opposed to Zionism and the Jewish State? Were the non-communist socialism of the West and in particular the New Left of the 1960's opposed to Israel because of inherited ambiguous feelings in regard to the Jews? Shlomo Avineri believed so. As the philosophers of the Enlightenment in the eighteenth century advocated a secular society and rejected Christianity and yet, unconsciously, carried forward the inherited negation of Judaism and things Jewish, so did some of the radical socialists of the nineteenth and twentieth centuries. Avineri analyzed the work of Bruno Bauer who wrote during the middle of the last century. Bauer looked upon Christianity as a stage in history that had been overcome in the new, secular age, but because he unconsciously adopted the Christian perspective, he regarded Judaism as a stage that preceded Christianity and hence as even more retrograde, more to be depised, and for this reason he could not favor the emancipation of the Jews in modern society. This sort of inherited contempt for the Jews as Jews pervaded the writings of the radical socialists of the nineteenth and twentieth centuries. The symbols inherited from the Christian theological tradition were still operative. Avineri thought that it was this symbolism that made the New Left so ready to apply the model of oppressor and oppressed to the analysis of the Middle East and look upon Israel as representative of Western colonialism and imperialism and the Palestinians as the champions of Third World liberation, while in reality—we quoted Avineri here earlier—it was a conflict between between two national movements. Avineri thought that socialism on the whole had great difficulty in recognizing the legitimacy of Jewish existence in a secularized, post-Christian world.

Paul Jacobs, an editor of *Ramparts*, took another point of view. He thought that the opposition of non-communist socialism to Zionism and the Jewish State had nothing whatever to do with inherited anti-Semitic presuppositions. He tried to show that the nineteenth and twentieth-century socialist rejection of Zionism as a legitimate movement of self-determination worthy of support, was derived from a different political analysis of the world situation. Socialists did not look upon Zionism as a movement of national liberation. One of the reasons for this was that until fairly recently the Zionists themselves did not think in those terms. They aspired to political sovereignty in Palestine to create a refuge for Jews fleeing from European anti-Semitism but did not regard this movement as a return to the homeland. Even the Bund, the Jewish socialist organization in pre-revolutionary Russia, opposed the Zionist movement. Zionism did not stress the class struggle; instead of struggling in their homelands for the socialist reconstruction of society. Zionists went to Israel to create a socialist state there. In the heated discussions between socialists and Zionists over many decades, no one ever mentioned that the socialist opposition could be partly due to anti-Semitism. Only when Hitler arrived and especially after World War II did the non-communist socialist movements support the political existence of Israel as a refuge for the persecuted Jews. But even then, the socialist movements were not interested in Zionism. The so-called New Left, created in the United States in the early 1960's, was mainly concerned with American power, American foreign policy, civil rights in America, etc., and paid next to no attention to the Middle East conflict. The occasional political criticism of Israel did not worry the Jews living in the State of Israel. It was only after 1967 that the American Jews began to look upon the New Left as the great enemy of Israel.

Paul Jacobs concluded that the critical stance adopted by non-communist socialism toward Israel was due simply to an application of socialist principles and in no way derived from ambiguous feelings regarding Jews.

The discussion remained somewhat inconclusive, especially since Avineri accepted much of Jacobs' analysis. What Avineri failed to see, however, was why socialism and Zionism should be by nature incompatible. While socialism transcends the nations, it does so only after they exist. This is why Marx supported the Polish, German and Italian nationalist movements in the nineteenth century. The refusal to recognize the Jewish aspirations for national self-determination as a way toward the socialist transformation of society. Avineri thought, was a bad case of double standard.

This discussion, while inconclusive, had some theological significance. For in a good number of the Protestant Churches in America, especially among progressive churchmen, the attitude of the New Left to Israel had been very influential. Avineri also mentioned the position of Daniel Berrigan, which combined the perspective of the New Left and the ancient Christian symbolism.

Pivot in Christian Theology

The Conference on theology after the Holocaust included the examination of other important topics such as the relation of Jews and blacks in the United States, the criticism of the Bible in the contemporary counter-culture, and the psychopathology of anti-Semitism in history. The Proceedings of the Conference have now been published. This article has been a personal account. It is not a summary of the important lectures and responses; because of lack of space, interesting and insightful material had to be passed over in silence. I hope that the authors will forgive me. I may not even have succeeded in presenting the ideas of the authors treated here with the stress and the nuances which are theirs. The reason that I took this risk was my intention to communicate the concern of the Conference to a wider audience and to promote among theologically-oriented Christians reflection on the Holocaust as a turning point in Christian self-understanding.

Political Theology in Canada

Has Christian theology a political responsibility? Does the Christian way of life imply socio-political options and commitments? These were the questions examined at a two-day Conference held at Saskatoon, in the Province of Saskatchewan, Canada, on March 10 and 11, 1977. How should these questions be answered in the Canadian context? The Conference was planned by the department of religious studies at the University of Saskatchewan. The moving spirit behind it was Ben Smillie, professor of social ethics at St. Andrew's College, Saskatoon, and well known in Canada as a politically committed theologian who seeks to bridge the old Canadian Social Gospel and the new political theology. There were about two hundred participants, most of them from Western Canada. A good number were from the East.

Before giving an account of the Conference, let me recall to the reader that Saskatchewan is the province in which the Canadian socialist party, the Cooperative Commonwealth Federation (CCF), was founded in 1933, supported by a populist movement made up of farmers and workers and elected to form the provincial government in 1944. The success of this socialist movement was a unique event in North America. The best known book on Saskatchewan socialism published in the 1950's was S. M. Lipset's *Agrarian Socialism*. While the New Democratic Party (NDP), the successor party to the CCF, is still in power in Saskatchewan, it no longer sees itself as a democratic socialist movement: it has become a social democratic party that resembles in style the other political parties in Canada. Many of the old CCFers in the NDP in Saskatchewan and the rest of Canada remember the days when their party stood for a radical critique of society and the replacement of the present economic system. Since the Social Gospel was strongly active in the CCF from the beginning, many Christian groups, especially in Saskatchewan have kept alive the old spirit.

This piece of Canadian history forms the background to the Conference on political theology.

The Conference was organized in university style. The invited lecturers presented their talks, others were asked to respond to them, and time was scheduled for questions and answers. One afternoon, workshops were held dealing with important social issues in Canada. The entire Conference was more academic and less action-oriented than it would have been, had it been organized through a process that involved the various regions of Canada and, in particular, the underprivileged groups. Still, the voice of the voiceless was heard again and again at the Conference.

The Drift of Modern Theology

William Hordern, a Lutheran theologian presently teaching at Saskatoon, gave the first lecture in which he located political theology in the development of recent Protestant thought. In the nineteenth and early twentieth century, Protestant theology had become "liberal." Protestant theology, open to biblical criticism and modern philosophical schools, had developed an immanentist view of God and identified itself with the progressive, evolutionary perspective of dominant Western culture. Theology then addressed itself first of all to educated people. It argued, in the words of Schleiermacher, with "the cultured despisers of religion"; it shared the concerns of the middle class.

Karl Barth, after World War I, repudiated liberal culture, liberal theology and liberal economics. Barth was repelled by the death-dealing aspects of modern society, and he insisted that God was not the spirit that made the modern world alive. God was the wholly other. God's Word was the judgment on the dominant culture. For Barth, this judgment included the repudiation of liberal economic theory which recommended that individuals pursue their own advantage and trusted that the market system would regulate the well-being of the community. A system based on the promotion of selfishness cannot produce justice. Barth thought that the aims of socialists were identical with the aims of Christians. But since Barth did not admit God's presence in any historical development, he did not hear God's voice in the protest movement of the European proletariat. Still, Barth's rejection of contemporary culture did create support for the socialist imagination of society. Neo-orthodox theologians, Hordern told his audience, soon forgot the political edge contained in Barthian thought and made the otherness of God the reason for regarding theology as superior to economic concerns.

Most of the Social Gospel theologians, according to Hordern, were still liberals. Why? They shared the optimistic, evolutionary, immanentist trend of liberal theology and hoped that through human effort the Kingdom of God could be established on earth. They lacked a sense of God's otherness and of the brokenness of the human condition. Some listeners thought that this critique applied only to certain preachers of the Social Gospel; it did not apply, for instance, to the Canadian Social Gospel of the 1930's. Neo-orthodox theologians, in any case, found the Social Gospel too trusting in regard to history and historical movements.

From Barth, Hordern moved to the theology of hope, mainly associated with Jürgen Moltmann. Here God remains the wholly other, but since God is at the same time the fulfillment of the promises, the horizon of history, the absolute human future, the divine has historical power. History remains ever open to the new. Social change, even radical social change, is possible. We are not forever caught in the earthly prisons; the unjust social order is not here to stay. This theology was critical of the political status quo and economic injustices, and it elicited political reflection. Still, the Latin American theologian, Rubem Alves, criticized the theology of hope for being too abstract. God was only the horizon of history, and he was not really present in the struggles of people for justice and peace. Maybe it was necessary to introduce again a stress on divine immanence, even though from a different perspective. The theology of hope, Alves argued, spoke of present injustices and necessary social change without analyzing the concrete form of social oppression. This theology did not help Christians to act and make strategies in an evil world.

Still, present in the theology of hope was the recognition that traditional theology entertained such an individualistic understanding of the divine promises that the social meaning of these promises had been overlooked and neglected. The Catholic theologian J. B. Metz devised a program to "de-privatize" Christian theology, i.e., to remove the individualistic bias from Christian teaching and recover the social dimension of the biblical message. Metz called this undertaking "political theology." His political theology clearly recognized that modern individualistic culture had so influenced the reading of the Gospel that Christianity had become a symbol system legitimating present-day society and its anti-social orientation.

From Metz's political theology, Hordern moved to the theological movements of the 1960's produced not by European thinkers but by Christian communities belonging to underprivileged and marginal people. Here the perspective of theology was wholly changed. No longer did theologians belong to the dominant culture and address members of their own class (believing that their concerns were truly universal); here theologians, identified with a struggling people, saw human history from the perspective of the conquered, the little ones, the poor. We have black theology which makes the institutionalized racism of America the all-pervasive sin over against which God is discovered as redeemer and liberator. In Latin America theologians discovered the international economic system, which produces dependency and impoverishment among their people, as the death-dealing bondage from which the Christian message promises deliverance. There are liberation theologies produced in the various parts of Africa. There is liberation theology produced by Christian women, conscious of the subjugation inflicted on them by Church and society. These various liberation theologies, Hordern explained, have taught all Christian theologians significant insights, of which he mentioned two.

There is first the recognition that we always theologize and philosophize from a particular social location. Our perspective is largely defined by our place in history. When thinkers belong to the dominant section of society, they are tempted to regard their perspective as "objective" and universal. In fact, they are in need of the protests made by people at other social locations, especially the oppressed, to recognize that their own perspective is limited and even marred by their own privileges. Theologians then discover that not only theology but preaching and piety have a social location; they usually reflect the culture of this location and protect the existing political order. Religion is inevitably political, even if religious people are wholly unconscious of this. Unless religion becomes self-critical, it is the bearer of ideological elements. Political theology has the task to examine the implicit political orientation of religious thought, language and piety, and then to test it with the Gospel. Does the Gospel provide us with norms for this task? Confronted with various perspectives of seeing the social reality, followers of the Gospel, Hordern thought, should opt for the perspective of the wretched of the earth, the powerless, the voiceless, the exploited. He held that this is the message of the New Testament. Jesus brought the good news to the poor, the burdened, the marginal. This perspective of the crucified one remains normative for the Christian community.

A second important insight derived from the liberation theologies has to do with the social impact of thought. In classical theology we used to distinguish pure truth from its application. In liberation theology it has become clear that thoughts, symbols, and any form of inwardness have built into them a bent toward action. Thought has impact on society: ideas and symbols mediate the social reality to us and steer our action. Hence it is impossible to speak of Christian truth in the full sense unless it makes people perceive the world as a place of sin and injustice and impels them toward transforming it. The final test of truth is liberating practice. Christian creed and Christian prayer are assimilated in an authentic manner only if they open our eyes to the sin, personal and social, create in us a sense of solidarity with the humiliated, and summon forth hunger and thirst for justice and the yearning for a more humane society.

Modern theology, Hordern tried to show, has taken a shift to the left. In a subsequent lecture, Dorothee Soelle, a Christian theologian from Germany, who is presently teaching at Union Theological Seminary in New York City, described how this shift has led a good number of Christians to a socialist position. But before reporting on her lecture, let us follow the shift to the left in the official teaching of the Catholic Church, summarized at the Conference in a response by Gregory Baum.

A Shift in Catholic Teaching

In 1965, Vatican Council II produced a document, *Gaudium et Spes*, that looked upon the modern world in a positive way and encouraged Catholics to take an active part in it. The Catholic Church declared itself in solidarity with the whole of mankind and defined as its mission to serve the human community and tighten the bonds that bind man to man and peoples to peoples in the creation of a just and peaceful world. *Gaudium et Spes* was written by bishops and theologians associated with the developed Western nations, and it reflected the optimistic view characteristic of the 1960's. The answer to the world's problems was development and expansion.

Three years later, in 1968, at the Medellin Conference, the Latin American bishops looked at the same modern world and tried to define the role of the Christian community in it, this time from a very different perspective, that of the underdeveloped countries. The Medellin Conference recognized that the development and expansion, promoted by the North Atlantic nations, was in fact creating a state of dependency and increased exploitation in Latin America. Latin America had become part of a worldwide economic system which oppressed the hinterland for the benefit of the metropolis. While the Western nations were becoming more prosperous, the third world nations were thrust more deeply into misery. The Medellin Conference recognized that in this situation the Christian community must be in solidarity with the poor and exploited and struggle with them for their liberation. This new Latin American perspective had a strong influence on the Catholic Church's official teaching, especially at the Third Synod of bishops held at Rome in 1971.

This Third Synod of bishops became a turning point for Catholic social teaching. In a document entitled *Justice in the World*, the bishops adopted positions that went far beyond Vatican II. They introduced the notion of "social sin" and declared that the Gospel of Jesus Christ redeems us from sin, including this "social sin." We are told that the Christian understanding of redemption includes "the liberation from all oppressive conditions of human life." Salvation, in other words, has a social dimension, and divine grace has a political direction. While Catholic theology has never wholly forgotten the social side of divine salvation, popular piety and congregational preaching have only too often presented salvation as God's merciful rescue action delivering individuals from the catastrophe decreed upon the world. Such a privatized view of salvation is wholly irresponsible in today's world. The Synod adds that "action on behalf of justice and participation in the transformation of society" is "a constitutive element" of the Gospel life. In other words, holiness has a social dimension. The Christian life includes a socio-political commitment toward the reconstruction of society in terms of greater justice.

With this teaching, the Third Synod of bishops rejected a distinction recently introduced into theology between the vertical and horizontal dimension of the Christian life. The vertical dimension, it is argued, deals with man's relationship to God and the horizontal dimension with his relationship to others and society as a whole. Following the logic of this distinction, it is man's primary vocation to worship God and relate himself to God interiorly; to assume responsibility for the human community is important but secondary. On the basis of this distinction, some Catholics have criticized the new ecclesiastical emphasis on social justice and social criticism. What counts first of all, they argue, is personal surrender to the invisible God. But in the light of God's self-revelation in Christ and God's self-communication in the Spirit, the two dimensions, vertical and horizontal, are inseparably intertwined and fused. The God whom we seek is present in us and in others as the source of new life and the remaking of society. Conversely, action on behalf of justice is not a self-willed effort but surrender and obedience to the divine Word. Social commitment is, therefore, "constitutive" of the Gospel life. The promised salvation includes "liberation from all the oppressive conditions of human life." The Gospel has a political élan.

After the Third Synod of bishops, the Canadian Catholic bishops entered into ecumenical relations with the other major churches in Canada—Anglican, United Church, Presbyterian and Lutheran—and created permanent inter-church committees whose task it was—and still is—to examine from a critical Christian point of view the social, political and economic problems of Canadian life. Basing themselves on the careful reports written by these committees, the Canadian bishops addressed the Catholic community in a number of important statements and, conjointly with the other Christian churches, submitted briefs to the Canadian government.

In a brief entitled "Justice Demands Action," submitted to the prime minister and the federal cabinet in 1976, the Canadian church leaders, including the Catholic bishops, asserted that they "stand in the tradition of the prophets" and recognize that "to know God is to seek justice for the poor and oppressed." The brief then explains that "the present economic order is characterized by the maldistribution of wealth and the control of resources by a small minority" and pleads for "an alternative to the present unjust order, a new international economic order." This reasoning is repeated by the Canadian bishops in their 1976 Labour Day Statement, "From Words to Action." Here the bishops give the same two reasons why the present economic system is unjust: it expands the gap between the rich and the poor, and it leaves the control of resources in the hands of the few. Again they ask for the creation of a more just social order.

Is there something new in these texts? In the past, Catholic teaching has often severely judged international monopoly capitalism, but on these occasions the ill effects of capitalism were attributed to the greed of the rich and powerful. If they and the rest of society became more generous, more just, more Christian, then these ill effects could be made to disappear. The brief passages quoted above seem to operate out of a different logic. They accuse the economic system itself of leading to the maldistribution of wealth, of producing a growing gap between rich and poor nations, and of assigning power to a corporate minority. These are presented as systemic effects of capitalism. They occur whether the men who run these institutions be saints or sinners: the ill effects are built into the system.

In the 1975 Labour Day Statement " Northern Development: At What Cost?" the Canadian bishops demand that the government not allow the industrial development of the Canadian north without consultation with the native peoples. For if the large corporations and the departments of government carve up the land with purely economic goals in view, they will destroy the matrix of survival for the native peoples. Why, the Statement asks, do corporations and government agencies act in this way? "The maximization of consumption, profit and power has become the operating principle of this society." This is not a reference to the attitudes of the men in charge of these institutions; it refers rather to the operational logic associated with them. Again, in a letter on world hunger, called "Sharing Daily Bread," the Canadian bishops suggest that for the distribution of food the free market is no longer adequate. Why? Because the free market following the law of supply and demand distributes food only to those who have the ability to pay. Food is not available to people without money. What we need, in the area of food distribution first of all, is the democratization of the economic system. The ideals of equality and participation must be extended from the political to the economic order. In the Church's official teaching, I conclude, certain new emphases indicate a shift to the left.

A similar shift, in much stronger terms, can be found in the documents of the World Council of Churches. For some Christians, a minority, this shift to the left has led to an identification with socialism. This is true especially in Latin America where even some ecclesiastical documents have recommended that the ownership of the means of production on the continent pass from private hands to the entire community. A group called "Christians for Socialism" was founded in 1971. At present the Christian Left is under great political pressure in most countries of Latin America. According to a recent pastoral letter of the Brasilian hierarchy (October 1976) Catholic men and women who witness to social justice and advocate a more just distribution of wealth in Brazil and other Latin American countries are publicly accused of being subversives or communists and often persecuted in criminal ways. Today, "Christians for Socialism" represents a movement widely spread in Europe, especially in Italy, France and Spain, but also in Germany. Dorothee Soelle, a German theologian, gave an evening lecture at the Conference, open to the public, dealing with this movement to which she herself belongs.

"Christians for Socialism" in Europe constitutes an ecumenical movement in the Christian churches. These Christians do not form a political party, nor are they identified with a political party. Individual members may well belong to political parties or be identified with secular movements, but as a Christian association they deal with specifically Christian issues. What are these issues? Dorothee Soelle developed two of them. First, there is the theological effort to discern in the Church's preaching and popular piety the hidden ideology protecting and promoting the present social order, and, second, there is the effort to show that no intrinsic contradiction exists between the Gospel and socialism.

Critique of Mainstream Religion

Let us turn to the first effort, the unmasking of popular Christianity as an expression of bourgeois culture. This is, properly speaking, the task of political theology. This theme returned again and again at the Conference. It was discussed by Guy Bourgeault in a talk on the Church's relationship to the working people of Quebec, and by Malcolm Spencer in a talk given after the Conference at the Institute of Saskatchewan Studies. To summarize the various contributions I will mention five ways in which the Christian message can be made into an ideology of the status quo. There is first of all the trend to distinguish between the vertical and horizontal dimension of human existence and give priority to the vertical. I have mentioned this trend above. Popular piety and congregational preaching often give the impression that what really counts is eternal life. What really counts is to lead a life that prepares us for eternal life. The world to which we belong is the background against which we work out our salvation in fear and trembling. This popular Christianity relativizes the importance of history, makes people accept the world as it is, and makes all of their religious energies serve live in another world.

Over against this, political theologians insist that the vertical and horizontal dimensions of human existence are inseparably intertwined and fused in Christianity. God is present in us and in others as enabler, as transforming agent, appointing us to be transformers of human life. We pray that God's will be done on earth.

Human history is not the background against which we seek our personal salvation; it is rather the proper locus of the divine self-communication in the redemption of the human race. To turn to God does not imply a turning away from people engaged in a struggle for justice. In the Christian perspective, the eternal is not over and above the temporal, but in and through the temporal as matrix, orientation, and horizon. Thus the religious energies generated by Christian preaching become available for the reconstruction of human existence on earth. The message of eternal life has historical consequences.

The second ideological theme of popular Christian preaching is a certain doctrine of divine providence which reconciles people with the world as it is. The suffering inflicted upon us by the conditions of society is regarded as part of God's unfathomable saving design: it is providential, permitted by God for the sake of a greater good prepared for us in the future. Hence we must learn to resign ourselves to the conditions of our lives, we must accept our lot in patience, and we must offer up our suffering, with Christ's sacrifice, to Almighty God and recognize its redemptive power for the eternal salvation of mankind. God is the Lord of history, and even if we do not understand his ways, we must accept the course of history as part of his providential plan. Such a view of divine providence, coupled with a particular notion of patience, keeps people from being angry with the injustices under which they suffer and from wanting to remake the social order in accordance with greater justice.

For political theologians, divine providence is God's redemptive will for the whole humanity. This providence manifests itself not in all events of history, but precisely in those moments and those movements that contribute to the redemption of humankind from the enemies of life. The privileged high points of this providence are of course the biblical events, Israel's liberation from the dark power of Pharaoh, and Christ's persecution, death and resurrection. These events are normative for the Christian Church. They enable us to discern other manifestations of God's providence in history, namely in the dramatic passages from oppression to liberation, from inequity to greater justice, from death-dealing powers to life in abundance. Divine providence does not encourage resignation but nourishes eager and impatient hope for the remaking of the world. Christian patience calls forth not passive submission to the misery inflicted by society but steadfast hope that society is destined to be different and can be changed. Dorothee Soelle spoke of "revolutionary patience," thanks to which Christians refuse to abandon this messianic hope even in the darkness of a reactionary culture.

A third ideological theme is a certain view of original sin. According to this view, we expect that human society will always be a place of injustice. Thanks to God's grace, individuals may enter into holiness and practice the love of neighbor, but society as a whole is so damaged by the inherited sin that there is no hope for it. Individuals can be transformed through conversion of the heart, but society has no heart and social structures have no consciousness, and hence it is impossible to apply the notion of conversion to the social order. Whenever important structural changes are introduced, due to the success of an historical movement, they will quickly be deformed by human selfishness and become a new source of human oppression. This is the condition of the fallen world. There will always be rich and poor, successful and unsuccessful, exploiters and exploited. The hope for the creation of a more just society is an illusion.

For political theologians, the doctrine of original sin means that the self-organization of man in social order and in human consciousness has been gravely distorted, contains discrepancies, and produces misery and oppression for the greater part of mankind. We are all heirs of this distortion, it is embodied in the world into which we were born, and it is alive in our heart. Still, the revelation of this inherited sin was accompanied from the beginning by the divine promise of salvation. Where evil abounds, divine grace abounds even more. First in Israel and then in Jesus Christ, God has manifested divine power and revealed the redemption of history from the power of darkness. History is the locus of redemption. The salvation promised by Christ and proclaimed by the Church has therefore a social dimension, it initiates us into personal as well as social transformation, it affects individuals as well as structures, and it nourishes our hope that the world can be a different place. True, we shall never wholly escape our human brokenness; however just a social order may be, it will still bear the mark of sin. But this should not weaken the Christian's hunger and thirst for justice and the common effort of remaking society.

A fourth ideological theme is a particular view of the divine lordship. In popular piety and ecclesiastical preaching God is often presented as the king of the universe, omnipotent in rule, governing the world from above. God establishes order through his will. The image of divine power is here drawn from a particular political system, the monarchy. The relation between the king and his subjects is here extended, in a certain analogy, to characterize God's relationship to humanity. Unless this perspective is modified by other viewpoints, the doctrine of divine kingship or lordship easily becomes a symbol which legitimates the existing structures of authority, secular and ecclesiastical, and protects all master-servant relationships in society. Such a view of the divine lordship defends the political status quo, whatever its injustices.

Political theologians insist that the affirmation of God as Lord in no way makes monarchy or other forms of one-man rule a privileged political system. Nor does it legitimate master-servant relationships. Political theologians begin reflecting on God as love, as truth and as life. God manifests divine power in compassion: God "rules" the world by summoning people to see clearly and enabling them to act courageously. God is "Lord" in the antithetical way of servant, enabler, and good shepherd. God rules the world from within the historical struggle by taking the side of the poor and powerless. God is "Lord" because the divine Word judges the world and its injustices; God is "Lord" because the divine victory in Jesus Christ, crucified and risen, announces and anticipates the ultimate divine victory in all who are humiliated, marginalized, persecuted and oppressed.

A fifth theme of popular Christian teaching, mentioned in Soelle's lecture as well as in subsequent conversations, is the ideal of unity and peace separated from the demands of justice. In the Church's preaching we tend to praise unity and peace, we propose an ideal of reconciliation that makes competing sections of society to be of one mind, and we advocate a notion of unity in the Christian community that overlooks the differences between people, produced by worldly inequalities. But such an ideal of unity, separated from the demands of justice, is an ideology that protects the dominant groups and their power and makes the people at the bottom submissive. The grave injustices in society cannot be forgiven and forgotten; they must be changed. The only unity that is in accordance with God's will is unity in justice, and in a sinful world this demands a significant shift in power relations. Reconciliation between various parties implies the conversion of all, and this demands on the part of some the restitution of excessive power and undue privilege.

In Christian spiritual literature, we often find such a stress on unity and peace that in cases of conflict we quickly blame the troublemakers. The governing bodies of society are perceived as the guardians of harmony, they are the representatives of God's will, and hence it is sinful to make trouble, to rock the boat, or to organize dissent. A certain Christian spirituality suggests that in a situation of conflict it is the powerless who are to blame. But Jesus was a troublemaker from the beginning. He was willing to disrupt peace and unity for the sake of justice and truth. The revolution brought by him demands conversion and change of life. He left us the unsettling words that the first shall be last and the last first.

Christians and Socialism

In the preceding paragraphs we have moved away from the contents of Dorothee Soelle's lecture and introduced the ideas of other participants at the Conference. What she defined as the first task of Christians for Socialism was really the task of political theology in general. The second task mentioned by her, this time proper to Christians for Socialism, is the demonstration that there is no contradiction between socialism and Christianity. At one time the Catholic Church excluded socialism as a Christian option. In 1931, in the encyclical *Quadragesimo Anno*, Pius XI condemned not only revolutionary, atheist communism but also what he called "mitigated socialism," i.e., democratic forms of socialism, even when they are not opposed to religion and do not intend to abolish all forms of private property: "No one can be at one time a sincere Catholic and a true socialist." Since that time, especially in the last decade—I have indicated this above—the Catholic Church's official position has shifted to the left. This does not mean, of course, that the Catholic Church has endorsed or approved of socialism in any of its forms. All the shift signifies, it seems to me, is that the question must be posed anew from a Catholic point of view.

Dorothee Soelle, as well as other speakers after her, especially Guy Bourgeault and Malcolm Spencer, tried to describe the varying positions toward society the churches have adopted in modern times. Ernst Troeltsch's and Richard Neibuhr's classification of the churches' attitudes toward culture and society in the course of history must be extended to fit the churches' positions in modern times. A threefold model is useful in this connection. There is, first of all, the *conservative* stance. Here the churches identify, consciously or unconsciously, with the interests of the dominant class and understand themselves as the defenders of the existing order. Here the churches exercise conservative and sometimes even reactionary political influence, even if they claim that they aspire to spiritual things and are above the historical order of politics and economics. Second, we find what may be called a *reformist* stance. Here the churches are moved by the plight of the poor, the disadvantaged and powerless, and out of a sense of compassion, they become advocates of social reform. In the twentieth century we can give many instances when Protestant and Catholic churches have adopted a reformist standpoint, pleaded with governments to modify public legislation and summoned the Christian people to assume political responsibility and work for a more just social order. Can Christian communities move beyond reform? What happens when Christians come to the conclusion that the present system is unjust, that its ills cannot be removed by repair and reform, and that it should be dismantled and reconstructed in accordance with new social and economic principles? "Christians for Socialism" is convinced that such a *radical* stance is what the present situation demands.

We recall that according to the Canadian bishops the present economic order is unjust because it widens the gap between rich and poor and assigns control over the resources to a small minority. What the bishops did not publish in this context was a careful, detailed analysis of how the present system distributes wealth in this country and in the world and of what groups or people in fact make the decisions in regard to the use of resources. This kind of empirical research is necessary if we are to judge whether a reform of the present system can remove the injustices, or whether we ought to strive for the reconstruction of the economic system. Contemporary political theology demands that such an analysis of the relationship of classes to income, wealth and power be made in order to perceive the requirements of justice. Socialists hold that the injustices of social life can be overcome only if access to resources and the production of goods are made to serve the common good.

According to Dorothee Soelle, "Christians for Socialism" does not identify itself with any existing form of socialism. It has a vision of socialism that corresponds to well-defined Christian requirements. In particular, it rejects the Russian style, it has no use for authoritarian models, it repudiates the concentration of power in the party or state bureaucracy, it criticizes the purely "scientific socialism" which understands itself in terms of economic necessity, and it favors utopian trends in socialism, not to the detriment of a scientific analysis, but combined with it as source of new vision and on-going self-critique.

What is the theological foundation to which Christians for Socialism appeals? This is an important question. At the end of the nineteenth and the beginning of the twentieth century, some representatives of the Social Gospel used, without adequate distinctions, the ancient biblical language of the arrival of God's kingdom; they gave the impression that the historical movement for social reconstruction ushered in God's kingdom on earth. This unprotected language was severely criticized by Christian thinkers. Reinhold Niebuhr in his argument against the Social Gospel showed that such a naive anticipation of God's kingdom underestimated the sinful reality of the world, created unrealistic expectations, and left Christians without any theological principles for criticizing their own political struggle. Christians for Socialism does not follow this theological route. It rather sees itself confronted by a society profoundly divided between rich and poor, between those who in varying degrees profit by the present system and those who in different measures are excluded from the goods of life and condemned to poverty. With whom shall Christians identify—with the rich or with the poor? Or shall they remain neutral? Christians for Socialism holds that there is enough evidence in the New Testament that the followers of Jesus must identify themselves with the aspirations of the poor. The guide in the political arena is this identification with the marginalized, the underprivileged, the humiliated. Christians for Socialism does not regard the coming of a socialist society, however enlightened, as the final age of the world; on the contrary, by adopting the perspective of the underprivileged they have available a political guide and an on-going critique in the formation of any society, including a socialist one. The central mystery of faith in the perspective of Christians for Socialism is the death and resurrection of Jesus Christ. God's victory in the humiliated and marginalized Jesus provides a new perception of society as a field of conflicting parties, produces an identifcation of believers with the humiliated and marginalized sections of society, and creates the hope that evil and injustice will not prevail in the long run. This is the theological foundation that enables Christians for Socialism to discern God's liberating presence in social struggles and historical movements.

A Secular Viewpoint

Invited to the Conference were two secular scholars, the philosopher Kai Nielson from Calgary and the economist Abraham Rotstein from Toronto. Kai Nielson spoke against political theology as he upheld a socialist position. As an atheist he defended the view that religion has no sound rational foundation and consequently that theology, including political theology, is a useless undertaking. For Kai Nielsen there is not enough evidence for affirming God's existence. The claims made by religious people over the centuries do not stand up when examined critically. They cannot be verified in the manner by which we normally test the validity of affirmations. Hence the presumption is that there is no God.

The speaker then applied the same sort of reasoning to the

political arena. He first described capitalism as the economic system in which decisions regarding the use of resources, production and consumption are made by a few people, the owners and controllers of the large corporations and he analyzed the deprivation and exploitation which this sytem imposes on the major section of the population. Then he defined socialism as the economic system where the decisions regarding the use of resources, production and consumption are made by men and women appointed by the people and responsible to them, and explained that this is possible only if the instruments of production are publicly rather than privately owned. A reasonable human being confronted with the choice between these two systems finds rational evidence for the superiority of socialism: only socialism can meet the needs of the great majority of the population. Capitalism is irrational. Hence the presumption is that one must be a socialist. Nielsen explained that the communist countries which lay claim to socialism have in fact systems of state capitalism and bureaucratic domination, and hence do not live up to his definition of socialism.

Kai Nielsen's rational and utilitarian approach to the problems of human existence was severely criticized at the Conference. Ben Smillie, who responded to Nielsen, felt that the rationalistic approach, almost indistinguishable from philosophical positivism, was itself an instrument of dehumanization. It separated people from their feelings, their intuitive responses to reality and even their indignation vis-à-vis the great misery in the world. It produced a one-dimensionality of life in which there was no room for the profoundly human passions, for religious experience, for ecstasy.

Reason is of course useful and indispensable, but it is sent to work in a particular direction by the perspective in which reality is seen. It is ultimately this perspective which counts. Christians get their perspective from certain historical events, from the history of Israel and the life of Jesus; divine revelation opens for them a perspective on the world. Reason operating in this direction may reach toward the divine. However, hardly anybody at the Conference was in the mood to argue about God's existence and defend the validity of religion. One person made the following observation. Since, in the history of Israel and the life of Jesus, God stands revealed as helper of the poor, defender of the defenseless, liberator of the oppressed, and just judge set over kings and princes, the big divide among the people of the world is not between those who believe in a divinity and those who don't, but between those who are in solidarity with the poor, the defensless and the oppressed, and those who aren't. These two dividing lines, let me add, produce two different maps of the world. Conservative Christians prefer the first map which unites all believers in God against atheists, agnostics and doubters. The Christians at the Conference tended to attach more importance to the second map which unites all those who favor social justice and take the side of the humiliated and marginalized. Where is the God of Israel to be found—among those who profess belief in God, or those who hunger and thirst after justice?

Questioning Messianic Hope

Professor Abe Rotstein, an economist at the University of Toronto, did not present an analysis of Canadian society. While at the University of Saskatchewan, he did give a lecture to the department of political economy on the new Canadian nationalism, but at the Conference on political theology he gave a paper analyzing the structures of rhetoric of Luther and Marx. He showed that Luther, relying on St. Paul, presented the human world, its evil and its promised transformation in a rhetoric identical in structure (not in content, of course) with Marx's view of historical transformation. The mediator between Luther and Marx is Hegel. Luther began his preaching by describing human existence as a form of slavery or bondage where men were slaves to sin and death. Thanks to Jesus Christ, this slavery to sin will be replaced by a new and glorious slavery: Christians become slaves of Christ, and they are now in an exalted bondage to him. The next step in the transfiguration of human life is the transition from the exalted slavery to participation in lordship. Christians now reign with Christ. This is Christian freedom. Lastly, there emerges the new community where people live together in freedom and equality, with the kingdom of God to be established as the final stage of the drama of redemption. Rotstein called the eager expectation of this radical transformation "apocalypticism." It has its roots in the ancient Scriptures.

According to Rotstein's detailed analysis of biblical and theological texts as well as Hegelian and Marxian literature, the stages of transformation found in Lutheran preaching are present in Marx's presentation of the world's historical process. First human existence is described as a slavery. Oppression reigns. In particular, the new class of workers produced by the industrial revolution, devoid of legal protection and organizations of defense, live in servitude. But thanks to the dialectics of history, the proletariat becomes the privileged class through which justice shall be brought to the whole of society. Their servitude is therefore glorious. They become the agents of revolution. At that moment the servants shall become lords. The revolution will place authority and responsibility for society in the hands of the workers. The proletariat shall be, at least for a time, the ruler of the new social order. Lastly, there emerges the perfect community where all domination, including the state, will disappear and people will live together in freedom and equality.

What conclusions did Rotstein draw from the parallel rhetoric? He concluded, first of all, that the Western radical tradition, especially in Karl Marx, is the continuation, in a secular key, of the ancient apocalypticism that had been partially integrated into the New Testament and handed forward in the Christian religion through some significant figures such as Luther. Though the Christian message of God's inversion of the world in the creation of the new humanity was quite different in *content* from the Marxian message of the inversion of the world in the creation of the classless, egalitarian society, the *rhetoric* of the latter was wholly derived from the former.

Was there also a practical conclusion? Here Abe Rotstein's paper was not so clear. Since the impatient expectation of total transformation has so often been disappointed and, at other times, become the source of struggle, violence and a new form of enslavement, and since the final situation after the victory of the messianic, apocalyptical ideal is often worse than the original state, is it not necessary to question whether built into this rhetoric

is not an illusion? Especially in the 1970's, after the eager hopes of
the 1960's have disappeared and the political and cultural left has
been decimated in North America, should we not start thinking
about the remaking of human life is non-messianic, non-
apocalyptical terms? In any case, Abe Rotstein's paper could be
understood in several ways.

Patrick Kieran, professor at the School of Social Work,
Halifax, who responded to Rotstein, understood the paper in a
positive manner. It demonstrated, he thought, that Christians and
Marxists agree, against the liberals, that present society can be
transformed. Kieran felt that the word "apocalypticism" had been
used rather too broadly and might usefully be replaced by the
notion of "transfiguration." When the stages of transformation are
understood as the description of a long historical process, then the
expectation of transfiguration, whether in Christian or in Marxist
terms, challenges the view almost universally held in our society
and repeated ad infinitum and ad nauseam that the social order will
never change, that there will always be injustices, that it is useless
to hope and work for the coming of a new society, that people
always remain selfish and ambitious, and that however perfect the
conditions of life may seem, the old misery will soon start all over
again.

Liberalism, Pat Kieran explained, was an attempt on the part
of European thinkers to find a foundation for social consensus after
the unity of world view and religion had broken down. Religious
upheavals and religious wars had created conditions of chaos.
What is possible in this attempt to find a ground for social agreement by abstracting from values and common vision? Liberalism
was such an attempt. It tried to unite people through the minimal
neutral link between them, their common reason. On science, all
could agree. Science was to provide the common synthesizing
perspective. All that was required for the making of a peaceful
society was the scientific consensus of individuals, one by one.
Liberalism, then, was a remedy for the unresolvable conflicts in
which communities with different world views were engaged: it
promoted a new individualism where each man favors his own. In
this context the government is no longer understood as the pro-
moter of the common good; the government is seen simply as the

protector of the rights of the individual citizens and their property, which is the source of their self-reliance.

This is the social framework in which modern capitalism thrived. Freedom in this situation meant absence of government interference and revolt against any restraining, socially-oriented vision, such as religion, that kept people from dedicating themselves exclusively to their own pursuits, especially the increase of their property and with it their power in society. Eventually liberal society became reform-minded. But social change was understood in terms of improving the lot of individuals, especially the poor, and here modern liberal society has produced admirable examples of welfare legislation. However, the social project as such could not be changed. This is unthinkable for liberals. Individualism, private property, scientific consensus, value neutrality: these constitute the structure of reality. Against this inheritance, Pat Kieran explained, both the biblical and the Marxist traditions insist that transfiguration is possible. It is possible to change the social project.

Abe Rotstein's paper could also be interpreted in a more negative manner. While Professor Nielsen proposed atheism in its rationalistic form, Rotstein's paper could be read as proposing atheism in a socio-existential form. The great stories of hope contained in the Scriptures, which have nourished the vision of Jews and Christians and, after a secular transposition, of humanists and socialists, may be an illusion; they may in fact have done harm. This means that there is no ultimate horizon of history. There is no meaning in history which transcends it. There is no dynamics operative in the lives of people which is bigger than they are, carries them beyond themselves, opens them to new visions, and generates in them the hope that their destiny is to be a community of brothers and sisters. Rotstein's paper could be read to say that there are no divine promises operative in human history. This may not be Rothstein's position, but his paper could be understood in this sense. While Nielsen's atheism is a theory that deserves the attention of philosophers, a socio-existential denial of transcendence in history has a powerful impact on ordinary people, on their personal lives and their political engagements. The Conference provided the occasion to look these issues straight in the face. The foundation of political theology, as Dorothee Soelle insisted, is faith.

What Is the Canadian Context?

Neglected at the Conference was the specifically Canadian context. Most of the papers were of a more theoretical nature, treating a general theme. No one tried to analyze the social and economic reality of Canadian society which is after all the context in which Canadian Christians do their theology. How does the Christian Gospel tie into the life-and-death questions of Canadian society? The proposal that received most attention at the Conference was that the main enemy of human life in Canada and the world was the structured injustice of economic exploitation. We recall that this was the view of the Canadian church leaders. The greatest danger to the world today is the economic system that increases the gap between rich and poor and permits the few to control the resources. What the church leaders did not do, and what nobody at the Conference attempted to do for the whole of Canada, was a careful empirical analysis of what this maldistribution of wealth looks like in detail, which are the groups and classes that are favored, which are the exploited sections, and who makes the decisions regarding resources, production and consumption. Such a class analysis is necessary to understand the Canadian context of political theology.

The only speaker who engaged in class analysis was Yves Vaillancourt, professor of political economy at Montreal, who drew a careful picture of Quebec society at several significant moments of its history. During the troubles of 1837, the ordinary people, then still largely peasants, were under the domination of the merchants, landlords and public officials, then, needless to say, largely English. The bishops at that time, in response to promises for ecclesiastical protection made by the rulers, decided to act as the defenders of the power structure. They condemned rebels and dissidents and counseled the people to obey the constituted authority. Guy Bouregeault read from the ecclesiastical documents published at that time. Yves Vaillancourt continued the class analysis for other crucial moments in Quebec history, such as 1917 and 1945. In each case he first analyzed the structure of the power block and the popular masses, determining their relative size, their respective material interests, and their language. Then he examined the intermediary sector, made up of clergy, intellectuals, soldiers, and salaried professionals, who were able to choose whether to identify with the interests of the power bloc or the populus. He showed that the hierarchy, because of privileges granted to the Church, prevented the more independent-minded lay leaders, especially the intellectuals, from exercising leadership in Quebec. It was only during the so-called Quiet Revolution of the 1960's that a development took place in Quebec that had occurred in Europe a century earlier.

In this context, Yves Vaillancourt showed the ambiguity of the Quebec nationalist movement. Does the middle class which governs this movement pursue the interests of its own class? (For instance, does the business elite, through greater national independence, aspire after leadership positions in industry and finance presently denied to it?) Or is the movement governed by men concerned with a more just distribution of wealth in Quebec? Do they hope that greater independence will enable them to rectify the economic and social injustices from which the Quebec people have suffered in the past? The Parti Quebecois suffers from the ambiguity that affects all social democratic parties. In whose favor do they steer the country? For those who look upon North American society from a socialist perspective, it is not easy to decide whether greater independence for Quebec or closer association with the rest of Canada in a modified federation would be of greater benefit to the popular sector of society.

The importance attached to class analysis led the Conference to deal with the socialist tradition. The participants from Saskatchewan with their memories of the CCF philosophy and the radical Social Gospel felt very much at home in this. Some Conference participants felt at ease with Marxist language; others wanted to retain an approach and a language that remained more closely linked to the Canadian socialist tradition. It is reasonable to distinguish between Marxism as a tool of analysis, as a political strategy, and as a philosophy of history. But the Marxist-style class analysis has become so much part of sociological methodology in general that social thinkers make use of it without adverting to its Marxian origin. There seems to be no good reason why persons relying on Marxism as a tool of analysis should think of themselves as "Marxists." Pius XI was no "Marxist" when he analyzed, in his encyclical *Quadragesimo Anno*, how capitalism has led to the creation of monopolies, how it tends to control governments, and how it has produced what he called "the new imperialism of money," exercised by corporations that reach beyond national boundaries and escape the control of national governments. The use of Marxist analytical tools has become universal today.

Still, there was an interesting discussion at the Conference on the differences between various forms of socialism, especially between a Canadian and a more strictly Marxist socialism. In one public argument, the features characteristic of Canadian socialism were spelled out. Canadian socialism in the 1930's and 1940's followed the British labor movement in its attachment to the parliamentary system. Second, since in some parts of the country, especially Saskatchewan, the CCF was rooted in a populist movement made up largely of farmers, Canadian socialism understood itself from the beginning as an alliance between farmers and workers and hence tended to avoid the term "proletariat" which in Marxist language refers to the industrial labor force. Third, Canadian socialism was heir to a strong liberation tradition: it defended the freedom of expression, the freedom of association, and other constitutional liberties. The parliamentary and libertarian trends, one might mention, were not simply political stances; in Canada they were firmly rooted in the religious traditions of Protestantism. Moreover, while Marxists usually appealed to "scientific" arguments analyzing the contradictions in the present system, Canadian socialists also provided "moral" arguments against capitalism and demanded the reconstruction of society in the name of the biblical idea of justice. To this we must add the achievement of Canadian socialism in the 1930's and 1940's in building a party organization that embodied the democratic, populist and libertarian ideals, remained in touch with the grassroots, and attempted to overcome the bureaucratic ills associated with the traditional political parties. Some participants of the Conference felt that Canadian socialism today, while making use of scientific analysis, should—at least in English-speaking Canada—use concepts and words that reflect this democratic, populist, libertarian and biblical heritage.

The question was raised in the public discussion whether democratic socialism really deserves the name of socialism. The democratic socialist parties of Britain, Scandinavia, Germany and France as they reached for electoral victories advocated not socialism but social democracy, and when they were voted into office they sought to reform the capitalist system rather than replace it with a new economic order. What they tried to create, largely without success, was capitalism with a human face. Other participants added that the revolutionary socialism of Eastern Europe has for the most part given way to state capitalism and bureaucratic domination, and in this way betrayed the socialist idea. There is no socialism in the world that can be imitated; if a just social order is to exist in Canada it must be created anew.

Is this possible? Is the new possible in history? Some people think that nothing new takes place in history, that history is the endless repetition of identical structures, including the structures of oppression. However, others hold that history is open-ended. In particular, Christians believe that history is open. Why? Because God is redemptively present to it! Again we are pushed back to the question of faith. Are there divine promises operative in human history—yes or no?

During the discussion one point was made more than once, namely that it is a mistake to create an inevitable opposition between reform and radical change. While there are reformist positions that seek nothing else than the improvement of the present system, there are other reforms that seek to introduce into the system elements at odds with its essential character, that tend to transform the system into something new. These latter are sometimes called "non-reformist reforms" or "system-transcending reforms." A good example in Canadian history is the cooperative movements in the 1930's and 1940's which sought to improve the lot of farmers and fishermen, but which by introducing cooperative ownership created a new approach to private property and led people to a spontaneous critique of capitalism. In the concrete order, therefore, a socialist movement must advocate reforms, choosing for itself concrete objectives that can be reached in the present order, as long as these reforms bear within themselves elements that bring to light where the present system fails and nourish the vision of an alternate society.

Capitalism or Technocracy?

What is the nature of our bondage? Sin takes many forms, personal and social, but the question is whether there is a principal bondage to which the others are in some way subordinated. This is how Roger Hutchinson, professor of religious studies at Toronto, summarizing the Conference at the end, formulated the crucial issue. The great number of participants, I think, regarded economic oppression, the growing gap between the rich and the poor, and the cultural consequences of the present system as the principal bondage which pervades all aspects of human life and makes other more damaging forms of oppression, be they racist, sexist, or whatever. To defend this view, they could refer to recent ecclesiastical documents in the Catholic and Protestant traditions. These participants held that it is the Church's task to marshal scriptural and liturgical resources to make the Christian people stand against contemporary capitalism. It was in this context, as we noticed above, that the discussion of socialism and Marxism was inevitable.

But there were other participants who did not think that economic injustice was the principal source of the dehumanization of contemporary society. They realized, of course, that there is great misery in the poor sector of society, which includes the major part of the third world, and that suffering is great among the marginalized groups of society, such as the native peoples of Canada; but they insisted that malaise and alienation also pervade the successful sector. Abraham Rotstein said that modern industrial society demands an ever-increasing apparatus of technology, and that it is this all-pervasive technology that impoverishes the substance of human life. Technology creates dehumanizing conditions of life and alienates people from the depth of their human existence. Life becomes pragmatic, quantified, thin and gray. The same view was voiced in other contexts by Vern Wishart from Edmonton and Jim Penna from Saskatoon. The power of technology and bureaucracy is so distorting an influence that any highly industrialized society whether capitalist or socialist, will produce human self-alienation. The human bondage in the modern age, they hold, is deeper than economic exploitation.

This position is well known. The classical formulation, at least among sociologists, is found in Max Weber. "Rationalization," as he called the trend created by science and bureaucracy, leads modern civilization into the "iron cage," "the icy polar night"—a tedious, empty, gray, dehumanized existence. This malaise with modern industrial society was characteristic of German intellectuals at the end of the last and the beginning of the present century—Simmel, Scheler, Spengler, Heidegger, to mention a few. Germany, we recall, became industrialized only in the 1880's, and the subsequent shift in social power and the rise of a new class appeared to the German elite as an expression of vulgarity and a threat to high culture. Even the socialists of the Frankfort School expressed this enormous contempt for mass culture. Could it be that the vehement critics of modern industrial society in Germany were, in part at least, lamenting the waning of an elite society? To what extent is their rejection of modernity an ideology of decline?

Be this as it may, in the 1960's the radical students adopted the Weberian rather than the Marxian critique of contemporary society. They looked upon "technocracy" as the modern agent of dehumanization. They turned to the classical sociologists, such as Weber and Michels, who had analyzed the dehumanizing effects of bureaucracy in government, industry, business and—last but not least—political parties, including the German socialist party. Weber thought that a socialist revolution would lead to the dictatorship of the bureaucrats (Beamte). The Conference did not pay sufficient attention to this important critique of modernity.

Today there are additional reasons for scaling down the size of our industries: the ecological crisis and the exhaustion of resources. But when one asks how it is possible to gear down large-scale industrial society, introduce more craftsmanship and smaller-scale technology into the productive process, and replace mass production by less efficient but more humane industrial procedures, the answer would seem to be the one already mentioned: control over the means of production and the power to plan a more human mode of making and distributing goods—basically a socialist project.

While the issues discussed at the Conference made us repeatedly come up to the brick wall of present reality and reminded us that in Canada only a minority of men and women ask these questions and seek new answers, the spirit at the Conference was joyful. Christians at the boundary always enjoy themselves when they come together: they experience fraternity (sisterhood), they find others who share their anguish, they make plans for expanding the network of renewal, and they nourish one another's faith that God is graciously present to the world and that, therefore, in every serious human struggle something new and marvelous being born.

The Impact of Sociology
on Catholic Theology

Sociology is a complex field of study that can be divided in accordance with its various fields of interest: there is a sociology of institutions, a sociology of religions, a sociology of knowledge, and so forth. But it is also possible to divide sociology in accordance with the methodologies employed in its exercise, each of which implies a distinctive approach to the social reality. To examine the methodological diversity in sociology brings out the conflictual nature of social science and suggests that in the sociology departments of our universities are fought out many ideological controversies in regard to the sociological enterprise.[1]

Let me add to this confusion and introduce the following distinctions between sociologists. There are some sociologists who try to use their science to give an adequate understanding of the social reality under study. They wish to render an empirically tested account of this social reality, explain it in terms of its causes, and possibly find in it the verification of some wider theoretical perspective. These sociologists, whether they be positivists, functionalists or phenomenologically-oriented, want to know society as it is. There are, however, other sociologists who regard it as their task to study society in order to change it. These sociologists are sensitive to the inner contradictions of the social reality, the dysfunctional elements that undermine the social system and/or that make life unlivable for many of its members, and in their analysis of the given reality they study how it has come to be so damaging and what are the forces that tend to change it. The first group of sociologists adds stability to the social reality, while the second group initiates people into a critical perception of society and thus makes a contribution to the process by which society is transformed.

Since theologians serve the word of God which judges and recreates the face of the earth, they are constantly concerned with changing the human reality. It is for this reason that the second group of sociologists are particularly appealing to them. In this paper I want to deal with the contribution of sociology to the understanding and transformation of consciousness, with what some authors like to call "the sociology of knowledge." In Part I, I shall point to the events in the Church's life that have made theologians turn to sociology, in Part II, I want to present the important sociological discovery of the historicity of truth, and in Part III, I shall deal with the social foundation of error and the critique of ideology.

I

In the nineteenth century a new world was being created.[2] Through growing industrialization in certain parts of Europe, culture and society underwent visible changes. We find rapid urban developments; we observe a new social mobility; people are torn away from their towns and villages and move into the new cities; two new classes are being created, the working class, unprotected by any legislation and living in miserable conditions in the cities, and the successful bourgeoisie, the owners of the industrial and commercial enterprises, who became the creators of a new urban culture, of new values, of a new style of government. This growing industrialization was accompanied in some places by changes in the political order. Democracy, or the ideal of democracy, made people aware that society was not a given to be received and protected, but a reality made by people and therefore capable of being dismantled and transformed. Should it not be possible to devise a social order that is more rational, more egalitarian, more efficient, leaves more room for personal freedoms and grants men the opportunity to climb on the social scale? When these things were happening in various parts of western Europe, perceptive people were aware that a new world was in the process of being made. There was a great difference between the old world they had inherited and the new world that was in the making. The reflection on these two worlds and the systematic comparison between the old and the new produced what was later to be called sociology.

Whether we turn to Tocqueville, Comte, Marx or Toennies, we find comparisons between the old and the new. These scholars tried to devise categories or models (ideal types, as they were later called by Max Weber) that would make them more observant of what had gone on in the past and what was happening in the present, that would enable them to systematize the difference between the old and the new and discover causal connections between the institutional changes and the transformation of culture. Sociology was created by this comparative method. It tried to clarify the difference of which every perceptive person was aware; it tried to devise terms of comparison that would allow people to sort out their own experience, render an account of their past and prepare themselves for the problems of the future.

While there are great differences among the sociologists mentioned above, they all agreed that the institutions in which people live have a profound effect on their consciousness and its cultural expressions. In various ways the sociologists tried to show how the transformation of the processes of production and of political organization changed people's awareness of themselves, their values and ideas. This, I suppose, is the basic sociological insight. The institutions to which we belong create a certain kind of consciousness in us. Some sociologists call this social determinism. They do not deny personal freedom and creativity, but they claim that the expressions of this freedom and creativity will inevitably bear the marks of the society in which they have been produced. Looking at a great painting we are able to tell the century or even the decade in which it was made and determine the part of the country where it originated. The social reality (the *Realfaktoren* as Max Scheler called them) creates consciousness and its cultural expressions (the *Idealfaktoren*). This special sociological insight is, of course, only part of the story. For there are indeed moments in history when consciousness in turn affects the structures of society. The relation of mind and society is dialectical. But the second element of this dialectic in no way invalidates the first. The specifically sociological insight remains that institutions create consciousness and its cultural manifestations.

Here is a first conclusion regarding the impact of sociology on Catholic theology today. Contemporary Catholic theologians are open to sociology because they have experienced the old and the new in their own history and are bound to compare them and to relate them to one another. I do not think I am exaggerating here. Catholics have gone through a significant transformation of church life. What has changed in the Catholic Church through Vatican II is not only public policies in regard to ecumenism, mixed marriages, responsible parenthood, religious pluralism, social responsibility and collegiality. What has also changed is the Catholic self-understanding.

The older ones among us are able to read again the spiritual books that guided our lives fifteen or twenty years ago, the articles we then published, or possibly the text of the sermons we then preached. We have here empirical evidence for making a comparison between the old and the new. This empirical evidence is important. We cannot simply rely on our memory. To make it more comfortable for ourselves our memory often tries to soften the contradictions in our personal histories. We are in need of documentation to make a valid comparison. In our theological studies we are constantly confronted by the difference between the old and the new. Reading about the development of doctrine and the mutations of the Christian faith in the past seemed to us very theoretical. We then thought that we had acquired the definitive form of Catholicism. Now we know what religious transformations feel like. We realize that what is being changed is people's self-understanding so that the inherited religious symbols and the traditional religious language acquire a new meaning for them.

Thus we are bound to go on comparing the old and the new and thereby turn to questions that are of interest to the sociologists. We become sociologists without being aware of it, like Tocqueville and the other perceptive observers of social and cultural change in the nineteenth century. For we must explain to ourselves how it is possible to change as much as we did and yet affirm the continuity of Christian truth. The theories that explain the development of doctrine in philosophical or psychological terms no longer seem convincing to us. We realize that social changes have produced the changes in the order of ideas. What happened was that the changes in the Church permitted us to participate in a new way in the culture and society of North America. Before, we belonged to a Catholic subculture in North America, drawing our intellectual life from the neo-Scholastic tradition of Europe and living in structures that protected the purity of this tradition and assured the survival of Catholicism in a hostile environment. After Vatican II with its new teaching on Church and world, we were ready to enter the mainstream of North American life. Seminaries moved to the university campus, Catholic theology was being taught in secular religious studies departments, and the style of life that theologians adopted was determined by their academic pursuits more than by the ecclesiastical tradition. We wanted to look like others and speak like others—not to be conformed to their image but rather to offer critical words and words of hope that could be heard. What has changed are the institutions in which we live and the education we require for theology.

I do not wish to insist that all this was due to Vatican II. Andrew Greeley has given good arguments for the view that these changes would have taken place in American Catholicism even without Vatican II. For it was the rise of a vast section of the Catholic population to higher education, to greater income and a higher social status that made the Catholic community in America leave the structures and the education characteristic of the immigrant church to enter the mainstream of American society. In his book *The New Agenda* Greeley contrasts the old and the new in terms of the immigrant Church versus the religious aspirations of the middle class.[3] Vatican II facilitated these changes, but it did not represent the source of the impetus. (The question could well be raised to what extent the teachings of Vatican II themselves express the liberal aspirations of the widening Catholic middle class in the industrialized nations of western Europe and North America.)

Because Catholic theologians have experienced the old and the new, they are bound to ask questions about the relation between the two. While they acknowledge the difference between the old and the new, they also want to protect the continuity of church life through these changes and hold on to the uniqueness of the Gospel. The traditional theories of doctrinal development that stress the unity and self-identity of truth do not leave sufficient room for the experience of the contemporary theologian. What has changed is not just doctrine but the perception of the Gospel. Jesus Christ means something else to us today than he did fifteen years ago. At the same time, theologians repudiate the idea that their old perception was not truthful and that only the new one is faithful to divine revelation. No, both were true. There were obviously distortions in the old manner of perceiving the Gospel, but there are probably also distortions in the present mode, distortions which are still hidden from us. Theologians find themselves asking the question of the sociologist: How can we account for the difference in truth and values in various cultures without falling into relativism?

Because sociologists take for granted that knowledge is socially grounded and hence varies with the social conditions in which people live, it is sometimes supposed that they must be relativists. I am sure that there are sociologists, not reflectively inclined, who are satisfied to establish how ideas are related to their social base and leave it at that. They then create the impression that truth and values depend purely and simply on the conditions of society. More reflective sociologists (Alvin Gouldner speaks of "reflexive sociology") realize that to establish the social foundations of ideas is only part of their task. They must also raise the question of the unity of truth and the abiding nature of values through social change, since if they do not undertake this sort of reflection, they not only undermine religion and philosophy, they invalidate sociology as well. For sociologists move into diverse cultures and societies trusting that they can apply their methods and their logic to study these; they have the confidence that conversation and observation are possible; they take for granted that there exists some common human bond between diverse peoples and ages that transcends culture and that could be strengthened by communication. Since a relativism of truth would undermine the very project of sociology, sociologists seek some sort of foundation for the unity of truth.

Karl Mannheim, one of my favorite sociologists, distinguished between "relationism" and "relativism."[4] Relationism refers to the particular sociological insight that knowledge and forms of the mind are related to, and dependent on, the social conditions in which people live, while relativism designates the skeptical outlook on life that invalidates all abiding truth and values. Relationism in no way questions that within each society it is possible to distinguish between truth and falsehood, good and evil; to accept the historicity of mind does not lead to skepticism. According to Mannheim, relativism is grounded in a social experience of hopelessness. It is found in successful classes or groups that have lost the sense of their own destiny; such people have learned to shrug their shoulders. A rising class or a group that wants to free itself from oppressive structures does not remain agnostic about what is right or wrong. It is not surprising that relativism prevails among the intellectuals of Western society. But sociologists who want to protect the validity of their own scholarly enterprise must try to overcome the dominant skepticism.

Catholic theologians today are open to the concerns of sociology not only because they have experienced the contrast between the old and the new but also because they are confronted in their own Church with a manifold image of truth. We always knew that religion varied from one culture to another even if we did not attach any theological importance to this. Italian Catholicism was different from the religion in which we participated at home. Every country has its own piety, its own religious style, its own idea of holiness, and within each country religion varies according to social class. At one time we thought that it was possible to enclose these various religious trends into the same theological system. We thought that there was one theology for the entire Catholic world. Today this dream has been shattered. We feel increasingly dissatisfied with the theology that comes to us from other parts of the world. Part of our heritage is, I suppose, to get enthusiastic about the ideas and methods that come to us from overseas. Even Protestant theologians, more firmly rooted in the American experience and the American intellectual tradition than we, have sometimes succumbed to this sort of enthusiasm in regard to German theological thought. Catholics have displayed a good deal of such enthusiasm. We sometimes endorse the liberation theology that comes to us from Latin America, even though this theology, more than any other, understands itself as grounded in a particular cultural and political situation and derived from a sociological analysis of this situation. On its own terms, liberation theology in North America would make sense only if it were based on an analysis of the complex reality of American society and its relation to the rest of the world. While we find some of this enthusiasm among Catholic theologians, we also find an increasing awareness that North American Catholics must develop their own theological reflection. (Let me add that the interesting and original theological reflection that has taken place in Quebec, within a very particular cultural and religious tradition, remains curiously unknown even among English-speaking Catholics in Canada.) We are confronted today with theological pluralism.

Let me add at this point that we have never paid sufficient attention to the plural character of religion within the Catholic Church and in particular to the nature of American religion. Sociologists from the days of Tocqueville on have realized that the Christian religion fulfills important functions in American society that differ from its European equivalents, even if the set of doctrines held should be the same. Catholic theologians have never paid any systematic attention to this difference. Because the Catholic Church in North America recited the same creed, celebrated the same sacraments and taught the same theology as it did in Europe, they thought that the meaning of these religious words and gestures were the same. It was again Andrew Greeley who, over the years, has insisted on the special character of American religion and the need to take this seriously in theological reflection and pastoral policy. He has been accompanied in this, albeit from a different perspective, by Rosemary Ruether.

Modern Catholic theologians are confronted with the problem of the one and the many in their own theology. Again they share the concerns of the sociologist. For while social scientists recognize the great diversity among different societies, they presuppose nonetheless that they are able to study these cultures and come to some sort of valid understanding of them. I have mentioned above that reflective sociologists are very much aware that a meaningful encounter with other societies is only possible if one presumes some common bond between people. Sociological study is possible only if we trust that we are able to listen to others, interpret their actions and make some sense of them, and eventually establish a bridge of communication between them and us. What we presuppose here is some underlying sharing in what may be called human nature. When sociologists use this word—it is rarely enough—they do not think of a definable human nature, the dimensions of which are known to philosophers (or the Holy Office). Sociologists think of human nature as still a-building. It is the common ground presupposed in the encounter with other cultures, and on this common ground it should be possible to widen the range of what can be shared. Despite the diversity of societies, reflective sociologists are concerned about our common humanity.

While there is often a certain reductionist trend in sociology that seeks to reduce human life to measurable dimensions or, worse, to a single measurable dimension, the classical sociologists regarded themselves as guardians of the human. The question they had in mind when they studied society was the discernment of those elements of society that damage the humanity of its members. Emile Durkheim invented the word *anomie* to signify the loneliness and the anguish that modern, urban, individualistic society inflicts on its people. He tried to detect the "pathological" trends in society which undermine the common social matrix that undergrids the well-being and moral integrity of the people. Max Weber analyzed the effect of modern bureaucracy—and the quest for an ever more efficient bureaucracy—on human life and spoke of "the iron cage"[5] in which we may all soon be caught. Modern technology and bureaucracy, "technocracy" in the jargon of the 1960's would eventually result in "the disenchantment of the world."[6] Weber held that modern society would, in the long run, make human life flat, gray and pragmatic: the great human passions would disappear and man's humanity would be diminished.

After the time of Max Weber, the spirit of technocracy

analyzed by him entered into the exercise of sociology itself, and some critical sociologists claim that when this happened sociological research and sociological literature contributed to the dehumanization of modern life. The reductionism mentioned above could easily attack the substance of the great events that create human life—birth, childhood, marriage, etc.—and instead of sociology acting as guardian of the human, it could become an element of culture that undermines it. It is not surprising that we have at this time a strong reaction against this technocratic trend among some sociologists. With the help of phenomenology, these sociologists try to show that the knowledge of the everyday world is primary and that all specialized, technical knowledge, including science and sociology, is derived from this primary knowledge and makes sense only when this relation is understood.[7] Scientific sociology is always an abstraction. Ethnomethodology tries to show how much the human reality is distorted by use of the scientific methodology. These efforts to make sociology again the guardian of the human are sometimes called "wild sociology," as in John O'Neil's little book *Making Sense Together*.[8] Wild sociology wants to enter the conversation by which people make sense out of a troubled world and find the ground for common action.

Sociologists, then, be it explicitly or implicitly, accept a common humanity in their studies. If they are reflective and critical sociologists, they are conscious of this and realize that their vision of what humanity is and is meant to be, enters into the very exercise of sociology and affects the conclusions of their research. Sociology should be value-free in the sense that sociologists must free themselves from bias and prejudice, but in a deeper sense the exercise of sociology is inseparable from human values; it is never value-free. The sociologist, then, like the modern Catholic theologian, is faced with the problem of the one and the many.

After showing that contemporary Catholic theologians are confronted by questions that incline them toward sociology, I wish to indicate two lines along which sociological thinking has made an impact on Catholic theology: the first has to do with the historicity of truth and the second with the historicity of error.

II

For sociologists, truth is historical. Consciousness is historically constituted. All ideas reflect the social and political circumstances in which they are produced. As I have indicated above, this is the proper and specific insight of sociology. It follows from this that the history of ideas and the development of doctrine will have to be studied by taking into account the changing social reality. Karl Mannheim distinguished between two ways of studying the history of ideas.[9] According to the first way, the scholar tries to detect how one idea has emerged from the preceding one by a process that can be accounted for in philosophical or psychological terms. This has been the general approach adopted in the study of the Church's doctrinal development. Theologians have tried to trace the history of doctrine along the line of ecclesiastical teachers, thinkers and witnesses and understand the evolution of doctrine that took place largely in terms of intellectual development. This method abstracts from the social and political circumstances in which ideas emerge. Mannheim calls this purely intellectual approach to the history of ideas "ideological" because it disguises not only the social foundation of these ideas but also the place of the scholar in the society of the present.

The other method for studying the history of ideas demands that the scholar turn from the idea to the people, the class or the group who originated it and held it—Mannheim calls this the carrier (*Träger*) of the idea—and then examine the social conditions of this carrier and in particular the tensions that these conditions generate. If the people who hold a particular set of ideas— the carrier, in other words—undergo significant socio-political changes, they will generate new thought out of the new situation, and hence the passage from the old set of ideas to the new cannot be understood unless the socio-political changes of the carrier are taken into account. Ideas are instruments by which a people or a group deal with their real problems. Hence as these problems change, people will think new thoughts derived from previously held ideas in such a way that they, the people, shall again be able to deal effectively with their lives. Ideas change because changes have taken place in their carriers.

This principle is exemplified in the creation of sociology during the nineteenth century as well as in the passage from the old to the new in the consciousness of contemporary Catholic theologians. I made this point at the outset of this chapter. The creation of a new industrial and democratic world in the nineteenth century provoked the reflections that eventually became sociology, and the passage of American Catholics from a subculture to the mainstream of American life has significantly modified theological thinking. The principle that ideas change because changes take place in their carriers is not a reductionist formula. It does not exclude intellectual creativity and freedom. It simply acknowledges that the work of creativity and freedom has a social foundation.

Biblical scholars have often adopted the second mode of historical research. Their attention to *Sitz im Leben* made them aware of the social grounding of religious teaching and ready to understand the development of religious ideas in terms of the changing social and cultural circumstances. Theologians have rarely applied this second mode in the study of doctrinal developments. The great exception remains Ernst Troeltsch who combined theological and sociological competences in the writing of his major work, deceptively entitled *The Social Teaching of the Christian Churches*. [10] While this work is in many ways outdated, it is so singular that it still remains of great interest. Contemporary theologians are beginning to write articles and monographs analyzing the socio-political base of certain doctrinal shifts, but there is no major sociologically oriented work so far, shedding light on the christological and trinitarian developments in the Christian Church.

The social foundation of ideas or the historicity of truth is implicitly recognized in ecumenical dialogue. For here Christian theologians of different traditions come together to study their doctrinal agreements and disagreements in the hope that a better understanding of the historical conditions under which these positions were defined will enlarge the common ground between the churches. Even religious doctrines are instruments by which churches, relying on the Gospel, try to solve their actual, historical problems. The meaning of doctrinal controversy can only be understood if we take into account the *Sitz im Leben* of the various positions. What religious concern did the various groups want to protect? What element of the truth did they feel was being . threatened? Or, on a more secular plane, what social or political necessity, interest, or preference influenced the formulation of doctrine? What hidden agenda was operative in these controversies? (What, for instance, is the sociology of knowledge of the famous controversies about grace and free will? Theologians are only beginning to ask such questions.) If these social foundations are clearly understood, then the diverse positions may not appear as far apart as they did before, for behind the various emphases may well lie a common intention of remaining faithful to the Gospel in very special, historical circumstances.

St. Augustine never realized that in his struggle against the Donatists he dealt with a marginalized people, ethnically apart from the dominant class, heirs of a different language, and enemies of the Roman Empire which had pushed them away from the fertile land in the plains to the inhospitable mountains. This oppressed group found it impossible to forgive bishops who under great political pressure had been willing to worship in the state religion of Rome. The Romanized Christians of the plain found this easier to forgive. How would St. Augustine have formulated his defense of sacramental efficacy, whatever the personal dignity of the minister, if he had realized that the passion of his opponents was rooted in political reality and that his own style of thinking was linked to his Roman culture?

In ecumenical dialogue theologians try to grasp the religious and social conditions of the churches which have contributed to the divergent doctrines. In the early literature emanating from the World Council of Churches, these conditions used to be called "the non-theological factors" of Christian disunity. According to the sociology of knowledge, this distinction between theological and non-theological factors is too neat. For the non-theological, social and political factors create a certain consciousness, the framework in which the Gospel is experienced and expressed, and thus they flow into every formulation of doctrine. If this

sociology-of-knowledge approach were consistently used in ecumenical discussion, one might be able to show that the divergent
doctrinal positions were adopted by the churches who ap-
proached the Gospel from a perspective determined by their own
history, and that therefore the positions which at first appear
contradictory may in fact be reconciled—without weakening or
watering down the Christian message.

This approach raises the question of the unity of truth. How
can we defend the truth of the Gospel and still hold to the authenticity of its various historical formulations? This is the problem of
"historicism," in which sociologists have been as interested as
historians and philosophers. Since sociologists insist that all truth
is historical, are they still able, we ask, to acknowledge that some
truth transcends the culture in which and by which it was formulated? If the answer to this question were no, sociologists would
have to abandon their science. Usually sociologists assume that if
the truth is abstract enough, if it deals not with reality but with an
ideal order, then such transcendence is possible. Such cultural
transcendence is found in mathematics and it may also be found in
the natural sciences. Yet even here some sociologists go on ques-
tioning under what social conditions science was first developed
and what social conditions must obtain so that science achieves
cultural power and generates an ever wider application to human
life. Who knows? Perhaps modern science is so closely linked to
the technological, bureaucratic society that what appears to us as
its universality is rather the sign of the cultural victory of the West
and hence represents a universality of power and aggression. But
is there a truth transcending culture apart from mathematics and
the natural sciences?

Sociology, as I mentioned above, presupposes the possibility
of universal human communication and hence inevitably edges
toward metaphysics. Karl Mannheim was very much aware of
this.[11] In his sociology of knowledge he insisted that all truth was
historical. But if we look at the critical edge of this truth and the
orientation it induces in human life, then one might imagine a
truth that is universal—even if it could never be possessed except
perspectively. Mannheim thought that in every society people

wrestle with the problems of their lives and learn to distinguish between truth and error, right and wrong. In this social quest truth appears as a critique of the current notions and the orientation of social and personal life. If we compare the various sytems of values and ideas, we may find that they are quite different, but if we set them into their socio-political context, we see that they perform a similar function: they criticize oppressive trends and practices, they promote human life, they reach out for wider communication. It is not unreasonable to suppose that from a vantage point not yet available to us (and possibly never to be available to us) these various systems of truth and values are perspectives of a single truth. Mannheim held that unless sociologists acknowledged such a drift toward humanization and the presence of a universal dynamics in man, they would either undermine the entire work of sociology by a total relativism or else reify one historical system as the final and total truth. While the sociology of knowledge convinced Mannheim that all truth is historical, it also made him affirm the unity of truth in a common, relational orientation. Mannheim realized, of course, that this brought him to the edge of metaphysics, but he preferred not to develop this line of thought.

Truth as critique and orientation appeals to theologians who seek an understanding of religious truth that allows them to affirm the self-identity of the Gospel and its manifold historical formulations. As long as the notion of religious truth was drawn from neo-Scholasticism it was impossible to account for the passage from the old to the new and to reconcile the historicity of Christian doctrine with its transcendent unity. But if religious truth is critique of an existing culture and orientation toward renewed life, then it is possible that one and the same message acquires different meanings in various historical circumstances. Theologians have turned to hermeneutics, the theory of interpretation to be able to read and reread the biblical message out of different sets of presuppositions and hence reconcile the unity with the plural form of the Christian Gospel.

This is not the place to discuss theological hermeneutics. Since I am interested in the impact of sociology on theology I wish to make two remarks in this connection. First, the hermeneutical circle is also of interest to the sociologists. In the important controversies between sociologists who try to assimilate sociology as much as possible to the natural sciences and sociologists who insist that the human sciences (*Geisteswissenschaften*), including sociology, have a specific methodology, the latter have attempted to clarify the hermeneutics involved in the exercise of sociological research.[12] While natural sciences take for granted the separation of subject (the observer) and the object (the observed), except in some limiting cases, the human sciences—including sociology—acknowledge an interrelation of subject and object. Both the social scientist and the social action studied by them have been produced by the same history. The social scientists do not stand on neutral ground; they find themselves in a position that has been affected by the object they intend to study. In other words, they find themselves within the hermeneutical circle and before they can read correctly the empirical data they have collected, they must determine the precise place which they occupy in this circle. They must discover how the social action they study has affected their own self-understanding, and, conversely, if they study events more or less contemporary to them how the world with which they are identified has affected the object of their research. From Wilhelm Dilthey and Ernst Troeltsch to the contemporary critical sociologists of North America (C. Wright Mills, Robert W. Friedrichs, Alvin Gouldner, John O'Neil to mention a few), the struggle of sociology against the illusory ideal of value-neutrality and the quest of sociology for a new kind of objectivity are expressed in a body of literature that deals basically with hermeneutics, even if this particular term is not used.[13]

My second remark has to do with a principle of interpretation used in sociological research that would be helpful in theological studies. Since sociologists hold that consciousness and its cultural expressions are created by the social reality (in the sense explained above), it is possible to understand a particular social event in two ways: first, there is the meaning which the social event has to the actors involved in it, and, secondly, there is the meaning the event has, possibly unknown to the actors, as an expression of the wider social reality with which the actors are identified. Karl Mannheim calls this second "documentary meaning."[14] It is possible to study football in terms of the meaning which the players assign to the game, but it is also possible to study football as an expression of the socio-economic reality to which the players and the spectators belong, an approach that might account for the extraordinary power football holds over the imagination of contemporary society. Since the social institutions in which we live create a certain mind-set or consciousness, more is expressed in people's self-expression than their personal intention: the society expresses something about itself in the words and gestures of its members, even if this remains unknown to them. When idealists talk of the *Geist* of a community that expresses itself in works of art and literature, we may object to the metaphysical implications of their language, but we have to admit that it accurately records the sociological reality.

If we apply this principle to the reading of biblical literature, then we must take into account two distinct meanings of a text, one the literal meaning which is intended by the author and the other the documentary meaning which expresses something of the sociologically defined community to which the author belongs. In other words, there is a hidden meaning in a biblical passage that transcends the literal sense. The same principle can be applied in ecclesiology to give more precise meaning to the reliance of Catholics, including the Catholic theologian, on the wisdom produced in and by the community. Catholics have stressed more than Protestants that in the search for the understanding of the Gospel the theologians are not alone and that they should not surrender themselves fully to their own insights unless they are supported in this by a significant section of the believing community. In other words, the believing community itself is involved in the discernment of Christian truth. This position makes good sociological sense. For if consciousness is created by society, then the ideas people have reflect the common institutions and the socio-political conditions in which they live. A reading of the Gospel can be authentic only if it is shared by many. This explains, moreover, why the same religious development takes place in a good number of people dispersed in the same society, even though there is no direct communication between

them. Only if theologians are confirmed by a significant movement in the Church do they know that more expresses itself in
their interpretation of the Gospel than their own conscious insights: what they think also expresses something of the community's wrestling with its own conditions of life.

Theologians, I have said, try to solve the problems raised by
the passage from the old to the new, and by the one and the many,
through the application of hermeneutics to normative texts.
There is, however, another way of dealing with these
problems—a way, derived from the sociology of religion, that
does not contradict the preceding way but parallels and supple-
ments its. Beginning with Emile Durkheim, many sociologists
have come to understand religion as a set of symbols that offers
people an interpretation of the whole of reality, dominates their
imagination and their hearts and orients their action in a certain
way. Durkheim and some of his followers did not believe in God,
and hence there was a reductionist tendency in their brilliant
analyses. They presented religion as the sacred canopy protecting
society and hinted that its creation was due to nothing but society's quest for stability. Other sociologists used the same symbolic understanding of religion non-reductively. Robert Bellah
distinguishes two trends in the sociological approach to the study
of religion as symbol system—"symbolic reductionism" and
"symbolic realism."[15] By symbolic realism he means the view
that does not simply regard religious symbols as a reflection of
society and its aspirations but acknowledges them as possessing a
creativity of their own (and hence as remaining open to a
metaphysical interpretation).

Christian theology is able to make use of the approach to
religion derived from symbolic realism. For it is possible to regard
divine revelation in Israel and Jesus Christ as the manifestation of
God's hidden gracious presence to human history (this is shared
by much of modern theology) and look upon this revelation not
primarily as truth addressed to the mind but as stories and symbols through which the believing community interprets reality,
understands itself and its mission, and opens itself to the divine
self-communication. It is possible, in other words, to regard divine revelation as symbolic.

The so-called Modernists, we recall, tried to look upon divine revelation as symbolic. They did this to overcome the rationalistic understanding of religious truth operative in the theology of their day. However, the Modernists did not derive their understanding of symbols from the incipient social sciences contemporary to them. For them symbols were signs addressed to the memory, recalling significant events of the past and hence exercising power on people's emotions. Symbols communicated religious sentiment. We note that the notion of symbols, derived from the sociology of religion, is quite different. Here religious symbols are the form of the imagination, through which people lay hold of reality, understand themselves, their origin and their destiny, and move forward in creating their history.

Does this symbolic understanding derived from sociology neglect the noetic component of divine revelation? This is usually the first question that theologians ask. It seems to me that this approach does relegate this noetic component to a subordinate position. What divine revelation communicates directly is new consciousness. Through the story of Israel and the life and personality of Jesus the believing community comes to see reality in a certain way and by remaining faithful to this it eventually re-creates its history in keeping with the divine promises. God acts in the community's history through the revealed symbols. In order to protect these divinely revealed symbols and repudiate false interpretations, the Christian community tried to lay hold of these symbols in a conceptual way and thus produced a set of doctrines. But these doctrines by themselves do not mediate the divine revelation. They initiate people into divine salvation only if they are grasped in their connection with, and dependence on, the revealed symbols. By putting primary stress on the noetic component of the Gospel, we have obscured the power of divine revelation; we have separated doctrines from the symbols they were meant to affirm and transformed them into conceptual information (usually quite unbelievable) about the divinity. By making use of the sociology of religion, the theologian is able to recover a broader, more action-oriented understanding of divine revelation and discover meaning and power in the Christian religion that has often been overlooked.

This is the approach we find in the writings of the sociologist Andrew Greeley.[16] While his writings are occasionally marred by outrageous generalizations and angry polemics against somebody else's position, his constructive effort to join theology and the sociology of religion in the interpretation of the Christian Gospel for modern society has been original and successful—and deserves the serious attention of theologians. As I have written elsewhere, I regard this application of symbol analysis to the understanding of the Gospel as the most fruitful trend in American theology.[17] Greeley has worked out his concept of symbol in line with the sociological studies of Talcott Parsons, Robert Bellah and Clifford Geertz, and after he applied this concept in a thological way to the interpretation of the Christian religion, he found himself, possibly to his surprise, very close to Paul Tillich's theological use of the symbolic. Greeley often adopts the Tillichian formulation that the Christian symbols shed light on human life and history, that they disclose the basic ambiguity of existence and reveal the divine graciousness operative at the heart of it. Christian symbols make known the hidden structure of reality; they reveal the divine judgment on the world and the hidden divine life present to the world, grounding and orienting the forward movement of life and history. (This recalls my earlier remarks on truth as critique and orientation.)

The constructive theological work of Rosemary Ruether, the most important section of which exists so far only in manuscript form, also uses symbols as the central instrument for interpreting the meaning and power of religion. Her understanding of symbol, however, is derived not from the sociology of religion, even if it is not in contradiction with it, but from her original training in classics and the study of ancient religions.

How does the symbolic understanding of divine revelation help theologians to solve the problems raised by the one and the many and the passage from the old to the new? Symbols have many meanings. In different cultural and socio-political situations the Christian symbols speak different languages. Since these symbols reveal the ambiguity of life and since the face of evil changes in various societies, the symbols will produce new meanings as the societies undergo significant changes. We touch here upon the extraordinary creativity of religion. Andrew Greeley, following his sociological method, trusts that symbols are resourceful; they give rise to many meanings. When the Christian community finds itself in a new social and cultural situation, the inherited symbols associated with the inherited meaning may at first fail to make sense or fail to illumine the life in which people actually find themselves, but as Christians wrestle with their religious inheritance in the new situation, the identical symbols will produce new meaning. They will eventually shed critical light on the concrete form of life and bring people in touch with the divine mystery present to them and carrying them forward. In his *The New Agenda*, Greeley uses this approach to explain the shift from the old to the new in the recent American Catholic experience. In other writings of his he has applied this method to interpret the covenant story and the Jesus story to our times. What remains constant and unchanging in the Christian religion are the symbols revealed in Israel and in Jesus Christ; what changes is their meaning. The formal function of these symbols remains the same in all ages and societies, yet their actual meaning undergoes significant transformations. While Andrew Greeley does not treat this approach in a speculative manner, his method offers a new and original way of reconciling the unity of the Gospel with its changing manifestations.

III

We now turn to another line, along which sociology has had an impact on Catholic theology. The first line had to do with the historicity of truth. The second one, which I wish to discuss in the remaining pages, has to do with the historicity of error.

Every age and every group of people produce their own form of blindness. This is an insight that is shared by those sociologists who have been willing to enter into dialogue with Karl Marx. Each group of people, through a largely unconscious process, creates an understanding of reality that legitimates its power and privileges. This, in Marxian language, is ideology. Ideology is the distortion of truth for the sake of social interest. We are all subject to some false consciousness. The sinfulness of the world, to use theological language, affects the very structure of human reason. This basic Marxian insight, which is so appealing to Augustinian theologians with their stress on the universality of sin, has been lifted from its original Marxian context and applied in a variety of ways in sociological approaches that have nothing to do with Marxism. Max Weber, who followed Marx neither in the view that economics is the primary social variable nor in his political eschatology, was quite willing to admit that the ideas of people and their religion always tend to fulfill a particular legitimating function in regard to their power and privileges. Max Weber did not reduce the meaning of ideas, culture and religion to this legitimating function, but he was willing to detect in them the ideological moment.

Let me add that a similar unconscious trend to produce false consciousness is also described in Freudian psychoanalysis, for there we are told that operative in our lives is the trend to build "defenses." To the extent that we are afraid and unwilling to deal with our instinctual conflicts and the unintegrated aspects of our personality, we build defenses—by a process of which we are unaware—that prevent us from seeing ourselves and the world as they really are. None of us is ever completely free of false consciousness even from this point of view. Even here we remain in need of on-going *metanoia*.

In sociology and psychology, then, we find a significant intellectual movement that looks upon error in human life not as accidental; error is just as profoundly rooted in our history as truth—and often just as revealing.

What is the relationship of ideology and religion? For Marx, religion was purely and simply false consciousness, even though he also wrote that "religious distress is at the same time the expression of real distress." "Religion," he continued, "is the sigh of the oppressed creature, the heart of a heartless world, the soul of soulless conditions."[18] Sociologists of religion did not follow Marx in seeing religion almost exclusively as ideological defense of the existing power relations. In three famous chapters of his *The Sociology of Religion*, Max Weber examined the relation of religion and class and showed that religion always had different layers and trends, some of which were conservative and some critical.[19] Weber readily admitted that there are situations where one and the same religion serves as the legitimation of the ruling class and the consolation of the lower classes. Since Weber's time a good deal of sociological research has been done on the social function of religion. While some sociologists put more emphasis on those aspects or trends of religion that legitimate the social and political status quo—religion as sacred canopy—others have focused more on prophetic and innovative religion, following Max Weber, and brought out the radical potential in the religious traditions.

Theologians can no longer stand back from the ideological critique of the Christian religion, to which the sociologists have led them. The time has come that we too must acknowledge the historicity of error. In the past we tended to attribute to human weakness the failings of the Church and the failure of the Christian religion in some situations to ally itself with the historical movements for truth and justice. We were of course ready to admit that we and our ancestors were fools and sinners. But today we can no longer regard these failings and failures as unfortunate and regrettable accidents. We must ask whether they were produced by the discrepancies built into our institutions and the identification of religion with the interests of the dominant classes. The worst we have done is closely linked to the best we have inherited. This is, alas, the human condition.

The power of ideological distortion of the truth impressed itself on me many years ago when I studied the anti-Jewish trends present in the Christian religion and their link to the formation of Western culture. Christians became contemptuous of the Jewish people not because they, the Christians, were sinners and failed to live up to the Christian call to love; they learned to despise the Jews and denigrate their religion because of the ideological framework in which the Gospel was proclaimed. Woven into the most precious things we have are the distortions, produced by social interest, that eventually translate themselves into institutional forces of destruction. The defense of the Christian claims against the synagogal reading of the Scriptures produced a Christian language that made the Jews appear as an inferior people and, as Rosemary Ruether has recently shown in her *Faith and*

Fraticide,[20] eventually led to the negation of their social existence altogether. Contemporary theologians, I repeat, find it impossible to stand back from submitting their religion to an ideological critique. This is what I mean by the historicity of error. Theologians believe, moreover, that it is ultimately the Spirit of God who leads them to engage in this critique.

How can ideological distortion or false consciousness be overcome? From a sociological point of view, false consciousness cannot be overcome by science or philosphy. New thinking alone will not do. Since the particular forms of blindness are rooted in the societal reality of the people struck by it, what is necessary is that they resituate themselves in regard to this society. What is needed is commitment and action. Ideas change when their "bearers" undergo significant societal changes.

From a theological point of view, we have to say that the process of conversion, commitment and action by which people are delivered from ideological distortion is summoned forth by God's Word and moved by God's Spirit. Hence theologians are quite willing to examine critically their own tradition, even if they find discrepancies built into its language and its institutions that seem to threaten the integrity of the whole. We have to be willing to feel the ground shake under us. Marx believed that by identification with the most oppressed class, true consciousness becomes available to people. This is not enough, for wherever people are situated, they are in need of an on-going critique. Christians want to add to the Marxsian formula that it is through identification in faith with the oppressed and crucified man Jesus that they begin to detect the structures of domination in the several institutions to which they belong and thus move toward overcoming the layers of false consciousness.

Let me add that this view of the historicity of error has introduced vehement controversies in the social sciences. The sociologists who defend the value-free nature of social science suppose that the error in sociological research is due to mistakes in measurement and failures in the use of logic. To gain more reliable results the social scientist must refine his measuring instruments and perfect his conceptual tools, sociologists who repudiate the value-neutrality of social science add that error in sociological research may also be due to an ideological distortion of the researcher's consciouness. What may be required, as we suggested above, is that scientists discover their actual place in the hermeneutical circle, and this may demand a raising of consciousness. Today sociology departments are divided on this methodological issue.

Contemporary Catholic theology has opened itself to the historicity of error. Theologians on the whole have been willing to submit their religion and even their theology to an ideological critique. I already mentioned the scholarly effort to discern and come to grips with the anti-Jewish ideology operative in the Christian tradition. Much work has also been done on the anti-feminist ideology of biblical religion, Judaism and Christianity. An outstanding example of this research is *Religion and Sexism*, a collection of several articles on the image of women during various periods of Western religion, edited by Rosemary Ruether. These studies show that the images of women, drawn from several distinct traditions, were various forms legitimating the existing structures that subjugated women and excluded them from public life.

We can think of many other examples of ideological deformations affecting the Christian religion. The question has been raised whether the tradition of monocratic power in the Catholic Church, according to which all ecclesiastical institutions are hierarchically ordered and government is exercised on every level, including the highest, by a single man, is grounded in a divinely revealed disposition or whether it is an ideological trend through which the monocratic episcopate that evolved more or less accidentally in the early Church was able to legitimate its claims and powers. This is an important question, for the experience of authority mediated to people through their religion has a profound effect on their social and political ideals. Sociologists have often pointed out the interaction between democratic structures of the Protestant churches and the democratic ideals of the political order. The question has been asked in Catholic theology whether the centralizing power of the papacy is a historical development guided by the Spirit, as it is usually supposed, or whether it is an ideological development that should be overcome. A growing number of Catholic theologians have adopted the latter view.[22]

In this context one should mention the issue raised by Max Weber and Ernst Troeltsch according to whom the so-called Protestant ethic has contributed to the creation of capitalism and remains its legitimation.[23] The Protestant religion is here seen as creating hard-working, individualist, self-reliant men who appreciate free enterprise and honest competition as the basis of economic life. According to Weber and Troeltsch these ideals were at odds with the older Christian tradition which placed the community at the center of people's awareness and presented individual life as a participation, albeit at a rather fixed place, in the life of the community. Weber's and Troeltsch's thesis has been confirmed by sociologists working in North America—for instance by Richard Niebuhr in the United States[24] and S. D. Clark in Canada.[25] According to Bryan Wilson, the British sociologist, it has been the genius of Protestantism to supply every rising class with the religious motivation and inward power to climb on the social and economic scale.[26] According to Will Herberg and Andrew Greeley this ethos is not confined to Protestantism in America; it is equally shared by Catholics and Jews.[27] It would appear, then, that the religion we have inherited is the inward spirit of what is excellent in capitalism, summoning people to the virtues necessary to make the system work and proscribing as sin the outlook and attitudes that undermine it. We note that this theory was by no means first proposed by Marxist sociologists. On the contrary, it represents a central theme in the sociology of religion. Ernst Troeltsch believed that the churches that have become successful, in whatever age, have allied themselves with the dominant classes and created a fusion between cultural ideals and reliaious aspirations.[28] At the same time, Troeltsch held that Christianity would again and again produce critical religious movements that tend to undermine the dominant values and provide people with a new vision of social life. In our days Christian theologians have taken these studies seriously and try to examine to what extent our inherited Church life is the legitimation of the prevalent economic system and its political consequences.

The " political theology " of Germany and "liberation theology" of Latin America are particularly sensitive to the historicity of error. According to these theological trends, in order to proclaim the Gospel it is necessary to make a sociological analysis of evil and injustice in society, then criticize the inherited religion to the extent that it legitimates these ills, and finally, relying on new commitment and religious experience, formulate the Christian message as God's promise to deliver the people from the sinful and demonic forces that distort their humanity. I mentioned above that American Catholics are sometimes overenthusiastic in regard to theologies produced in other parts of the world and try to incorporate these into their own thinking without first examining how they can be applied in North America. If theologians want to develop a critical theology for North America they will have to turn to social studies to clarify the structure of evil on this continent. Under the impact of sociology, Catholic theology is turning more consistently to the discernment of ideology in religion and culture. It has been suggested that consciousness-raising is the blameworthy invention of Paolo Freire; as a matter of fact the raising of consciousness is deeply rooted in the sociological tradition. Thanks to the influence of this sociological trend, there are a growing number of theologians who hold, with Edward Schillebeeckx, that unless we are committed to the emancipation or liberation of mankind, we are unable to free ourselves from ideology and formulate in a credible way the Christian message.[29]

The saving message of Jesus Christ intends to deliver people from false consciousness and appoints them to transform the world. This is not sociologically demonstrable, but this is what Christians believe. Jesus has come to deliver people from all of the enemies of life. This is the prophetic text with which Jesus introduced himself: "The Spirit of the Lord is upon me, because he has appointed me to preach good news to the poor; he has sent me to proclaim release to the capitives and recovering of sight to the blind, to set at liberty those who are oppressed, to proclaim the acceptable year of the Lord" (cf. Lk. 4:18-19). While this perception of divine redemption has not been formulated with its political implications prior to the impact of sociology on theology, the foundations of this wide view are amply present in Scripture and the Catholic tradition. In Jesus Christ God has acted on behalf of all of humankind; in Jesus Christ God has united himself not only with one man but through him with the entire human family; in Jesus

Christ God has revealed that there is a single destiny for all men and women, Christian and non-Christian alike. Jesus came to usher in a new age. Jesus is the instrument of God's kingdom which is promised to us at the end of time but which is anticipated by us in special moments of our history when we pass from sin to grace, from oppression to freedom, from blindness to sight. In the past, under the influence of individualistic cultural trends, we have often privatized the Gospel, i.e., we have often understood the Christian message as if it were addressed only to individuals Today, largely under the impact of sociological thinking, theologians are recovering their Christian foundation: they recognize that the Gospel has meaning for persons as well as societies. One of the tasks of contemporary religious thought is the deprivatization of the Christian message.

The impact of sociology on Catholic theology that I have examined in these pages lies in the application of two principles— the historicity of truth and the historicity of error. These two principles must be jointly applied in theological research and reflection—and this is not always easy. It is very difficult to decide whether a certain aspect of the religious tradition should be interpreted as an authentic expression of the Gospel in a given situation or as an ideological deformation of the truth. In his book *Infallible?* Hans Küng presents two interpretations of the teaching of Vatican I on infallibility.[30] This teaching may either have been the only way in which the Church could affirm its reliance on divine guidance in a culture in which truth was regarded in highly rationalistic terms (historicity of truth), or it may have been an ideological distortion of the Christian message on divine guidance, prompted by the quest for more papal power and ecclesiastical security (historicity of error). Küng does not decide between these two theories of interpretation. A one-sided emphasis on the historicity of error would eventually undermine all sources of wisdom inherited from the past, and a one-sided stress on the historicity of truth would lead to a theological method that could reconcile with the Gospel any and every development, however strange, in the life of the Church. Here again theologians are confronted by problems that also preoccupy sociologists. Shall they study societies mainly in terms of what they contribute to human well-being or rather in terms of the damage they do to people? Is there a set of criteria that enable sociologists to make such a decision in each concrete case? Or do they depend in this decision on a choice that is not derived from their science at all?

It is my view that sociologists (and the theologian) should approach the object of their study from a perspective that promises to make their work a contribution to the humanization of life. This raises many important issues which contemporary sociologists are no longer able to avoid. Social science, too, must serve the emancipation of the human race.

NOTES

1. G. Baum, "Sociology and Theology," *Concilium* 91 (New York: Herder & Herder, 1974), pp. 22-31. Cf. C.W. Mills, *The Sociological Imagination* (New York: Oxford University Press, 1958).

2. R. Nisbet, *The Sociological Tradition* (New York: Basic Books), pp. 21-46.

3. A. Greeley, *The New Agenda* (New York: Doubleday, 1973).

4. K. Mannheim. *Ideology and Utopia* (New York: Harcourt, Brace & World, no date), pp. 78-79, 85-87.

5. M. Weber, *The Protestant Ethic and the Spirit of Capitalism* (New York: Charles Scribner's Sons, 1958), p. 181.

6. M. Weber, "Science as a Vocation," in *From Max Weber*, ed. Gerth and Mills (New York: Oxford University Press, 1958), p. 155.

7. The important author who introduced phenomenology into North American sociology is Alfred Schutz. Cf. his *The Phenomenology of the Social World* (Evanston: Northwestern Univeristy Press, 1967).

8. J. O'Neil, *Making Sense Together* (New York: Harper & Row, 1974).

9. Mannheim, *Ideology and Utopia*, p. 268.

10. E. Troeltsch, *The Social Teaching of the Christian Churches* (New York: Harper & Row, 1960).

11. Mannheim, *Ideology and Utopia*, pp. 88-94.

12. Cf. G. Baum, "Science and Commitment: Historical Truth According to Ernst Troeltsch," *Journal of Philosophy of the Social Sciences* 1 (1971), 259-77. (Reprinted in this volume.)

13. The search for a new "objectivity" is found especially in the Frankfort School of social thought and its followers in North America. Cf. Martin Jay, *The Dialectical Imagination* (Boston: Little, Brown and Company, 1973).

14. K. Mannheim, "On the Interpretation of 'Weltanschauung,' " *Essays on the Sociology of Knowledge* (London: Routledge & Kegan Paul, 1952), p. 44.

15. R. Bellah, *Beyond Belief* (New York: Harper & Row, 1970), pp. 246-57.

16. A. Greeley, *What A Modern Catholic Believes About God?* (Chicago: Thomas More Press, 1971); *The Jesus Myth* (New York: Doubleday, 1971); *The Sinai Myth* (New York: Doubleday, 1972).

17. Greeley, *The New Agenda*, Foreword, pp. 11-34.

18. *Marx and Engels on Religion*, intr. by Reinhold Niebuhr (Schocken Books, 1964). p. 42.

19. M. Weber, *The Sociology of Religion* (Boston: Beacon Press, 1968), pp. 80-137.

20. R. Ruether, *Faith and Fratricide* (New York: Seabury Press, 1974).

21. R. Ruether, ed. *Religion and Sexism* (New York: Simon and Schuster, 1974).

22. Cf. P. Misner, "Papal Primacy in a Pluriform Polity," *Journal of Ecumenical Studies* 11 (1974), pp. 239-62.

23. M. Weber, *The Protestant Ethic and the Spirit of Capitalism*. For a collection of articles discussing the Weber thesis, see S.N. Eisenstadt, ed., *Protestant Ethic and Modernization* (New York: Basic Books, 1968).

24. H. Richard Niebuhr, *The Social Sources of Denominationalism* (New York: Meridian Books, 1957).

25. S.D. Clark, *Church and Sect in Canada* (University of Toronto Press, 1948).

26. Bryan Wilson, *Religion in Secular Society* (London: Penguin Books, 1969), p. 42.

27. W. Herberg, *Protestant, Catholic, Jew* (New York: Doubleday, 1955); A. Greeley, "The Protestant Ethic: Time for a Moratorium," *Sociological Analysis* 25 (1964), pp. 20-33.

28. Troeltsch, *The Social Teaching of the Christian Churches*, p. 331.

29. "In contemporary society, it is impossible to believe in a Christianity that is not at one with the movement to emancipate mankind": Edward Schillebeeckx, "Critical Theories and Christian Political Commitment," *Concilium* 84 (New York: Herder & Herder, 1974), p. 55.

30. H. Küng, *Infallible? An Inquiry* (New York: Doubleday, 1971), pp. 151-6.

Spirituality and Society

Spirituality is not simply a hidden reality. It takes place in the heart, and in this sense it remains invisible to others; at the same time, interiority in any of its forms translates itself into a personal stance toward society and other people, and in this sense becomes socially visible. Associated with any spirituality is a particular attitude toward the world. Inwardness issues forth in action, it has an impact on society, and for this reason sociologists have always studied spirituality as a significant factor in the making of the social world.

At the beginning of this century Max Weber proposed and defended the famous thesis that the inwardness of a certain Calvinism, especially in its Puritan form, had an important impact on the creation of modern society, characterized by industrialization, big business and technology. Weber showed that this particular Christian spirituality translated people's religious energies into purely secular activity, into work and dedication, and for this reason had a special affinity with the spirit of the new capitalism. The Protestant ethos, Weber held, gave sacred legitimation to worldly dedication, private enterprise, and the coolly "rational" style of life appropriate to the new class of manufacturers and merchants. The Protestant ethic strengthened the section of the population that became the creators of the modern, "rational," industrial and technological society, characterized by hard work, personal discipline, and self-promoting individualism.

No spirituality can be understood—this is the view of sociologists—unless one takes into account the social context in which it emerges and the impact it has on society. Since inwardness, be it religious or secular, translates itself into an ethos and a stance toward world, it cannot be fully grasped and evaluated unless we situate it in the concrete historical conditions in which it

129

flourishes. Any study of modern Christian spiritual trends and of the so-called new religions must be accompanied by a sober analysis of the conditions of modern life and the various *ethoses* or visions of life that characterize contemporary society.

In this lecture, then, I wish to describe four characteristic *ethoses,* well known to all of us, and then raise the question how Christian inwardness is related to these. Since the topic is large and the space available to me limited, these reflections are largely of an introductory kind.

Ethos I: The Work Ethic

Ethos I refers to the work ethics already mentioned in a previous paragraph. Max Weber thought that it was an original creation of Protestantism. What counts in this ethos is dedication, personal responsibility, hard work, the rational organization of one's private life, and the careful restriction of those aspects of life, such as the emotional and the "irrational," that interfere with the industrious, productive life. Ethos I demands that we achieve, that we prove ourselves in success and that we become reliable and efficient personalities. At one time Ethos I was a religious attitude, but as modern society became more pervasive its secular institutions, such as the schools, mediated the Protestant ethic to people without religious inspiration. The work ethic thus became the dominant secular ethos of industrial society.

We see the characteristics of Ethos I more clearly when we compare it with other kinds of spirituality. As a pre-capitalist, pre-industrial religion, Catholicism created spiritual styles appropriate to its society, with emphasis on contemplation and celebration rather than on work. Weber himself contrasts the difference found among Protestant and Catholic workers in Europe as late as the end of the nineteenth century. When a factory owner promises more money for piece work to Protestant workers in England or Germany, they will work harder so that by the end of the day they will go home with a thicker pay envelope. But if the factory owner promises more money for piece work to Catholic workers in Spain or Poland, the workers will do less work—because by noon they will have earned enough money for the day and feel justified taking it easy in the afternoon. Weber makes it clear that in an aristocratic society, religion cannot make hard work a central virtue nor can it condemn laziness as a social vice. Why not? Because the aristocracy does not work. The aristocracy was often engaged in fighting and defending their territories and in many instances they were also involved in administrative tasks, but their social existence was not defined by work, either manual or mental, as it was for the lower classes. Since dominant religion tends to identify with the concerns of the ruling class, pre-capitalist Catholicism did not understand the Gospel as a call to work. In feudal Europe, every stratum of society had its own appropriate ethos and it was the genius of Catholicism to reconcile these various *ethoses* in the vision of a single, stratified society, based on mutual respect and cooperation. Needless to say, when Catholics came to live in modern industrialized society they were socialized into Ethos I. Sociological research has shown that in the United States Catholics exhibit the same dedication to achievement and self-promotion as do Protestants.

We come to understand Ethos I better if we study the difficulties experienced by people from a tribal background who enter modern, urban industrial society. Tribal life produces solidarity and cohesion and inspires a conservative attitude toward the structures of life. In tribal society human life is close to nature and its rhythms. When people from such a background find themselves in the city, they become wholly disoriented. They are at first quite unable to become industrious, efficient, responsible, self-promoting workers. They find it hard to keep a job. They are not inwardly geared to industrial life. Moreover they suffer from the dissolution of the kinship ties; they become lonely, dislocated people without the inner resources to engage in the competitive struggle for economic survival that characterizes modern society. Sociologists have shown that these people have found in religious sects, Christian and even non-Christian, a spiritual home that mediates to them Ethos I and empowers them to survive and in many instances, to thrive in modern industrial society. The sects are important socializing agents. Here the people who have newly arrived in the city find a spiritual tribe; they experience close personal ties, a little like the kinship solidarity they experienced in the past. In the sect they are allowed to express their emotions. At the same time the sectarian ethos to which they are introduced makes strict moral demands on them: they become strict with themselves, and learn how to be dedicated, reliable, and punctual; they become good workers; they learn how to live well, save their money, and constrain their sensuality. At the same time, the sects provide an outlet for the emotions in prayer meetings and worship services: they welcome the "irrational" side of life. Here the believers are allowed to express their feelings, to sing and shout, to move their bodies and reach out after ecstasy. These services provide an escape from the cruel discipline which modern society demands of people. At the same time, the sects limit these forms of spontaneous self-expression to definite intervals. When Monday morning comes, the members are again ready for the factory. They have been empowered once again to get through the week with Ethos I.

This socialization of people into modern society can be observed in African and South American societies. In earlier times the entry into industrial society was a European and American phenomenon. When the peasants of Europe had to move to the city to become workers, they underwent a very similar process. In fact Bryan Wilson, the British sociologist, thinks that it has been the genius of Protestantism to help various groups of people to enter modern society and in fact, by providing them with the appropriate work ethic, to enable them to rise to higher levels in that society.

Ethos II: Consumerism

In classical capitalism the central issue was production. Needed in society were dedicated workers on every level, in the factory, in the office, and in management. But in late capitalism the central issue has come to include consumption. Since technological perfection enables us to produce an enormous number of goods and since our industries are managed to increase the profit of the owners, we find ourselves with an overflow of commodities. Who is going to buy all these things? What counts in late capitalism is, therefore, the extension of the market. This has political consequences. To gain access to cheap resources and create new markets overseas, the highly industrialized countries expanded their political influence on the other continents: they either incorporated distant lands into themselves as colonies or created close ties with them by integrating them into an economic system controlled by them. But the extension of the market also has cultural consequences. Since we have to start buying more commodities ourselves, we start dreaming of an ever increasing standard of living, we desire to spend more money on improving the house in which we live, the clothes we wear, the food we eat and the leisure which is ours. We become consumers. Pleasure, physical comfort, having a good time, expensive hobbies, all styles of life prohibited by Ethos I, exercise an important economic function in late capitalist society: they consume products.

The new ethos is so important for the functioning of the present society that mass media and advertising companies try their best to make us into consumers. We desire new things all the time. A certain social pressure, the expectation of other people, and a subtle blackmail exercised by society make us into ever eager customers; we buy more things than we really need, we spend money we cannot afford, and we often find ourselves in debt. We are taught to dream of leisure, of long weekends, of free time to spend money and buy new pleasures.

One should add here that in the technological society of today the division of labor in the productive process has become very complex. The great majority of people perform insignificant jobs; they only deal with a tiny aspect of production, and they are cut off from the total process so that they never see the whole picture. For this reason, the vast majority of people in our society have tedious work. And because work is boring, devoid of creativity and imagination, people dream more intensely of their leisure time, after five o'clock, on the weekends, and above all on the brief vacation once a year. These periods have to reward us for the tedium of life. Then we become swingers, spending money lavishly on enjoyment and comfort. Ethos II makes us into pleasure seekers.

It is worth mentioning here that young people have become an important market for our industries. If they can develop their own taste in music and clothes, in styles of entertainment and expensive equipment such as cameras and stereos, they will buy and consume the commodities produced by our industries. It may even be important to introduce children to Ethos II. While they have no direct access to money, they could be made to persuade their parents to buy them clothes, toys and equipment that give them pleasure and mark them off as superior to those children whose parents cannot afford these things. In the middle class, Ethos II is quite capable of making parents spend money they do not have so that their children will not feel inferior among their peers at school.

Ethos II promotes what I will call "expensive hedonism." Further on we shall examine how the various contemporary *ethoses* are related to pleasure. For the moment we want to point out that Ethos II generates a conflictual approach to life since for the great majority of people it has to be coupled with elements of the work ethic. Production must still go on. We still have to earn the money we spend. The work ethic remains the ideal from 9 to 5. In the office or at the work place we still must be dedicated, efficient, responsible, and self-promoting, but this dedication to work now no longer defines our entire existence. We no longer discipline our lives as we used to in Ethos I. For as soon as the office hours are over, we want to move into the joy of living. Sometimes a few martinis can be of help here. But if we cannot enjoy ourselves in the evening, then at least there is the weekend when we have occasion to spend money on a good time. Ethos II is conflictual because it contains a double message: be dedicated in the day time and be a swinger at night and on the weekend. Can we really do this over a long period of time? Some people become troubled by headaches and anxieties, and they begin to use tranquilizers and medicines of various kinds to keep up the pace. While these irritations lay the foundation for a large drug market useful for the expanding economy, they often have debilitating consequences for personal life.

Ethos III: Person Growth

With Ethos III we enter a world that is very familiar to us. This inward stance is defined by openness, dialogue, the quest for authenticity and personal growth. Here people recognize that they have potentials as yet undiscovered and unused. They feel that this lack of personal development is largely due to strictures imposed on them by society, and that they could develop, explore their powers, and realize more fully their destiny if they were open to the new, engaged in trusting conversation and cooperation with others, and defining the norms of personal life not in accordance with the inherited code but in terms of personal authenticity and loving human relations. Ethos III has emerged in the twentieth century thanks to the influence of the psychotherapeutic movement, existentialist thought and personalist philosophy. It finds expression in our educational theories, in our cultural ideals and even in our present religious aspirations.

If we read contemporary literature carefully, we observe that Ethos III appears with two contrasting emphases. When some people speak about openness and personal growth, they recommend an ideal of self-realization that places the self at the center of the imagination. The quest for personal fulfillment beyond the limits of traditional behavior appears here as a gentle and sophisticated individualism. Moving forward toward the exploration of our hidden powers, we tend to be interested above all in ourselves.

There is, however, another vision of Ethos III, one that recognizes that self-centeredness in all its forms, even in the most sophisticated, is a barrier preventing us from following our destiny. If self-realization places the self at the center of the imagination, then it locks us into a prison and prevents us from fulfilling our true powers. The more sensitive trend in Ethos III realizes that maturing persons are enabled to forget themselves and become present to others. The ideal of self-realization does not put the self into the center of the imagination: on the contrary, the quest for authenticity and sustained openness to others frees people to leave themselves behind, lose themselves in a reality that is greater than they, and ultimately serve the ultimate value that sustains the loving community. For religious people, self-transcendence made possible through personal growth leads ultimately to the surrender to God in which human life finds fulfillment of its hidden powers. With this accent, Ethos III is not a self-indulgent ethic, a subtle narcissism; it is rather our entry into our destiny. Openness, growth, exploration, and fulfillment in this context presupposes our hidden potentiality to transcend ourselves. Christians believe that the human movement toward self-transcendence is due to God's grace.

Ethos III, then, is not without its ambiguities. Today a growing number of Christians situate themselves within this ethos. They interpret the Christian Gospel as a call to personal growth and a power unto self-transcendence. They understand the divine presence to human life as a liberating power enabling people to live their humanity to the full, explore their hidden potentialities, transcend their damaged resources and enter upon a creativity of ever new proportions. These Christians approve of the unconventional life, they recognize that many old customs and rules must be broken, but they trust that in following the quest for authenticity they will be delivered from self-centeredness and forget themselves in the expectation of God's kingdom, to use the ancient biblical expression. A good deal of modern theology and contemporary spirituality are written from this viewpoint. Ethos III influenced certain sections of Vatican II. At the same time, this Christian literature provides also critical principles that enable us to discern and overcome the ambiguity of Ethos III.

To what groups in society appeals Ethos III in its secular or religious form? I suggest that they are mainly salaried people whose work is interesting. Salaried people are somewhat removed from the competitive climate of the modern economy. Even though growing unemployment and layoffs have recently made life more competitive in institutions serving the public—I am thinking of teaching and social work, for instance—still salaried men and women are largely protected from the pressures that characterize the world of production and business. Some of these salaried people have interesting work. (Interesting work, let me add, is a great gift which, alas, is only enjoyed by a small minority in our society.) Interesting jobs are those that serve other people: this includes positions in schools, social work, ministry, community organization, communications and the arts, etc. It is to these people, I suggest, that Ethos III appeals. The harassed businessman, the exhausted laborer, the overworked housewife—the majority of the population, in other words—do not know how to make sense of the quest for authenticity and openness to being.

They are often condemned to use all their energies just to survive. Ethos III is critical of Ethos I and Ethos II. For if personal growth becomes a way of life, then the work ethic of achievement and production appears as damaging and the hunt for commodities and expensive pleasures as inauthentic. Ethos III in fact implies a criticism of modern industrial society. From the viewpoint of Ethos III, contemporary society appears as an impersonal, technologically defined and bureaucratically controlled machine that does not allow the people who participate in it to grow and find their authentic human destiny. Ethos III, therefore, encourages a certain politics of personal growth. The people identified with this ethos want to increase the participation of the many in the decisions made by the few. They favor decentralization, shared responsibility, and the involvement on all levels of participants in the societal process. A participatory society would allow people to become more truly human through their daily activities. This politics of personal growth, one should add, is highly idealistic, not to say unrealistic, for the people with real power never permit others to share in it. People with power seem to cling to it. For this reason it is only at some universities, in some schools, in some social agencies—in other words, in institutions apart from the economic and political sector—that this participatory approach to organization has been tried. Despite the promising statements made at Vatican II, the ideal of greater participation has not yet modified the exercise of power in the Catholic Church. The jurisdictional order is still strictly from the top down, even though the ideals have become collegial.

Ethos IV: Emancipation

With Ethos IV we move into a different world. This ethic has emerged among groups and peoples, oppressed by the dominant society, who are struggling for liberation. In North America, best known among these is the black movement. Here people have become aware not only of the inferiorization inflicted upon them by the dominant structures of society but also of the distorted self-image and the concomitant passivity which this oppression has induced in them. The power of domination works through political and economic institutions, but it also achieves its goal through the creation of a particular kind of imagination. Oppressed people can be made to feel that they find themselves at the lowest level because this is where they belong. Emancipatory movements, therefore, while reaching out for political goals and economic power, have a spiritual task; they promote a new self-understanding. Black is beautiful. These movements also create a heightened sense of solidarity. One is fully justified, therefore, to speak of a special ethos associated with liberation movements. In some radical literature, authors have adopted the term "the raising of consciousness." They see the task of the liberation movement to make the oppressed group aware of their inferiorized situation, permit them to experience the anger they have long felt for the oppressor but were unable to express, teach them to affirm themselves in pride and become conscious of their social power, and transform the people into a single-minded community dedicated to their collective emancipation.

We find this ethos among the blacks in North America. But similar movements exist in other parts of the world directed against the consequences of the colonial system and imperialism, whether political or economic. Ethos IV finds expression in the women's movement. Other disadvantaged groups in North America, marginalized by the established institutions, are presently exploring the meaning of Ethos IV for their situation. We think of the native peoples, and we recall the Mexican Americans and Puerto Ricans in the U.S.A. and the movement for Quebec independence in Canada. But the present system excludes from self-determination and the goods of life not only ethnic communities and women but also a large section of the population, the lower section—that is, the people whose lives are ruled by economic necessity and whose powers are constantly exploited for the profit of others. Many Americans and Canadians are today engaged in a quest for emancipation from the contradictions of the present economic order.

That modern society needs liberation from the present economic system—i.e., the late form of capitalism culminating in the economic dictatorship of the transnational corporation—is today not only the view of radical political thinkers, but also the growing conviction of moderate social observers. We could invoke here the teaching of popes and bishops. In a recent public statement, the Canadian bishops have reiterated the now common Catholic position that the present economic system inevitably widens the gap between rich and poor nations and produces an unjust distribution of wealth. Ethos IV is, therefore, not confined to groups marked by colonial exploitation or by sexual and cultural oppression; it exists also in the mainstream of North American life among those who recognize the inadequacies of the economic system that, to quote again the Canadian bishops, "maximizes power, profit and consumption."

Ethos IV is critical of the three *ethoses* previously described. Ethos I is too individualistic. To work hard, achieve and look after one's own promotion may work in the middle class: among the oppressed such an ethos would undermine the sense of solidarity necessary for the emancipatory struggle. The successful among the oppressed groups and classes are often tempted by Ethos I; they are tempted to move ahead, climb on the social scale, break their tie with their original community and become self-promoters along with the other successful people in society. The black community, to give a single example, is often robbed of its natural leaders because blacks who do well as organizers or academics are quickly hired by white institutions, move to a new neighborhood, and lose contact with their black brothers and sisters. In a recent "Black Theology Project, Atlanta '77," this temptation was spelled out in detail. The same document also warned the struggling black community against the modern style of life we have called Ethos II. The striving for commodities and expensive pleasures destroys the meaning of the liberation movement. Ethos IV, then, must supply a spirituality, secular or religious, that prevents the struggling people from identifying with the worst features, especially the egotism, of the dominant society.

Ethos IV is also critical of the ethic of human growth. For while this ethic opposes human domination of others and dreams of human passage from the realm of necessity to the realm of freedom, it seems to presuppose a certain middle class status and a salaried position plus interesting work. In a situation of oppression, ideals such as authenticity, openness and personal growth seem very far away. Dialogue is possible only among equals. Oppressed groups, on the other hand, must learn the politics of confrontation. Since many of them are struggling for basic justice, the sensitivity to a highly personalized bourgeois conscience does not appeal to them. Ethos IV is characterized by a more radical rejection of society's dominant values. It advocates a transvaluation of values. Since the norms and ideals of the dominant culture, including the churches, tend to legitimate the existing order with its oppressive structure, the liberation movement wants to invert them. The first shall be last and the last shall be first. Ethos IV adopts a language of negation and inversion to raise the awareness of the oppressed people and strengthen the bonds of solidarity. Ethos IV sustains them in their protracted struggle by offering a utopian vision of the future society.

Ethos IV assumes different forms in different liberation movements. The emancipatory ethos exists with contrasting emphases. In some radical literature, the movement for liberation is exclusively concerned with the suffering people at the bottom and visualizes their eventual entry into the position of power. In other radical literature, more congenial to Christians, the liberation movement is concerned with the suffering people at the bottom as well as the powerful at the top. For this literature, going back to Hegel's famous analysis of the master-servant relationship, shows that the exploitative relationship between the dominant and the dominated not only damages the people at the bottom but also dehumanizes the people at the top. The masters, too, are estranged from their true humanity, and for this reason the inversion of the established order will not only free the oppressed but also allow the oppressor to enter more deeply into his or her humanity. In this literature, the oppressed do not look forward to occupying the place of the oppressor; on the contrary, they look forward to a new order where no group will define itself by the power it wields over others. In this form Ethos IV anticipates the eventual overcoming of man's exploitation of man.

Christian Spiritualities

After this brief description of four *ethoses* found in contemporary society, we must ask how the Christian Gospel is related to them. We have already made several observations on this topic. The Christian churches have shown that the Gospel can be understood as God's call and appointment to live within Ethos I. Ethos I, let me add, exists with contrasting emphases. For it is possible to live a life of dedication, frugality, and achievement joined to an overriding egotism and indifference in regard to others, yet it is also possible to follow the work ethic and emphasize personal responsibility within a margin defined by Christian or humanist ideals of mutual help and common concern. When Christian spirituality endorses Ethos I, it has always sought to correct the spirit of self-promotion by an emphasis on public welfare. Liberal society itself, one might add, discovered already in the nineteenth century that the owners of industry and commerce should be interested in improving the social conditions of the poor and the workers because only through social reform, it was argued, would society become stable and the lower classes make enough money to become customers and consumers in the market economy. Here egotism is tamed by enlightened self-interest. In this context, even without special Christian inspiration, Ethos I has its own reformist dimension.

In North America today we observe a growing return to Ethos I. We find this in the traditional churches as well as in the expanding evangelical movements. People are troubled by the disorder in society, they are torn apart by the conflicting values with which they are confronted, and because of this experience of normlessness—Barbara Hargrove uses the term "anomie" for this—they turn to a religion that gives clear definitions of right and wrong, defends the existing order of things, and offers them peace as useful, hard-working citizens. Anomie strengthens conservative religion. Yet it seems to me that today Christians can identify themselves totally with Ethos I only if they repress the critical, prophetic tradition of the Gospel. At this time, church leadership is most sensitive to this prophetic mission. I have mentioned the Canadian bishops; I might equally well have turned to other church leaders among the major denominations in Canada and the United States. We find the same prophetic spirit at the World Council of Churches and in the social teaching of the papacy. Here the present order is criticized, not legitimated. Because of this remarkable leadership the Christian churches cannot simply return to Ethos I; they also promote other spiritual stances, stances connected with Ethos III or Ethos IV.

The return to Ethos I is today advocated by some secular thinkers and politicians. While they themselves are not religious, they hope that the churches will return to the work ethic and the old virtues so that American society will become more stable and recover its aggressive self-assurance. They prefer stability to justice. An example of this is the recent book by Daniel Bell, *The Cultural Contradictions of Capitalism*. The author shows that present society is being torn apart by two antithetical trends: the industrial system demands hard work and dedication, yet the cultural movement favors the search for pleasure and happiness. Bell does not notice that modern pleasure-seeking is largely induced by the economic system itself and the need for ever increasing consumption. He equates what I have called "expensive hedonism" with the quest for enjoyment. How can we return to a stable society? he asks. How can the industrial society again become a smoothly running machine without endless complaints, disruptions and upheavals? What we need, Bell thinks, is to stimulate a cultural movement that will persuade people that happiness is not so important. But what cultural forces are there that counter the human quest for enjoyment? Bell thinks that religion is today the only force that could make pleasure appear undesirable and persuade people to give up the search for self-fulfillment and sacrifice the search for personal happiness. For this reason Bell advocates a return to conservative religion. What we need is Ethos I.

In this context, let me examine the relationship of the various *ethoses* to pleasure. This is important since in the Christian tradition there has been a strong tendency to slander pleasure and persuade people that there is something wrong with it. Fortunately there have also been other, corrective trends in Christianity. Ethos I, as we indicated above, is cautious in regard to pleasure.

To the extent that pleasure interrupts the work routine and hinders us from becoming achievers, it should be avoided. The only pleasure recommended is one that refreshes us and sends us back to work with new vigor. Ethos II, as we saw, promotes all the pleasures that money can buy. It fosters a materialistic outlook on life where all qualities are transformed into quantities and the measure of reality is its price. Marx called this "the fetishism of commodities." This expensive hedonism has a clearly defined economic role, namely to increase consumption. In Ethos III pleasure plays a different role altogether. For here pleasure is affirmed as an expression of the liberated person. It is welcome as a way of growth and fulfillment. Ethos III, however, creates its own critique of pleasure to the extent that it impedes personal growth. Ethos III recognizes that the search for pleasure can be a flight from the important things in life, from self-knowledge, from love or personal responsibility. Not all pleasure then is welcome, but only that pleasure which flows from the freedom of the heart and the expansion of the personality. In the Christian churches, Ethos III, properly formulated in theological terms, has done much to give pleasure a theological status in the Christian life. Such a counterweight against an ancient suspicion of pleasure has been badly needed.

In the ethics of emancipation, it seems to me, pleasure again has a different meaning. For the oppressed people, pleasure is a foretaste of the freedom toward which they move. Black people have written about the pleasure of dancing. They have explained that in a world which despised them and which at all levels assigned them an inferior place they found that dancing was their true home. There they expressed their freedom, there they enjoyed themselves, there they did what they could nowhere else in society—create their own beautiful world. In the literature of oppressed groups we find that the moralism of the established society which prohibits pleasure, including sexual pleasure, is seen by the people struggling for liberation as part and parcel of the big No which society says to them on every level. The dominant morality appears to them as part of the oppressive order. Again, pleasure here becomes a moment of anticipation. Liberation movements become restrictive in regard to pleasure only when they are successful. When the national revolution has been successful, when the new nation struggles for increased production and prosperity, we usually observe a return to a more traditional morality and the restriction of pleasure. What counts in the new society is hard work, and what is needed for this is Ethos I.

It is important that Christian teachers not prejudice people against pleasure. The negative attitude of the past has made many Christians haters of life rather than lovers of it. Today we must find an affirmative approach to pleasure. We need ascetical principles that enable us to discern the personal and social meaning of pleasure. A few years ago, the Canadian Catholic bishops wrote a beautiful pastoral letter on hunger in the world and its implications for the Canadian people. In one section the pastoral letter dealt with the political aspects of the problem and made daring recommendations to the Canadian government including, as the most startling, the abolition of the free market for the distribution of food. Why? Because the free market distributes food only to people with the ability to pay, while what is necessary is to distribute food to all people. God has created food for all, not just for people with money. In another section, the same pastoral letter dealt with the personal response to world hunger. Here it advocated the search for a simpler, a more modest life-style in the developed countries. In this context the bishops said that we have become too greedy in regard to food, too eager to satisfy our sensuousness; we should reduce our enjoyment at meals and think more of the hungry world when we are at the table. Since I was greatly moved by the pastoral letter and at the same time had difficulties with the way in which the bishops recommended the simple life, I took the liberty of writing to them. The Church, I argued, should not engage itself against pleasure. We have made people feel guilty about sexuality in the past. If we now make them feel guilty when they enjoy their meals, we pit the Gospel against our nature as God created it. The instincts were created to be our friends, not our enemies. If, therefore, it is necessary in today's hungry world to tell people that the simple life is more truly evangelical and that simple food is to be preferred by us in the developed countries, above all for its symbolic meaning, revealing our solidarity with the whole human family, then we must do this not by making people feel guilty about the pleasure of eating but rather by arguing that is is possible for us to enjoy simple food, good bread, cider and cheese, as much and even more than others enjoy gourmet food tainted as it is by its symbolic connection with elitism and economic privilege. We are in need of a spirituality that reveals to us how pleasure, gratuitous pleasure (not commodities), nourishes the Christian life.

Christian spirituality, we conclude, can locate itself in Ethos I and, as we have seen above, in Ethos III. It has no use whatever for Ethos II. But Christian spirituality can also find a context in the ethos of emancipation. Both the Old and the New Testaments provide a prophetic spirituality that judges the existing system, yearns for the coming of a new order and prays for the transvaluation of values. "The first shall be last and the last first." "Thy kingdom come!" "The powerful shall be pushed from their thrones and the lowly will be exalted; the rich shall be sent away empty and the poor will be filled with good things." In fact, a very good argument can be made that the secular emancipatory movements, including Marxism, have derived their passion and their basic vision of history from these biblical sources. In the sixteenth century the Anabaptists brought to life the radical biblical tradition with its apocalyptical overtones and created a theological language of judgment, of struggle, and of hope that nourished movements of resistance or revolt. This language never disappeared anymore from the West. It was to this language that the oppressed or exploited turned, even though in most cases mediated through secular agents. Today Christians are finding their way back to Ethos IV.

If Christianity is so pluralistic, what is the task of the religious educator? Some people think that religious education and public preaching should be indentified with a single ethos. It seems to me that this would not be an adequate policy in the long run. The Christian Church is too multiform at this time. What is necessary, therefore, is to present Christian teaching as providing spiritualities for several responsible stances in life, Ethos I, III and IV. This pluralistic approach is liberating in itself since it presents the Gospel not as a finished system imposed on us by the Church but as an open-ended tradition. It depends on the social background of individual students and on their personal development (including the special call of grace) what Christian ethos they wish to embrace. This seems to me the only realistic policy for religious education in North America. The attempt to make Ethos III or IV normative will produce a powerful opposition from the advocates of Ethos I, and since they are likely to be in a majority, they could threaten the survival of the alternative *ethoses* in the Church's official teaching. In many instances, the account of Ethos IV in the Church and a description of the social conditions in which this ethic emerged will profoundly affect students, especially if this approach is not made normative for them. Only after living with the new ideas for a while in a non-threatening situation do many of us become moved to action and capable of assimilating these ideas as our own.

Have these four *ethoses* left enough room for the classification of the new religions? I am not quite certain of this. We have already mentioned the return to conservative religion among vast numbers of people afflicted by society with anomie. There is, however, another affliction—again I follow Barbara Hargrove—which can be called "alienation." Here people feel that society estranges them from their own powers, their inner meaning, their true human destiny. Alienated people of this kind are attracted by many of the new, non-conformist religions, many of which are influenced by Eastern spirituality and put an emphasis on comtemplation. These young people swim against the stream, they oppose the dominant values, they reject the work ethic of society and the achievement orientation of their parents. Does their spiritual stance create a new ethos? Do we find here the emergence of a new force? Since these movements are so new, it is difficult to reply to this question. Some groups like the Moonies, which at first give the impression of being counterculture and standing in judgment on our society, turn out to be supporters of Ethos I and protectors of the virtuous society, preferring stability to justice. Other groups that appear countercultural, when confronted with the problem of organizing a large movement, easily turn to models drawn from the business logic into their movement, a logic that runs counter to the original inspiration. Transcendental Meditation, we hear, has become a big business; it is packaged and sold at a reasonable profit. But where does non-organized mysticism stand? Seventy years ago Ernst Troeltsch concluded in his sociology of the Christian religion that mysticism in any of its forms remains on the whole restricted to the comfortable classes, the classes whose main problem is not economic survival nor the tedious drudgery of every day. Maybe this is still true today. The question arises, therefore, whether the power of the present-day society is so strong that the new religions, especially when they become big movements, find themselves driven to the dominant conservative religious ethos, Ethos I, unless they move closer to the therapeutic and existentialist wisdom of Ethos III or the more radical social yearning for the realm of freedom associated with Ethos IV. As a tentative conclusion I propose, then, that the three spiritual stances define the possibilities of contemporary spirituality: Ethos I, III, and IV.

Sociology as Critical Humanism

In this essay I wish to present sociology as a critical humanism. I realize, of course, that this is not the sociology that university students necessarily meet in social science departments.
Dominant in many sociology departments is the spirit of positivism. Many students studying sociology at a university get
the impression that social science creates an attitude to society
which eliminates social ideals and moral commitment and promotes a detached and value-free approach to contemporary social
problems.

The Spirit of Positivism

Before turning to the sources of classical sociology and examining the humanism of the founders of modern social thought,
let me clarify what I mean by the spirit of positivism. By positivism I refer to the attempt on the part of the social sciences to
assimilate as much as possible the scientific method derived from
the natural sciences. What does this mean? It means, first of all,
that sociologists will try to "measure" social action in some way,
and to do this they must translate all qualities into quantities.
Mathematical logic can be applied to human action only to the
extent that it is quantified. Sociologists following the spirit of
positivism will therefore search for quantitative data, and whatever cannot be numbered will have to be neglected by them.
Second, sociologists who want to follow the scientific method in
their research will propose hypotheses as causal explanations of
social behavior and then try to verify these with the help of exper-
iments, empirical observation and complex mathematical reasoning. What is presupposed here, and this is the third characteristic of
positivism, is that social behavior is determined by fixed laws

which researchers are able to discover. As physics discovers the laws operative in the physical universe, so can sociology disclose the laws of society. According to positivism, then, society is not a human project in which people are involved as participants; it is rather a fixed system determined by social processes independent of people's intentions, dreams and creativity. Fourth and finally, since they search for laws implicit in social behavior, positivistically-oriented sociologists think that it is possible to predict what will happen in society. According to them, predictions is the highest achievement of the social sciences. Because of this, these social scientists feel that sociology deserves to be called a science in the strictest sense.

For the founders of sociology whom I wish to discuss in this chapter, human action was never simply behavior, never simply external action to be observed from without and grasped in quantitative terms. Social action was always *behavior plus meaning*. It is not enough to take into account the observable behavior of people; it is equally important to understand the meaning that the actors assigned to their behavior. And while quantitative methods are useful and in fact indispensable for the study of behavior, they are useless when it comes to the understanding of meaning. What is required here are methods of interpretation, thanks to which sociologists can come to understand what social action means to the actors engaged in it. Positivism supressed the question of meaning.

Let me indicate very briefly the harmful consequences of the spirit of positivism. The following remarks are by no means derived from my own critical reflection. They are derived from a body of sociological literature critical of positivism. Even in periods when positivistic sociology ruled the intellectual climate at universities, there were always the few, the exceptional scholars, who repudiated the dominant trend and tried to clarify its dehumanizing impact on society. The sociologists who come to my mind as I am saying this are Karl Mannheim in the Germany of the 1920's and C. Wright Mills in the United States of the 1950's. The list of such names could easily be prolonged.

What then are some of the dehumanizing consequences of the spirit of positivism? Most apparent is the fact, verified in personal experience, that the purely quantitative approach reduces the human being to diminished proportions. Positivism is a form of reductionism. In its attempt to understand society, positivism only considers the measurable dimension and wholly overlooks the aspect of meaning, intention, freedom and vision. From this it follows, secondly, that society is no longer seen as a creative process in which people participate often out of resources of personal freedom. Society becomes a fully determined system in which people, as the constituting units, are moved to action according to determinable laws. Lost is the vision that the social process not only produces and reproduces society but also affects the persons involved in it and significantly modifies their self-understanding. Positivism is not open to changes in people's perception of themselves. Imagination and consciousness have no effect on what takes place in society.

The ideal of positivism is perfect objectivity; this is the third problematic consequence. As scientists study the physical universe by abstracting from their personal feelings and seeking perfect detachment, so will positivistically-oriented sociologists separate themselves from their spontaneous reactions to the social events they study. Scholars should not get emotionally involved in the objects of their research. If they want to achieve reliable results, they should shrug their shoulders, assume a value-free stance, and disregard the actual relationship which links them to the objects they are studying. The social scientist who follows the spirit of positivism is able to study the social injustices of contemporary history without responding with moral indignation.

Sociologists steeped in this spirit will teach their students to shrug their shoulders. In a certain sense, of course, all sociologists want to be "objective"; all want to separate themselves from personal bias and preferred cultural ideals, all want to be objective in their research in the face of the pressure which government or church authorities put on them. On the other hand, sociologists who repudiate positivism insist that in order to understand social action we need the right perspective; not every perspective that observers may adopt reveals the truth. Some sociologists insist that the best angle for discovering the truth about society is accessible to researchers only through a commitment to human emancipation.

The fourth debilitating effect of positivism, related to the preceding, is that it makes scholars disregard the actual historical relationship to the objects they study. How has the world with which the scholar is identified affected the social action he now studies? And, conversely, how has the object of research affected the scholar's own history and the formation of his consciousness? The stance of objectivity that positivistic sociologists adopt makes them blind to the historical links that tie them to the object of their research. Positivists think of themselves as value-free. But because they do not engage in critical reflection on their own situation and their intentionality, they are unable to discover how their supposed objectivity is actually produced by an identification with the dominant values of their own culture. The claim of value-neutrality is only too often a disguise; it hides the scholars' endorsement of the dominant cultural norms. It is impossible to study social action without being guided in one way or another by a vision of what human life is meant to be. Implicit in all social research is a philosophical (or theological) anthropology. Our symbols of what human life is destined to be shape our responses to people and society and affect the social perception of reality.

After this all too brief description of the spirit of positivism, I wish to turn to the central idea of this essay. What I want to show is that originally sociology was a critical humanism. The founders of sociology—in this lecture I will refer to Alexis de Tocqueville, Karl Marx, Emile Durkheim and Max Weber—were men who sought objectivity in the sense that they tried to overcome inherited prejudices; at the same time they were men committed to values. They were humanists. When I insist that they were critical humanists, I claim that they were not content with human life as they found it in modern society; they suspected that dehumanizing forces were at work in society; they created sociological science to analyze these destructive forces and to examine whether there were trends in society that promise to remake human life and permit people to reach their full human potential. What we find in the founding thinkers of sociology is a humanism painfully aware of the threats to human well-being in liberal, industrial society. While these thinkers were on the whole not religious and while, with the exception of de Tocqueville, they never mentioned God, they did ask questions about human life that have a curiously theological ring to them. This, at least, is the way in which their writings have impressed me.

Alexis de Tocqueville

Let me begin, then, with Alexis de Tocqueville, the French aristocrat who traveled to the United States during the first half of the nineteenth century and wrote the celebrated study *Democracy in America*. De Tocqueville tells us that he went to America to examine the new egalitarian society that had been initiated in Europe through the French Revolution and that had progressed in a more peaceful way, with fewer obstacles, in America, the land without aristocracy. As a conservative of sorts, de Tocqueville was afraid of the new liberal society. At the same time he thought that every social upheaval that had taken place in Western history over the last seven centuries had in fact promoted greater equality among people, and he could not but see in this orientation the providential drift of Western history. De Tocqueville believed that God was operative in this movement toward greater equality, even if it went against his own personal taste. He hoped that from his study of American society he might be able to foresee what people's life would be like in Europe under the impact of the new revolutionary ideas. When he went to the United States, he tells us in his introduction, he looked for the "image" of America, that is, for the most typical forms of life, because he felt that the most typical will remain and develop while the episodic and accidental will eventually disappear. He realized, of course, that this method of looking for the typical could introduce distortions into a sociological study, for it could lead an observer to exaggerate the regularities in American life. However, he was willing to take this well-calculated risk. What he wanted to present to his readers was not a description of American life but a typification that would enable him to anticipate what life would be like as the historical development continues. History has validated de Tocqueville's genius in the application of this method, for to this day *Democ-*

racy in America remains an exciting book, whose insights are still verifiable by the reader's personal acquaintance with American life.

De Tocqueville was above all impressed with America's democratic institutions. Here he found an egalitarian society in which people were allowed to create the conditions of their social existence. He observed the mobility of American life, the ease with which people moved from one town to another, and, more remarkably, the freedom which permitted the financially successful to rise to higher social classes (and the losers to drop to lower ranks). In America everyone is free to pursue his own interests. Coming from a traditional, more cohesive, aristocratic society, de Tocqueville was disturbed by the individualism produced by the American system. He found that egalitarian society destroyed the inherited social cohesion, released people from solidarity with others, urged them to care for their own careers, and fostered the dominance of the commercial and competitive spirit in every sphere of life. Egalitarianism—that is, the equality of all citizens before the law—weakened the people's attachment to their traditional communities. Thus society inevitably came to be an aggregation of individual citizens held together by the power of the government.

De Tocqueville analyzed American cultural life in great detail. What interests us at this point is his critical humanistic question. He searched for the forces operative in democratic society that threatened the well-being of people. Where did he see the dangers implicit in democracy? De Tocqueville spoke above all of two trends which, when combined, could create conditions of tyrannical oppression in democratic society, the kind which the world had never seen. What were these trends?

First de Tocqueville tried to show that egalitarian society inevitably leads to highly centralized government. Since egalitarianism dissolves traditional communities and atomizes the population as a mass of separated individuals, all cohesive and regulative power shifts to the government. The government becomes in charge of the various social responsibilities which in feudal society were exercised by many smaller groups and communities. Egalitarian society leads to a growing government bureaucracy. As this trend gains more momentum, de Tocqueville feared, the counter-forces in society, which constitute some sort of balance of power in the state, will disappear.

De Tocqueville even asked himself the question that was to be crucial for Marx a few years later: Will the owners of the factories emerge as a new ruling class? In other words, will egalitarianism produce a new kind of domination, the domination of the owning classes over the workers? De Tocqueville replied to this question in the negative. (We recall that the industrialization of America took place only in the second half of the last century, long after de Tocqueville's visit.) He gave two reasons for this. In the first place he thought that industrial production and commercial enterprises were such unstable institutions that the people who make a great deal of money and join the power elite easily lose their money again, go broke, and drop from the upper ranks of society. Because of this instability, de Tocqueville thought, the owners of factories will not come to form an upper class. Secondly, de Tocqueville defended the idea that the highly centralized government will not permit the industrial owners to form an upper class. The government will eventually intervene by law to limit the power of the industrialists, control their production, and regulate their employment of money.

To this day, let me add, sociologists are still divided on the true nature of American society. There are those who, with de Tocqueville, claim that America has no ruling class, that it has only a set of individuals elevated to power, an elite as it were, which does not constitute a social class with clearly defined interests. Other sociologists, preferring Marx to de Tocqueville, recognize in America a ruling class—the owners and directors of corporations, distinct from government, and yet in most instances protected by it—which exercises great power and successfully promotes its own class interest in the world.

De Tocqueville's first fear for democratic society, then, was centralized government. His second fear was the power granted to public opinion in egalitarian society. Since one person is as good as another, people do not look toward authorities to learn wisdom and clarify their ideas. Each person is entitled to his or her opinion. Each person relies on the common sense available to people generally. This approach eventually makes people attribute great authority to public opinion. What everybody holds and repeats, produced by the opinions of the many, acquires authority. As the majority determines the policy in democratic governments, so the majority also determines the ideas, the values and the taste of Americans. De Tocqueville was disturbed by this trend. He contrasted it with the low esteem in which public opinion was held in aristocratic society. In traditional society people looked for wisdom among the few. They turned to the exceptional persons dedicated to the pursuit of wisdom, and even these wise men were thought to draw their insight from a religious tradition or some other outstanding tradition of wisdom. In aristocratic societies public opinion was despised. If everyone holds it, if everyone agrees with it, if it is commonly accepted and expresses the mood of the marketplace or town hall, then it must surely be false. Wisdom goes counter to popular belief. In democratic societies, de Tocqueville thought, public opinion was granted so much power that people found it impossible to free themselves from it. They firmly believed that public opinion is the source of truth. De Tocqueville found an extraordinary conformity of mind and taste in America. The individualism that characterized the private lives of the citizens did not prevent them from agreeing easily on the values and ideals which define their culture.

De Tocqueville feared that one day the two dangerous trends in democracy will come together and constitute a new kind of despotism the world has never seen. He contemplates at length what will happen when central government is able to affect and steer public opinion. Then the laws and policies of the central bureaucracy will be accompanied by persuasive psychic pressures inducing people to comply with them. When the despotic reigns of past ages imposed heavy burdens on people, they were unhappy with their oppression and hated the tyrannical power. They obeyed the laws with clenched teeth. Yet the new despotism that threatens democracy may well be of a different kind. For people, influenced by a carefully planned public opinion, will gladly accept the rulings made for them, fit themselves cheerfully into the tight cage, and regard themselves as free and enlightened, even as they lose all access to critical thought and freedom of action. There are chapters in de Tocqueville's *Democracy in America* that anticipate the horrors recently depicted in a moving film called *Nashville*.

If imposed conformity and the loss of freedom are the dangers that threaten human life in democracy, what are the social forces that protect the well-being of people? De Tocqueville recommends here the counter-trends of social cohesion and traditional wisdom. What is interesting is that he sees these counter-trends above all in the form that the Christian religion has taken in America. While in the old Europe religion undergirded the linguistic, cultural or national unities of peoples and was embodied in established churches recognized by government, in America religion was pluralistic. There were many churches, none of them established. The denominations provided the American people with communities that taught them to overcome their cultural individualism and produced bonds of solidarity with wider groups of men and women spread over the entire country. These denominations created social cohesion against the atomizing trend of egalitarianism. Religion in America produced communities in which people overcame their isolation and learned to be selfless and concerned with the common good. Denominational religion provided views different from those of the government and fostered common action resisting the influence of the centralizing authority. De Tocqueville thought that religion also protected people from the tyranny of public opinion. For in each Christian church, the faithful were in touch with a great tradition of wisdom and on this solid ground were able to resist the pressure of the commonly held beliefs. Religion in America, in contrast to its role in Europe, was a source of personal freedom. De Tocqueville realized, of course, that religion was not the only counter-trend operative in society. He hoped that secular associations created by people with common interests would exercise a similarly freeing role in America. He felt that the health and well-being of people in egalitarian societies depend very largely on the network of citizens' associations, religious and secular, as a counterweight to government power and matrices for the taming of individualism.

Let me mention in passing that de Tocqueville's sociology of religion has had a great influence on sociologists since his day. We shall come back to this when we discuss Durkheim's critical humanism. Andrew Greeley's interpretation of American religion, persuasively presented in his book *The Denominational Society,* is an imaginative application of the Tocquevillian approach.

Karl Marx

Let me now turn to the sociology of Karl Marx. Again, our interest in Marxian thought is quite limited. What I hope to show is that at the center of Marxian social thought emerges the critical questions: What are the dehumanizing forces in society, and what social processes might possibly overcome these destructive trends and initiate people to a fuller humanism? I have no intention of dealing with Marxism as a social philosophy or a political movement. I make no reference whatever to the Eastern European nations who fraudulently call themselves socialist. What interests us here is simply Marx's sociology as critical humanism.

With other social critics Marx recognized that the application of steam power to the productive process (the industrial revolution) was creating a new social order different from traditional society. Marx paid special attention to the emergence of two new classes through the new factory system. There was first the new class of factory owners, joined by new commercial entrepreneurs, united by the common purpose of enlarging profit; then there were the new workers, men without property, obliged to sell their labor to survive in the life struggle. The workers were also united by a common interest, namely to escape from their oppressed situation. If they could become conscious of this common interest, they would form a social class and become the important instrument for the reshaping of society. Marx held that the conflict between these two new classes is the motor force that will determine the future of capitalist society. The older classes—the aristocracy, small merchants, craftsmen, peasants and so forth—would gradually disappear, leaving the new classes with diametrically opposed interests. We note that while de Tocqueville focused on the political conditions of life and derived from them the trends that changed human self-understanding, Marx concentrated on the economic conditions of life. In his view, the economic institutions determined the forms of social life and the structure of personal consciousness.

This new society, Marx insisted, gravely inhibited man's destiny to full self-expression. To clarify the damage to human life, Marx made use of an important term, "alienation," which he took over from Hegel's writings and to which he gave a new, even multiple meaning. Modern society, in his eyes, was alienating; it estranged people from their own depth, from one another and from nature itself. Marx's theory of alienation is complex, and to this day scholars argue about the way in which his various remarks on alienation can be harmonized in a single theory. What I wish to do is simply single out one important aspect. According to Marx, the alienation inflicted on people in modern, capitalistic society changes them significantly and makes them into egoistic creatures.

To be egoistic is, for Marx, not part of the human condition as such, nor is it part of human nature. Egoistic man is the creation of modern, capitalist society. The modern world destroys the social matrices to which people belonged, undermines the values they have inherited—all values disappear, Marx laments, except one, the cash-value—produces the isolation of individuals in new urban developments, and makes each person compete with his neighbor and promote his own advantage. Egoism affects the working class as well as the owning class. The worker finds himself surrounded by strangers with whom he must compete on the labor market, and as he himself becomes an item, a quantity, in the productive process, he begins to look upon himself and his fellow workers as objects subject to manipulation. The workers are condemned to this isolation until they recognize their common interest and develop solidarity. The owners of the factories are also estranged from their own depth. They too become egoists. For not only do they plan the production and distribution of goods in a way that maximizes their own profits, they also plan their entire lives, including their personal relations, so that they too serve the enterprise in which they are engaged. Man in the new society is defined by his career. His wife must serve him in the exercise of his entrepreneurial task, his politics must advance the interests of his class, and even culture and religion must protect and enhance the productive enterprise. Egoistic man, in Marx's eyes, is the form of modern alienation. In reality, Marx thinks, man is a "species being"—that is to say, man can only unfold his powers and talents in community with others and ultimately in solidarity with the entire human family. Egoism is the ultimate impoverishment of human existence.

In Marx's perspective, the owning class is more alienated than the workers. Why? Because while the workers suffer from the conditions of exploitation and through this suffering are called to open their eyes and recognize the alienation inflicted upon them, the owning class is more comfortable and hence its members are able to persuade themselves that they are happy. The distortion of perception is greater in the owning class. The owning class can hardly come to recognize the alienation the system inflicts on its own members; they have too much to lose. The workers, on the other hand, have nothing to lose but the chains that tie them to exhaustive and exploitative conditions; they are free to come to a realistic perception of their own condition. Through solidarity and organization the working class could become conscious of its true situation, recognize the alienation proper to capitalistic society, and reach out for means to overcome the institutional framework which is the source of their misery.

Alienation, we note, is inflicted on people through the competitive economic institutions that define their social reality. At the same time, alienation does not remain a form of material deprivation. According to Marx, the material deprivation translates itself into spiritual effects, of which egoism is the central one.

Can this alienation be overcome? Marx was profoundly convinced that if people laid hold of their lives, organized themselves in a movement, changed the economic institutions and democratized the ownership of the means of production, the power of alienation would be overcome. A cooperative, non-competitive life, delivered from profit-orientation, would enable people to recover their lost resources, experience themselves as a family, and realize the powers and potentialities that are theirs. Marx insisted that emancipation must be self-emancipation. People have to free themselves. Marx did not think that people would change if a superior authority replaced the present economic system with another; what changes people is precisely their involvement in the movement and the common effort to remake the social order. This common endeavor introduces people to the hidden resources of power within themselves and eventually communicates to them the sense of being a species-being, i.e., a community of equals in solidarity.

Marx's sociology is a critical humanism. It is worth noting that he thought transcendence is possible. He was convinced that the dehumanization from which we suffer in present society is not a part of the human condition, nor an element of human nature itself. Since it has been imposed on people, it can also be removed. We are not predetermined to remain prisoners on earth. We need not endlessly repeat the misery that mankind has known over the centuries. It is possible to overcome alienation. Later on we shall see that Max Weber, a German sociologist who wrote two generations after Marx, did not share this hope. He came to the conclusion that the dehumanizing process built into modern life could not be significantly modified; we are caught once and for all in the iron cage and any reform movement, even if of radical proportions, will only confirm the tyranny of industrial civilization. Marx, as we saw, was a man of hope. He thought that the possibility of transcendence was rationally grounded. Some of the power of Marxist movement comes, I think, from the appeal of this conviction.

Emile Durkheim

We shall now turn to Emile Durkheim and Max Weber, the social thinkers writing at the turn of the century who are usually regarded as the fathers of modern, scientific sociology. They were both moderate positivists, that is to say, they affirmed the scientific method and rejected every form of metaphysics. But because they were both brilliant and sensitive scholars, they realized that in order to understand social action and give a causal explanation of it, it is necessary to lay hold of the inner meaning the actors assign to their action. This method enabled the two scholars to gain great insight into the social reality of religion. While Durkheim was an atheist and Weber an agnostic, their method, even though scientific, led to an appreciation of the role of religion in the making of society that was remarkable indeed and remains to this day the starting point of any sociological study of religion.

The one point I wish to make in this address is that the sociologies of Durkheim and Weber were, despite the great difference between them, forms of critical humanism. Both sociologists were concerned about human beings; both looked for social processes that would deliver people from the destructive pressures that contemporary society inflicted on them.

Emile Durkheim, the Frenchman, stood in the tradition of de Tocqueville. He focused on the individualism characteristic of modern society and tried to show that the complex division of labor, brought about by industrial society, produces social mobility, horizontal and vertical, severs people from the social matrices in which they were born, and inserts them into a network of interrelations that are purely legal or contractual. What is destroyed by modern social institutions is the bond that linked people to one another and created traditional social cohesion. Prior to the democratic and industrial revolutions, people were bound to one another by common values, a common perception of the world, and a common religion. The effect of modern society was to destroy the rich social bond and replace it by the weaker ties of shared, short-range pragmatic interests. Durkheim felt that the social bond in modern society could be greatly strengthened if people only realized that through the complex interrelations of their separate efforts they actually produced a stable society and a new, social matrix of their personal existence. However, this realization does not easily emerge. The complex division of labor condemns people to isolation and individualism, without making them conscious of their actual interrelationship. Thus modernity undermines traditional values and estranges people from the social matrix, which was at one time the carrier of religion and high aspirations. What happens is that we easily find ourselves alone and exhausted.

Durkheim created a special vocabulary to express the dehumanization proper to highly developed industrial society. What threatens people in the city is anomie, the anguish produced by meaninglessness and isolation. Twenty years before Existentialist philosophers analyzed the anguish characteristic of modern society, Durkheim, the sociologist, already observed the phenomenon and tried to deal with it scientifically. Anomie is the symptom that reveals the illness of modern life.

For Durkheim, anomie was not simply a personal illness. It was a personal predicament that had profound effects on the social order. Durkheim understood the disorder of society, the breakdown of public morality, the unbridled ambition of politicians, the organized greed of capitalists, and the ever growing egoism of the population as the result of people's uprootedness. Anomie is, therefore, the number one enemy. We recall here that de Tocqueville thought that *political* institutions were the principal factors accounting for the form of modern life and that Marx regarded *economic* institutions as the key for understanding modern society. Durkheim followed neither of them. He focused on the complex division of labor created by industrialization and studied the productive process not (as Marx did) in economic terms of inequalities and exploitations, but in social terms of social dislocation and cultural decline. Students of these great social thinkers will eventually have to ask themselves which of these analyses of the human predicament in modern society is the best one. While de Tocqueville, Marx and Durkheim made remarkable contributions to our understanding of the human situation, as systematic thinkers they cannot all be right at the same time. This question, however, does not concern us in this essay. All I wish to establish is that classical sociology is a critical humanism.

How can the trend in society toward anomie be overcome? Durkheim certainly did not think that industrialization could or should be abandoned. What he hoped for, even if his ideas on its realization remained incomplete, was the creation of "intermediary societies," that is to say, cohesive communities situated between people and the state, in which groups of individuals recover a sense of fellowship and solidarity. In such intermediary societies people would become rooted again in a social matrix, overcome anomie, and rediscover their sense of life and destiny. But how can these new communities be created? Since Durkheim was personally convinced that Judaism and Christianity would not survive in modern society, and since he thought that these biblical religions were identified with previous stages of social life, it never occurred to him that religion in a pluralistic society might produce precisely the intermediary communities of which he dreamed. Durkheim vaguely suggested that professional societies might eventually become social matrices for overcoming anomie. This was of course quite unrealistic. What is interesting is that de Tocqueville's analysis of religion in the United States, undertaken fifty years before Durkheim's sociological studies, actually concludes that the significant function of denominational Christianity in America is to provide clearly limited communities with which people identify, in which they overcome the individualism characteristic of the age, and through which they are in touch with sources of wisdom that render them independent from the pressure of public opinion. While Durkheim never thought of the role that religion might play in overcoming of modern anomie, his proposal of "intermediary societies" actually provides the Christian thinker with a useful model for understanding the place of religion in the modern world. Implicit in Durkheim's sociology, and quite unbeknown to him, is an ecclesiology for the industrial age. This theme is developed in an original way by the American sociologist and religious thinker, Andrew Greeley, in his book entitled *The Denominational Society*.

Durkheim, we note, was not a radical critic of society. He sought redemption from the misery of the industrial age not by advocating structural changes in the process of production but by promoting the creation of new cultural forces. One may wonder whether Durkheim's program was realistic.

Max Weber

Let us finally turn to the sociology of the great Max Weber. Since Weber never produced a systematic sociology but instead stressed the unity of his method applied to the study of social action in diverse cultures and different ages, it is not easy to come to an overall evaluation of his sociological work. Sociologists are still arguing how "to read" Weber's contribution to social thought. One could make a case for the view that Weber was not a humanist but a debunker of humanism. It is true that Weber understood life as an inevitable conflict between contrary values or opposite world-views and that the thought that every commitment to one set of values or to any one world-view would inevitably neglect other values or other authentic world-views and hence necessarily produce a counter-movement trying to undo the original synthesis. Every humanism is partial, Weber held, and hence none of them can last for long.

Still, Weber has more to say than this. Since Weber concentrated a great deal of his research on the creation and development of modern Western society, it is possible and, I suggest, even inevitable to find in his writings the humanistic question, written in capital letters, regarding the forces in present society that inhibit and undermine the unfolding of human potential. What are the destructive trends operative in modern society? Weber gave an answer to this question which was related to the answers of other sociologists (some of which we have looked at above) but which focused on a very specific aspect. The archenemy of human life, according to Max Weber, was "rationalization" or, in a translation that is adequate, "rational planning." While the "rationalization" of life had been operative in history from the beginning, it was in the modern period, beginning with the expansion of manufacture and commerce and the emergence of the secular asceticism proper to Puritan religion, that rational planning came to be the dominant force in the creation of society, culture and even personal life-styles. What people in modern society sought, with unparalleled intensity after the industrial and democratic revolutions, was an ever greater coordination of the various aspects of social life, the ever greater intellectual penetration of reality through the combination of the various sciences, and the ever greater streamlining of personal life oriented toward achievement and efficiency.

All developments in modern society move toward greater rational planning and hence promote the growth of bureaucratic government. This is not the moment to give an outline of Weber's ample sociology of bureaucracy. He thought he could demonstrate that the impulse of modernity, namely to increase rational planning, inevitably increases the bureaucratic apparatus, and that even reform movements designed to free people from rigidity of bureaucratic government will eventually multiply committees, expand full-time staff, double the written reports and increase red tape, and in the long run make society an ever greater prisoner of bureaucracy. Weber held that in highly industrialized countries it really did not make much difference whether the economic system was capitalist or socialist; since both systems will be caught in the same bureaucratic prison, they will generate the same unfree, pre-programmed human existence. Weber felt that the movement toward greater rational planning was inexorable. He feared that we would all end up in "the iron cage." The rationalizing trend would condemn people to live a gray and tedious existence, caught in short-range goals and superficial interests, and destroy in them the capacities for the great passions, for art, for beauty, for religion. Weber spoke of "the disenchantment of the world." He regarded the waning of religion with regret, not because he himself was religious (he was not!) but because he saw in the loss of religion a symptom of the decline of culture and the undoing of humanism.

It is interesting to recall in this context that the radical students of the 1960's adopted the Weberian rather than the Marxist analysis of the world's ills. What they objected to was the dehumanization produced by technology and bureaucracy—in short, by "technocracy." They preferred to follow Weber, the conservative Prussian, in denouncing the impersonal, preprogrammed, collectivist and unfree form of life imposed by the technocratic system, and they showed little interest in Marx's analysis of alienation as the result of capitalist production and exploitation. One may wonder whether the fact that the young people came from affluent homes had anything to do with their choice. In any case, as the affluence of the 1960's faded away, so did the radicalism of the young generation.

What did Weber hold out as a remedy for the decline of Western culture and the destruction of humanism? Nothing at all. He did not believe in transcendence. Weber felt that "rationalization" was here to stay. Every new idea, every utopian dream, every charismatic movement that promises a change in the constitution of human life will eventually be undone by "rationalization" and disappear as an effective force in history. There is no room in the modern world for the utopian imagination. Weber foresaw what Herbert Marcuse was later to call "the one-dimensional man." People were caught in a single dimension; they were reduced to short-range, pedestrian purposes, and even the utopian dreams, critical of the system and proposing new ends, would be reformulated by cultural pressures to serve the purposes of the very system. For Max Weber, there is no transcendence. Operative in history was a tragic principle of evolution that moved people toward the end of their humanity in the perfect beehive.

Weber's view of bureaucracy is undoubtedly too severe. He did not pay attention to the contradictions in monocratic bureaucracies, and hence did not study the forces that make bureaucracies inefficient and eventually may lead to their breakdown. Nor did Weber pay enough attention to the group of people who control a bureaucracy. The nature of bureaucratic government is not simply defined by its own inner structure but also, and very largely, by the goals and principles for which it is set up. However deadening bureaucracy may be, there is no good reason, it seems to me, to regard rational planning as the number one enemy.

These brief reflections on the four founding figures of sociology have shown that from the beginning sociology was a critical humanism. The spirit of positivism which has entered sociology, and in many instances has come to dominate it, is not intrinsic to the sociological enterprise. In many sociology departments we presently find several trends that resist the spirit of positivism and try to recover the spirit of humanism characteristic of classical sociology. Students approaching sociology with faith and commitment to values need not experience social science as a cold shower cooling their enthusiasm; for if they get in touch with the classical tradition of sociology, they will discover it as a source of clarification and as nourishment for their Christian social longings.

Religion and Socialism

In this essay I wish to examine briefly how socialism has looked upon religion and then recall the moments, including the present, when religion has looked favorably on socialism. I shall not deal with the religious persecution of Christians and Jews in many of the so-called socialist countries, since whenever party-controlled bureaucratic governments leave no room for the participation of working people in the decisions that affect the production and distribution of goods, the countries do not deserve the name of socialist.

Marxism

For Karl Marx religion was ideology and false consciousness. He looked upon religion as a set of symbols that legitimate the power of the ruling class and console the oppressed with promises of eternal happiness. Only once did Marx acknowledge that under certain conditions religion could also be an expression of social protest: "Religious distress is at the same time real distress and the protest against real distress." However, he did not pursue this theme. For Marx religion was the powerful force that prevented people from recognizing their real situation in history. "The criticism of religion," he wrote, "is the premise of all criticism."

Are ideas, symbols and other cultural expressions simply ideological reflections of the material base? Marx did not think so, but he left himself wide open to such an interpretation. Against the dominant tendency to reduce Marx's dialectical view of history to an economic determinism, Georg Lukacs in the early 1920's wrote a vehement defense of the creativity of consciousness in the revolutionary process.[1] Class conflict demands class consciousness. To become aware of their position in society and discover their historical role, workers must have a glimpse of totality. They become class conscious of an historical mission only if they have a sense of the total picture. With this Lukacs became the important Marxist philosopher of art. Art, he argued, cannot be reduced to an element of the ideological superstructure, for it has a positive function in the revolutionary process. Art enables people to encounter totality; it raises consciousness and mediates elements of the total picture that enable people to lay hold of the meaning of their concrete historical situation. Lukacs might have applied the same sort of argument to religion, but he never did this because he thought that religious symbols dealt exclusively with heaven.

In the same decade another important Marxist thinker defended the creativity of consciousness. Antonio Gramsci, the founder of the Italian communist party, recognized the enormous importance of cultural and subjective elements in the revolutionary process. He vehemently argued against "economic determinism" on the one hand and against "idealistic voluntarism" on the other. Economic determinism holds that the capitalist system will destroy itself in due time by its inner contradictions and hence leads to political passivity, while idealistic voluntarism supposes that revolution is mainly a matter of power at the top and that therefore a well-organized party could execute a coup, place itself at the head of the state and legislate socialism from above. Against this Gramsci argued that the present system is held in place not simply by a strong government defending the interests of the owning class; it is held in place more firmly by cultural forces, by the symbols, values and sentiments shared by the people, that legitimate and confirm the existing order. Marxism has therefore a cultural task. The entry into socialism is only possible if political action is prepared and accompanied by a new cultural awareness of the working class. Revolutionary strategy, according to Gramsci, has to take into consideration where people's heads are. Socialism cannot be imposed by a powerful party; it can only be introduced if it is supported by a ground swell of recognition and involvement. Gramsci called this interpretation of Marxism "concrete voluntarism," noting that it demands the promotion of cultural socialism.

In this context Gramsci made a detailed analysis of the social function of religion.[2] He was, I think, the first Marxist to undertake such a task. He realized better than most sociologists of religion (with the exception of Max Weber) that religions are not unities, that they have different meanings and exercise different social functions on various levels of society. Religion has reactionary and progressive trends. Gramsci argued that in the genesis of European civilization Catholicism embraced many progressive trends. Catholicism had become "opium of the people" only after the Reformation and Enlightenment when it came to identify itself with the interests of a defeated class, the aristocracy. At the same time, Gramsci did not think it would be a realistic policy for the communist party to fight against the Catholic religion in Italy. What he tried to do was to unmask the political meaning of the Catholic movements supported by the hierarchy and look for progressive possibilities in Italian Catholicism. He mentioned in particular peasant movements at the turn of the century that backed their radical demands with religious conviction. In the quest for cultural socialism, Gramsci was ready for a dialogue with religion.

Marx's brief hint that religion could be a gesture of protest was explored by Ernst Bloch more than by any other Marxist thinker.[3] Bloch emphasized the role of consciousness in the revolutionary process and attached great importance to what he called the "utopian imagination," the imagination that transcends the given order, creates a longing for an alternative society and releases energy for social engagement. Bloch did not mean by utopia what Marx and Engels had meant. Utopias, he insisted, need not be ideological or idealistic. Actually they unsettle the inherited order if they are generated by people not in a quest for high ideals, but in the pursuit of their material interests. When the infrastructure is ready, newness enters history through the utopian imagination.

For Bloch, biblical religion was the major source of utopia in world history. In the Bible the impatience with the unjust world finds religious expression; in it the deliverance of Israel from Egyptian bondage becomes the paradigm of divine salvation; in it the prophets denounce the oppression of the poor and defenseless, proclaim the coming judgment on the nations and their kings, and promise the arrival of a just and peaceful realm in which all domination will be overcome. In the Bible emerges a language of inversion and negation, according to which "the first shall be last and the last first," "the rich shall be sent away empty and the poor filled with good things, the powerful shall be pushed from their thrones and the lowly shall be lifted up." Bloch shows how in the course of biblical history the "above" of God became more and more "a forward movement" and how in the apocalyptical sections of biblical literature the entire God language is translated into a judgment on the empire and the arrival of a new world. What held biblical religion back, according to Bloch, was the theistic misunderstanding. To the extent that the great utopia was hypostasized as a timeless divinity, biblical religion was prevented from releasing its power to the dialectical process of world construction. It is the Western revolutionary tradition, according to Bloch, that is the authentic heir of biblical religion. The churches betrayed their origin almost from the beginning. Only atheists, Bloch argues, can assimilate and translate into reality the biblical utopia.

Bloch's extensive study of religion has had considerable impact on Christian theology.[4] Marxism is atheistic, but it has become a partner in dialogue with religion.

British and Canadian Socialism

The relation of British socialism to religion has been quite different. British socialism was the pragmatic union of various socialist and labor trends, some of which stressed the economic analysis of society and welcomed elements of Marxist theory while others were moved more by the vision of a new humanity and by moral indignation at the inhuman misery produced by capitalism.[5] The economic trends moved easily in the direction of rationalism and came close to the utilitarian socialism of the Fabian Society, while the moral trends included religiously-based socialist groups as well as secularist societies hostile to religion. For the sake of creating a mass-based movement, the various organizations were willing to stand together in the creation of a new political party, the Labour Party.

The British rejection of capitalism and the quest for a socialist economy were on the whole inspired by people who reacted against modernity out of an attachment to elements of pre-capitalist society. While in Marxist theory socialist consciousness appears as the negation and transcendence of the mind-set created by capitalism, British socialism seems to have emerged as a reaction to capitalism on the part of people identified with older values and pre-industrial ways. The early Tory criticism of industrial capitalism, found in the writings of Ruskin and Carlyle, inspired Englishmen of a later generation to turn to socialism. Christian socialist movements, some apart from the churches and others within the Church of England (for instance, Frederick Maurice's experiment of 1848), rejected capitalism as a system at odds with the biblical vision of human society. People from towns and the countryside who were sucked into the industrial work force repudiated modern society as the destroyer of human values and turned to socialism. Many Britons believed that the values and dreams they had inherited which constituted the heart of the British tradition stood in judgment over capitalism and empire and demanded the reconstruction of society in accordance with the public ownership of the means of production, a planned economy for the well-being of all, and a cooperative society where all could participate in the essential social processes. Socialism wanted to save elements of the past which capitalism was destroying. This led to an open approach to religion.

The eclectic nature of British socialism has often been criticized as a lack of theoretical consistency. It is possible, however, to defend the British socialist tradition from a theoretical point of view. Marxism seems to demand that the workers look upon their national, religious and cultural past as essentially distorted. Workers have nothing to lose but their chains; they are not perceived as having roots to which they are attached and which deserve to be defended. They must be willing to have their mind-sets wholly defined by capitalism, to become economic persons and then to transcend this impoverished consciousness by collectively following their material self-interests in the creation of socialism. But can one really overcome capitalist culture by simply extending certain of its aspects, self-interest and scientific rationality?[6] In British socialism there is a strong sense that to overcome capitalist society the exploited classes must draw upon many historical resources in their struggle, including the dreams of childhood, the yearning of the poets, the highest hopes of their religion, the freedom symbols of their national tradition, and—for some—religious experiences that nourish solidarity. A socialist movement can overcome the capitalistic system only if the self-interest of the oppressed and scientific rationality can be linked to the pre-rational, elemental aspects of culture, suppressed by the bourgeois revolution, that feed the yearning for the fraternal (sororal) society. These pre-rational elements are of course ambiguous and by themselves are dangerous guides of action, but subjected to an ideological critique and linked to the quest for social equality, they bring vital energy to the social movement.

Canadian socialism, organized in the CCF (Cooperative Commonwealth Federation) in 1932, was a continuation of the same British socialist tradition.[6] Committed to socialism and the eradication of capitalism in the Regina Manifesto, the CCF was the pragmatic union of several farmer, labor and socialist organizations whose critique of capitalism was based in part on the inner discrepancies of the system and in part on its immoral and un-Christian character. In several of the organizations that joined the CCF there was a strong flavor of the Social Gospel. This was true especially in Saskatchewan, and later in Cape Breton.[7] In its literature the CCF argued that the present system stood condemned by the highest ideals Canadians had inherited, namely the Christian call for fellowship and cooperation and the British quest for true democracy. The CCF went out of its way to demonstrate that the public teaching of the churches on social justice was in accord with the program of Canadian socialism. Even though as institutions the churches were in fact identified with middle-class interests and supported the government as the protector of capitalism, the policy-makers of the CCF realized that under certain historical conditions religious symbols and religious sentiment give rise to solidarity and social activism among Christian people.

The Christian participation in the genesis and life of Canadian socialism has been studied in Richard Allen's *The Social Passion* and Roger Hutchinson's as yet unpublished dissertation on the Fellowhip of a Christian Social Order.[8] In his study on the Social Gospel in Canada from 1914 to 1928, Allen observes a recurring sociological trend: a group of radical Christians committed to socialism form a ginger group in the church; they exercise influence on church leadership and succeed in imbuing the entire denomination with greater social concern. In this process the original socialist position is watered down to a reformist stance. The members of the ginger group are then confronted with a choice: they either exercise leadership in the church's progressive movement and mitigate their socialist convictions, or they remain socialists and by doing so cut themselves off from the church altogether. In his study of the Social Gospel in the 1930's, Hutchinson found a similar trend. The Fellowship for a Christian Social Order was a group of Christian socialists, each personally involved in the CCF (some even in the CP), who tried to influence the Christian Church as a whole and who were constantly confronted with the question whether to stay with the church or leave it altogether. What is interesting in regard to the Fellowship is that it created an original theology from a socialist perspective that anticipated in many ways the socialist-inspired "liberation theology" produced in the 1960's in Latin America.

The Churches Today

From the end of the 1960's on, we find a decided shift to the left in the official teaching documents of the Christian churches (not in their actual political involvement). This is true in Protestantism of the World Council of Churches and the U.S. National Council of Churches, and it is true in Catholicism of papal and episcopal teaching.

Let me summarize some of the changes in recent papal teaching. (1) "The principle of subsidiarity," which protects small institutions from interference from on high and was used in Church teaching as an argument against socialism, has been complemented in papal teaching by " the principle of socialization" (Pope John XXIII) which demands that whenever small institutions are unable to fulfill their function, higher powers are obliged to intervene and coordinate their activities.[9] This principle encourages the move toward participatory socialism. (2) Pius XI and Pius XII rejected socialism in all its forms, including social democracy, because they held that its basic principles were false and would therefore eventually move socialism toward evil, even if the intentions of its leaders were good. John XXIII and Paul VI, on the other hand, made a distinction between the original principles of Marxism and the concrete historical movement derived from Marxism, which may in fact transcend the original elements inimical to Christianity.[10] Some Church documents specifically allow for collaboration of Catholics with Marxists in certain concrete circumstances. (3) In papal teaching the fear of the all-powerful government produced by state ownership of the major industries and economic institutions has been replaced by the fear of the all-powerful transnational corporations. Already in 1931, Pius XI suggested that this new "international imperialism of money" was the inevitable outcome of unrestrained capitalism.[11] Today papal teaching recommends strong government to curb the power of the transnationals and moderate the national economy.[12]

In Canada, the major churches created inter-church committees in 1971, whose task it was to examine the current socio-economic issues from a Christian social justice viewpoint and to advise the churches in regard to their own public policies. These committees (known by such strange names as GATT-FLY, ICPOP and TCCR and including Share Lent and Ten Days for Development) provided the churches with research and conclusions on which they were able to take strong stands on a number of public issues. In a brief addressed to the government in 1976, the church leaders declared that "they stand in the tradition of the prophets where to know God is to seek justice for the poor and the oppressed." The brief insists that "the present economic order is characterized by the maldistribution of wealth and control of resources by a small minority." After referring to issues such as international development, transnational corporations and the land claims of the native peoples in Canada, the brief concludes that the poor people today ask for "an alternative for the present unjust order" and demand "a new international economic order."

The Catholic bishops in particular have produced several pastoral letters dealing with social justice. In their joint letter on world hunger, *Sharing Daily Bread*, the bishops argue that no assistance given to the third world can alleviate hunger as long as we have the free market distributing food. Why? Because the free market distributes food only to people with the ability to pay, while God has created the fruits of the earth for all people, whether they have money or not. The reference is here to the ancient Catholic principle of the right to eat. In a pastoral letter *Northern Development: At What Cost?* the bishops plead with the government not to allow the development of the north without previous consultation with the native peoples. Why, the bishops ask, do we cause so much harm to people? Because, they reply, we are a society that makes decisions in accordance with "the maximization of power, of profit and of consumption." In the Labour Day statement of 1976, the Canadian bishops insist that social justice concerns and political action are part and parcel of the Gospel life. It is the task of Christians to listen to the poor and oppressed groups in society, to inquire into the causes of their oppression, and to struggle to change society so as to remove these causes. The bishops say that until now only a minority of Catholics follow this way of life, but they regard this minority as significant since it summons the whole Church to greater fidelity.

These documents are remarkable. It should be added, however, that the bishops who produce the documents do not on the whole engage themselves, either personally or collectively, to communicate this social passion to the ordinary, church-going Catholics. The documents remain powerless because they are not backed by the action on the part of their authors. Despite this new teaching, institutionally the Catholic Church remains identified with capitalist society.

Still, one must ask where this new ecclesiastical teaching comes from. What is its social foundation? No adequate study of this has yet been undertaken. It is my view that the new Social Gospel in the Catholic Church is related to changes that took place in large sections of the Catholic Church in Latin America.

Latin America

In the middle 1960's the third world countries began to realize that the "development model" proposed by the industrialized capitalist centers was detrimental to them. "Development" means integration into the international capitalist system where the third world countries find themselves at the periphery, enriching the centers to their own detriment. What they need is not greater dependency but liberation.

At this time we find in Latin America politicized Catholic groups, "communidades de base" or "grassroots communities," committed to the struggle for liberation. These groups deviated from the position adopted by the Latin American bishops at the time, the position that recommended "a middle way" between capitalism and socialism. This middle way, led by the progressive elements of the bourgeoisie, supported the Christian democratic parties. What was wrong with the middle way, the grassroots communities argued, was that in the long run it always sides with capitalism against socialism. The middle way is an illusion. The grassroots communities opted for socialism and cooperated with secular groups in the struggle for liberation.

Solidarity with the exploited and commitment to political action produced a new kind of Christian reflection. The Christian activists discussed at length what Jesus Christ and divine redemption meant to them in their daily struggle. These discussions were eventually recorded and collected, sorted out and put into a certain order—a process that produced "liberation theology." The theologians who had joined these communities of joint action began to produce a substantial theological literature from the new, socialist perspective.[13] What were the main themes of this theology? The theologians first unmasked the ideological character of mainstream Christianity and then brought out the radical meaning of the biblical message that emerges when the sacred texts are reread from the viewpoint of the oppressed. The theologians show that (a) the sin of which the Bible speaks includes "social sin" or systems of oppression; (b) the "conversion" to which God summons people includes the rejection of bourgeois ideals, a socio-critical stance toward the world and commitment to emancipation (c) the grace and holiness mediated by Christ includes the radical transfiguration of the competitive, profit-oriented economic system into a cooperative economy, planned to meet the needs of all; (d) God is not a sky divinity ruling the world from above but a presence in history calling people to new awareness and empowering them to assume responsibility for their future, personally and collectively; and (e) Jesus Christ, identified with the underprivileged and crucified by the empire, inverted the existing order by his resurrection, made the last first and the first last, and continues to be the inverter of class societies and the liberator of the oppressed.

These radical Christians had influence on the Latin American Bishops' Conference meeting in Medellín, Colombia, in 1968. Medellín approved the liberation trend in the Catholic Church. A small number of bishops even involved themselves actively in the liberation struggle. Best known among them is Bishop Helder Camara. The Latin American bishops, joined by other bishops from the third world, had an impact on the international synod held in Rome in 1971 which published an authoritative document, *Justice in the World*. This document declared that political action for justice was a "constitutive element" of the Christian life and that the divine salvation brought by Christ "includes the liberation from all the oppressive conditions of human life." This shift in social teaching, largely due to third world influence, affected the bishops in the developed countries. It was after the 1971 synod that the Canadian bishops decided to cooperate with the other churches, constitute the inter-church committees mentioned above, and address the Catholic people at regular intervals with the radical message of social justice.

It is worth mentioning that while contemporary Church documents repudiate Marxism as a philosophical and political system, they have come to acknowledge and approve (a) that Catholics are involved in (non-Marxist) socialist projects of various kinds, and (b) that they make use of "cultural Marxism," i.e., insights drawn from the Marxist tradition that are useful for social thought, including theology, and can be assimilated in socialist projects.

Over the last few years, the conservative bishops in Latin America seem to have gained the upper hand. A number of them are engaged in a vehement campaign against liberation theology, and in this struggle they seek the cooperation of European Catholic bishops and the Vatican. Their main theological advisor, Father Roger Vekemans, an organizer of considerable gifts, has recently been shown to have received vast sums of money from the CIA to promote his reactionary political influence in the Latin American church (cf. *The Washington Star*, July 23, 1975; *Le Monde*, July 25, 27, 28, 1975). In the fall of 1978 the Latin American bishops' conference is scheduled to meet in Mexico. If the conservative bishops have their way—which is by no means certain—the conference will condemn the liberation perspective and make Catholicism again a symbol system legitimating the existing order of oppression.

Ginger Groups

The trend described by Allen and Hutchinson in connection with the Social Gospel in Canada also seems to hold true for socialists in the Catholic Church and in Protestantism today. There are ginger groups of Christian socialists that try to raise the awareness in the churches and influence ecclesiastical policies. When they are successful in making the churches more socially concerned, the socialist principles are watered down in the process and the members stand before the decision whether to become the leaders of the new progressive movement in the Church despite the compromise, or whether they should stand apart from the Church to pursue their socialist engagement.

This dilemma is most clearly seen in the worldwide network called "Christians for Socialism," founded in Santiago, Chile in 1971, which sought to embrace Christians involved in a socialist action.[15] In Chile the majority of the members were identified with Allende's Chilean socialism. The network did not understand itself as an action group. It recognized that Christian members were already involved in various forms of action and that they belonged to different organizations and movements. What "Christians for Socialism" wanted to do was to clarify the Christian position, denounce the ideological content of dominant Christianity, show that there was no contradiction between the Gospel and socialism, and render a witness that could become important for the life of the Church as a whole. In Latin America this network has been largely destroyed. With the military coup in Chile and the coming-to-power of military dictatorships all over Latin America in the middle 1970's, the Church's situation had been radically changed. The Christians of the left are persecuted; organizations such as "Christians for Socialism" have become illegal. Even the official Church, with its new social teaching, often finds itself under attack, is subject to censorship, and sees many of its socially concerned leaders, priests and lay, sent to prison. The Latin American "liberation theology" survives today mainly in exile.

In Europe "Christians for Socialism" is strong in Italy, France and Spain, countries where Euro-Communism has embraced democratic principles and wants to unite the people in a common struggle. In these countries this means cooperation with Catholics. The Catholic left in these countries does not have the approval of the bishops; it is often criticized and the priests of the left are under some pressure. At the same time no attempt has been made so far to exclude these Christians from the Church. "Christians for Socialism" in Europe includes Catholics and Protestants. It wants to be a network that includes and unites in conversation Christian socialists of different political orientations.[16] All agree that what is needed is a new cooperative economic system, that the productive tools should be publicly owned, and that production and distribution should by planned by bodies responsible to the people. Some Christians follow an Althuserian Marxism, emphasize the scientific character of socialism, and think that this leaves room for the addition of Christian philosophy. Other Christians opt for a more humanist form of Marxism which acknowledges the creativity of consciousness and therefore leaves room for many unexplored aspects of the life of the spirit. Other Christians again belong to action groups that define themselves in opposition to bureaucratic centralized Marxism and seek new forms of participatory or self-governing socialism.

"Christians for Socialism" also wants to protect theological pluralism in its own ranks which include Catholics and Protestants. The members are aware that there are several theological ways to the socialist position: for instance, Paul Tillich's religious socialism of the 1920's, the left-wing reading of Karl Barth based on Marquardt's recent study, the social reinterpretation of Bultmann by Dorothee Soelle, Helder Camara's extension of Catholic social teaching in the direction of socialization. Gutiérrez' adoption of the philosophy of praxis as the natural wisdom with which to clarify the meaning of the Gospel, and Segundo's biblically-based approach of rereading history and society from the viewpoint of the poor, etc.

Is there a Christian left in North America? The impact of liberation theology is certainly considerable. The Latin American literature has been made available in English translation, thanks to the initiative of Orbis Books Publishers, supported by the Mary - knoll Fathers in the United States. In Quebec, Catholics have formed a network, called "Politisés chrétiens," which brings together involved Christian socialists in joint religious and intellectual projects. In the United States, a wide network organized under the title "Theology for the Americas" at first brought together Latin American and North American Christians[17] and then engaged itself in a variety of theological and educational projects dealing with oppression in North America, for the most part from a socialist perspective. In the United States and Canada there are groups of Christians, often predominantly Catholic, who have been radicalized by working as missionaries in Latin America and who now explore the meaning of the socialist commitment for North American society. There are study groups that explore the implications of "liberation theology" for Christians in the developed world, efforts often referred to as "political theology."[18]

However, in the United States and (English-speaking) Canada there is no clearly definable Christian left. The radical Christians who are in solidarity with the oppressed, criticize capitalism and involve themselves in social action are *not* united in a socialist perspective. There are socialists among them—some Marxist, others belonging to the Democratic Socialist Organizing Committee founded by Michael Harrington in the United States or to the NDP in Canada. But they also include Alinsky-style community organizers, Christian anarchists who seek an alternative life-style in intentional communities, radical environmentalists (in whose judgment socialism is oriented toward growth almost as much as capitalism), Christians involved in cooperatism, welfare liberals, and red Tories.

Does the Christian left have a future? It could be argued that as the class conflict becomes more intense, the churches will cease to be permissive in regard to their left-wing members and push them out. Others might want to argue that there is an inner contradiction between a religion that proclaims eternal life and the socialist commitment to the reconstruction of society, and that for this reason Christian socialists will sooner or later discover that they have no place in the Church. Others will argue, on the contrary, that the Christian Gospel implies a radical transvaluation of values and that under certain concrete material conditions (which can be analyzed) the Christian faith may unfold its world-unsettling and re-creative power and make a substantial group of Christians eager to join others in building a cooperative commonwealth.

NOTES

1. Georg Lukacs, *History and Class Consciousness* (Cambridge, Mass., 1968).

2. Hugues Portelli, *Gramsci et la question religieuse* (Paris, 1974).

3. Ernst Bloch, *Man on His Own* (New York, 1970); *Atheism in Christianity* (New York, 1972).

4. This is true especially of two influential German theologians, Johannes B. Metz (Catholic) and Jurgen Moltmann (Protestant). Bloch's new language was adopted in Pope Paul VI's letter *Octogesimo adveniens* (n. 37) which praises the emergence of new utopias. The Pope recognizes that utopias may provide an escape from concrete tasks, but "a forward-looking imagination" may also "perceive in the present the disregarded possibilities hidden within it, and direct it toward a new future."

5. Stanley Pierson, *Marxism and the Origin of British Socialism* (New York, 1973).

6. M. Christian and C. Campbell, *Political Parties and Ideologies in Canada* (Toronto, 1974), pp. 116-157.

7. Cf. S. M. Lipset, *Agrarian Socialism* (Los Angeles, 1971); G. Baum, "Social Catholicism in Nova Scotia: The Thirties," *Religion and Culture in Canada*, ed. Peter Slater (Waterloo, Ont., 1978), pp. 117-148.

8. Cf. Richard Allen, *The Social Passion: Religion and Social Reform in Canada 1914-1928* (Toronto, 1973); Roger Hutchinson, "The Fellowship for a Christian Social Order." Th.D. thesis (Victoria College, University of Toronto, 1975).

9. Cf. *Mater et Magistra*, n. 54.

10. Compare Pius XI, *Quadragesimo anno*, n. 117, with John XXIII, *Pacem in terris*, n. 159, and Paul VI, *Octogesima adveniens*, n. 51.

11. *Quadragesimo anno*, n. 109.

12. Cf. *Populorum progressio,* 29-32; *Octogesima adveniens,* nn. 45-46; *Justice in the World* (III Synod), nn. 12-13.

13. This point was developed in 1932 in Paul Tillich's *The Socialist Decision* (New York, 1977).

14. The best known authors are Gustavo Gutierrez, Juan Segundo, Hugo Assmann and Enrique Dussel.

15. Cf. my article "The French Bishops and Euro-Communism," *The Ecumenist* (Jan./Feb. 1978).

16. *Christians and Socialism: Documentation of the Christians for Socialism in Latin America*, ed. John Eagleson (Orbis Books, 1975).

17. *Christen für den Sozialismus,* ed. Dorothee Soelle (Stuttgart, 1975).

18. *Theology in the Americas*, ed. S. Torres and J. Eagelson (Orbis Books, 1976).

19. Cf. the article "Political Theology in Canada," *The Ecumenist* (March/April 1977) and "Religion and Politics in the Prairies," Institute for Saskatchewan Studies, Vol. 7, No. 2.

The French Bishops
and Euro-Communism

In June 1977 the Catholic bishops of France published an important declaration on dialogue and cooperation of Catholics with Marxism and Marxist political parties.[1] The pastoral declaration spelled out "the conditions and the limits" of these new associations in France. While these new directives apply to Catholics in the political situation of France, they contain principles of political theology that go beyond anything expressed in ecclesiastical documents so far and are therefore of universal interest.

New Developments

Why this new interest in Catholic-Marxist relations? The French bishops give two reasons for this, one of them connected with changes in the Catholic community, the other with the evolution of the Marxist movement. A great number of dedicated Catholics, the French bishops say, have become intensely concerned with social justice: they reject the present economic system because it creates a gravely unequal distribution of goods and life chances, and thus increases the gap between rich and poor at home and more especially between rich and poor nations in the world. These activist Catholics follow the lead of recent ecclesiastical documents that have expressed this criticism. Today the Church urges Catholics to engage in social action in order to create, in collaboration with others, an alternative society. It is here that Catholics are bound to encounter Marxists.

Marxism too has undergone an evolution. The French bishops refer to several developments in France. There exists first of all a new "cultural expansion" of Marxism: this refers to the growing influence of Marxist thought on philosophical reflection, on sociology, on literature and other forms of cultural expression. Marxism has a cultural presence in France that can no longer be overlooked. It is inevitable that Catholics encounter it and necessary that they respond to it in a critical and creative manner. The bishops readily admit, at a later point in the pastoral, that the evolution of Catholic thought itself has been greatly affected by such a response to cultural Marxism.

The bishops then mention "social Marxism." By this they mean the influence of Marxism on the organizations and associations that constitute French society, such as municipal governments, political parties, university faculties, parents' associations, citizen groups and so forth. Here too Catholics encounter Marxism: here too they must learn how to analyze various Marxist trends and react to them in responsible fashion.

Finally, and most importantly, there is what the bishops call "political Marxism," that is, the action of the Communist Party in France. The declaration recognizes the emergence of the new Euro-Communism. It mentions in particular that the Communist Party of France has made itself independent of Moscow, has left the old orthodoxy and repudiated "the dictatorship of the proletariat." The French Communist Party has formally declared itself in favor of the democratic process; it seeks to unite the French people, and it wants to join with other left-wing parties and with Catholics committed to social justice in the creation of a common popular front for the remaking of society. The French bishops do not discuss whether this change of policy represents simply a momentary strategy of the Communist Party or whether it reflects a definitive revision of the old Communist orthodoxy, defined by the Third International under the hegemony of Moscow. What the bishops do say, however, is that Catholics in France find themselves in a new situation where contact and association with Marxists is a daily reality. Christian activists recognize that social reconstruction is not possible without the cooperation of the Communists; and conversely the French Communist Party realizes that their revolution remains unrealizable unless they can count on the collaboration of Catholics. In this new situation the bishops want to provide theoretical norms and practical guidelines.

The declaration begins by recognizing that today Catholics, especially activist Catholics, follow different political options and are for this reason divided. In a recent statement by the Canadian Catholic bishops we find the same reference to the divergent strategies within the Catholic community and the tensions and debates which are consequent upon this.[2] The French bishops first mention the Catholics who have made "a socialist decision." These Catholics regard the present economic system as the principal cause for today's social ills, they work in a socialist movement, and while they make use of a Marxist social analysis, they repudiate the Marxist worldview and the Marxist mode of action. What is meant by the Marxist mode of action? Reading the entire declaration, one has the impression that the bishops here refer to the creation of an authoritarian party that regards itself capable of arriving at truth in a scientific manner, dominates the working class in its political struggle and, after the successful revolution, becomes the ruler of the entire nation. This is in fact the Leninist mode of political action which was adopted as the orthodox position by the Third International. Socialists, then, in the terminology of the French bishops, are identified with a socialist movement that makes use of cultural Marxism but rejects Marxist philosophy and Leninist totalitarianism. The bishops recognize that in recent years many Catholics have become socialists, and they have no objection to this as long as these Catholics strive to protect the Christian values of personal freedom and family life within their movement. None of the warnings contained in the substance of the episcopal declaration are addressed to Catholic socialists.

Let me point out that we have here a new and interesting development, the rehabilitation of the word "socialism" in church teaching. We recall that in 1931 Pope Pius XI repudiated socialism in all its forms, the revolutionary socialism of Russia called Communism as well as the moderate socialism of the social-democratic parties of Western Europe.[3] He said that no one could be a believing Catholic and true socialist at the same time. Pius XI admitted that the reform programs of the social democrats often resembled Catholic social ideals, but he judged that socialists, however moderate, were still inspired by false principles and that these principles would eventually take over, whatever the intention of the political leaders. Moderate socialism was the door of entry into communism. The effect of this fateful ecclesiastical decision in 1931, in a Europe and a world about to be threatened by fascism, has often been discussed. It is worth recalling that the English Catholic bishops quickly declared that the papal judgment did not apply to British socialism: the Labour Party was in no way outlawed for Catholics. But for the vast majority of Catholics all over the world socialism became a bad word. A Catholic could not be a socialist.

Against this background, it is interesting to discover in ecclesiastical documents the rehabilitation of socialism. The beginning was made by Paul VI in his letter *Octogesima adveniens* (n. 31). The French bishops recognize the socialist decision of Catholics and understand it as one of the responses of socially concerned Catholics to the injustices of the present economic system. In the recent statement of the Canadian Catholic hierarchy we also hear of socialism as one of the political options made by Catholics in response to the inadequacy of the present system. Some participate in socialist movements, the Canadian bishops say, trying to reconcile them with the teaching of Jesus.

Four Questions

The body of the French episcopal declaration deals with Marxism, that is, with philosophical and political Marxism. The bishops recognize that in recent years many Catholics have joined the Communist Party in France. They plan to be faithful to the Christian Gospel, even while they embrace the Marxist position. They want to be "fully Christian and fully Marxist." Some of these, the bishops add, claim to have discovered the power of the Gospel through their Marxist political involvement.[4]

This recent development worries the French bishops. They say that in the vast number of cases, Christian believers who participate in the Marxist movement, even if they have the intention of protecting their Christian faith, eventually attach less and less importance to it until it dies altogether. Secondly, the bishops are worried about this recent development because in the parts of the world where Marxism has been translated into political reality the Christian church is regarded as an enemy, there are no civil liberties, and totalitarian rule excludes any kind of pluralism in society. The possibility of a totalitarian regime in France frightens the bishops. In this context they admit that they are equally disturbed by the emergence of systematic anti-communism in certain countries, associated with an ideology of national security, sometimes even with the claim to protect Christian civilization, that is equally hostile to human rights, supresses political pluralism, and opposes the social meaning of the Christian religion.

The bishops are worried, then, and they warn Catholics of the threat of totalitarianism. At the same time, they do not forbid Catholics to cooperate with Marxists and join Marxist political organizations. What they want to do in their declaration is "to clarify the conditions and the limits of dialogue." They admit the possibility that the evolution of Marxism in France has been such that critical participation of Catholics is in fact possible. It all depends on how the Marxist organizations reply to the important questions posed to them by Catholics. We note that the French bishops follow here the approach to Marxism recommended by John XXIII and Paul VI—in fact, they refer specifically to these popes. For while Pius XI in the 1930's held that any Marxist movement must be judged in terms of its underlying principles and hence no historical evolution could ever make it acceptable to Catholics, Pope John XXIII and Paul VI introduced a distinction between the original principles of Marxism in an historical movement and admitted that an historical evolution could transform Marxism so significantly that Catholics would be able to enter into dialogue and cooperation with it.[5]

The pastoral declaration formulates four important questions. On the answer given to these questions will depend the attitude of Catholics to Marxist organizations. The first question has to do with economic determinism, the second with the nature of persons, the third with totalitarianism, and the fourth and most important one, with the recognition of religion and the openness to the divine mystery.

1. The historical materialism entertained by Marxists is often described as a philosophy that sees the evolution of man and his world as determined by his economic life, i.e., by the mode of production and the organization of labor. Man creates tools for dealing with nature and organizations for producing and distribut-

ing the goods he needs, and in doing so creates his own consciousness. Consciousness is therefore largely a reflection of the material conditions of human life. What then moves history forward? Why have people not remained in the earliest forms of economic organization? Historical materialism holds that built into the systems of production are inner contradictions which divide people into exploiter and exploited and initiate the inevitable undoing of the system. Thus one economic system replaces another. Today we stand before the final revolution: the contradictions of capitalism prepare its downfall; and the oppressed class, the proletariat, will assume power in the creation of a cooperatively-planned, non-competitive economic system where the means of production are publicly owned, a system which does not produce class division, which initiates people into a consciousness beyond egotism, and which removes all injustices from society and eventually makes all forms of domination, including the state, wither away.

This view of history, leaving aside for the moment the messianic dimension, is based on an economic determinism. Human consciousness at each stage is largely constituted through the existing economically-determined social relations. The driving force of history is the conflict generated by the contradictions in the economic system, and since these can be analyzed scientifically, it is possible at all times to come to a scientific knowledge of the historical situation and the evolution of culture. In such an economic determinism it is even possible to claim demonstrable truth in the order of strategy and policy.

In this view man has no independent creativity. Consciousness seems to be a pure epiphenomenon, a by-product of the economic evolution, with no significant impact on the creation of history. In this view, moreover, scientific analysis, usually in the hands of a political party, is the infallible norm of truth and excludes from society all pluralism and intellectual dissent. Since Christians must repudiate such an economic determinism both in the name of the creativity of consciousness and the freedom of pluralism, they must ask French Marxists whether or not they are commited to such an ideology.

2. The second question raised by the French bishops is related to the first: it has to do with the nature of the human person. In a

Marxism defined in terms of economic determinism, the person has an altogether subordinate role in history. In fact, man is here understood simply as the ensemble of social relations, and human nature is the product, the ever changing product, of the systems of production and the organization of labor. The subject of history is man collectively speaking. Personal consciousness is here simply an aspect of the wider collective consciousness, which is the reflection of the economic order and the class relations it produces. Persons are here seen as subordinated to the social processes that move history forward; they are not bearers of rights, they are not creators of their own imagination, they are not free subjects possessing an inwardness that stretches beyond the empirical order.

Again Christians cannot endorse such a view. The question they pose to French Marxists is, therefore, how they regard the human person.

3. The third question raised by the French bishops is related to the preceding: it concerns the freedom of persons in society. Marxism holds that the true understanding of the historical reality is accessible only to the oppressed class. The ruling class is blinded by its own interests; it entertains an ideological view of society, which justifies and defends its superior power and its disproportionate access to the goods of life. In the present capitalist system, then, it is the proletariat that is the privileged class, the class that has access to truth, that alone can make a creative contribution to the remaking of society. At the same time, the inferiorized position of the proletariat has weakened it, the alienation imposed on it has distorted its humanity; and for this reason it is only an elite among the workers—and those of another class who identify with them—that have access to true consciousness and can apply the critical, scientific norms. Truth is available to a small body of men, to the party, which exercises supreme rule in communist movements and in communist lands. This view of truth, and the related concept of the infallible party, are incompatible with pluralism, with civil liberties, with the recognition of dissent and with the openness to learn from the insights of other traditions. Thus Marxism by its own weight leads to totalitarianism. Here again, Christians must confess that they can in no way cooperate with such a political movement.

4. Finally comes the most important question: What is reli-

gion? For Marxists, religion is false consciousness. It is usually regarded as an ideology defending the existing power relations; at best, it is the symbolic protest of people subject to alienation, it is the projection of dreams that a suffering and oppressed people create to spell out their judgment on an evil society, to strengthen their resistance against it, and to offer the hope that the good things of life from which they are now deprived will be granted to them in another world. While religion is usually a reactionary force, under special conditions it may provide motivation for joining movements of radical protest. Yet even then religion has no lasting role. It is founded on illusion, not on reality.

To the extent that alienated consciousness is overcome through the reconstruction of society, religion wanes. Christians who work with Marxists to promote revolution, the bishops say, seem to prepare their own disappearance. Marxism has no concept whatever of the religious vocation of mankind. Concern with the ultimate and unutterable mystery that engulfs our being and carries us forward has no room in the Marxist understanding of things. Atheism is constitutive of Marxist philosophy.

Previous Church Teaching

These are the four questions the French bishops pose to Marxists. The bishops admit that there is much in Marxism that is attractive to contemporary Catholics. They mention the preponderance of the common good over private interest; they invoke the sense of solidarity which embraces the workers, the poor, the exploited with an élan that transcends the nation and includes the entire human family; they speak of the radical alternative Marxism offers to the present market economy, in which vast numbers of people have lost their confidence and which seems wholly unable to solve the problems of production and distribution in a hungry world. Since the French Catholics are constantly exposed to the attraction of Marxism, it is all the more important to ask the four questions mentioned above.

In the second part of the declaration, the French bishops offer a Christian reply to Marxism, a reply based on contemporary political theology and passages drawn from Vatican II and other ecclesiastical documents. They offer in outline a Christian understanding of history, in which the struggle against oppression and social justice is the central, divinely supported axis. But before we come to this, we must deal with two more issues, one of which we can treat very rapidly while the other must hold our attention for some time.

First, then, how do the arguments warning the faithful of communism differ from the arguments which the Catholic Church has used in the past to condemn Marxism and to repudiate both communist and socialist movements? The traditional arguments were threefold: first, the Church defended the private ownership of the means of production, at least when this production had not achieved monopoly power and interfered with the responsibility of government. Second, the Church repudiated class war and the use of class conflict to overthrow the existing order. And third, the Church deplored the materialist philosophy and, implicit in it, the militant atheism.

In the declaration of the French hierarchy, the question of private property is not even mentioned. Since monopoly capitalism of today has become so problematic, many people who do not even regard themselves as socialists wonder whether this system is not the principal cause for the present crisis. People fear that the market economy will lead to a chaos of production that shall leave a large part of mankind in a situation of misery. Secondly, the bishops do not invoke class conflict as an argument against Marxism. They recognize the existence of class conflict; in fact they quote Leo XIII who, in his days, acknowledged that modern society was divided between the powerful few and the dependent, poor and exploited masses.[6] Class conflict is only to be rejected if it aspires to the victory of one class over others and the establishment of an authoritarian regime is which they are excluded from the building of society. The declaration recognizes that class conflict carried on in a democratic manner does not seek to eliminate the owning class but rather assigns a new place to them in society. From the Christian perspective, the ultimate aim of class conflict is cooperation.

Finally, the traditional ecclesiastical argument against the materialism and atheism of Marxism has been greatly refined in the French episcopal declaration. The bishops explain the doctrine of economic determinism, the nature of man according to a Marxist view, the causes of Marxist authoritarianism, and finally the nature of Marxist atheism. What is new and remarkable here is, moveover, that these arguments are not presented as definitive judgments on French Marxism but rather as questions addressed to Marxist organizations, on whose answers will depend the actual Catholic attitude.

Inner-Marxist Conversation

What the French bishops unfortunately do not tell us is whether the questions raised by them are addressed to Marxists from outside their own tradition, or whether they have in fact arisen in inner-Marxist conversations. It is regrettable that the bishops do not examine this. For their declaration easily creates the impression that their description of Marxist philosophy and political practice exhausts the Marxist self-understanding. But if these questions are in fact debated among various groups of Marxists, then the bishops have in fact joined an existing conversation. I wish to show that at least the first three questions mentioned above belong to an inner-Marxist dialogue. Only the last question, the one about the divine mystery, is not raised in Marxist literature.

1. Is economic determinism the only interpretation of Marxism? While certain passages in Marx's writings and a strong trend in Engel's work encourage such a scientific, reductionist understanding of history, and while this view was regarded by some as the official position by the Second International before World War I, this interpretation has been challenged from within the Marxist camp. Important here is the Marxist philosopher and activist, Georg Lukacs, who in 1922 in his *History and Class Consciousness*, accused the official Marxist interpretation of neglecting the role of consciousness in the making of history and of thus misreading Marx's dialectical philosophy. He designated as "vulgar Marxism" the tendency to reduce Marx's historical materialism to some form of economic determinism. Lukacs tried to show that

man's perception of reality, his imagination and his decisions, critically affect the reconstruction of society and that the neglect of these subjective elements caricatures the original philosophy of Marx and undermines the proper understanding of the human subject. Marxism is a fully human quest for a truly human society and hence involves the renewal of consciousness. Lukacs challenged the crudely empiricist copy-theory of knowledge, widely adopted in vulgar Marxism, by showing that we can understand our own social position only if we see it in the light of a more total view of history. It is this confrontation with totality that allows us to know the social reality to which we belong and to devise a strategy toward changing it. Details can be known only in the light of the whole. Lukacs spoke of the dialectical relationship between society and consciousness. Consciousness has a creative part to play in the socialist revolution.

On this basis, Lukacs became the great defender of art and the freedom of the artist. Great art may not be looked upon, as vulgar Marxists do, as part of the ideological superstructure; great art, on the contrary, provides an encounter with totality and hence makes people perceive more clearly their historical situation and its hidden possibilities. (A similar kind of argument could have been made for the role and power of religious symbols, but Lukacs, thinking that all religious symbols have to do with heaven, never did this.)

In twentieth-century Marxism we find two distinct trends, the "cold current" (to use Ernst Bloch's terminology), the scientific, determinist trend, and the "warm current," the trend which emphasizes the contribution of consciousness and defends the relative freedom of human planning and willing in the context of the concrete historical conditions. The various forms of Marxism constitute different combinations of the cold and warm currents. In this connection, one must mention the work of Antonio Gramsci, the founder of the Italian Communist Party, who died in the prisons of Mussolini in 1937 but whose thought continues to influence Italian communism. Gramsci argued with great vehemence against the theory of economic determinism. He proposed a voluntaristic understanding of Marxism. The logic of history, inscribed in the contradictions of capitalism, does not lead automatically to revolution; revolution takes place only if people recognize their historical situation, stand together in solidarity, and involve themselves consciously and freely in the collective project. Gramsci recognized the importance of cultural factors in the remaking of society. He believed that the introduction of a socialist economy could never work if it were imposed from above by an authoritarian government; what is necessary is that it be built up from below, that it correspond to a new awareness widely spread among ordinary people in city and country, and that it be carried forward by the collective involvement of the great masses. From this, Gramsci argued for the importance of the subjective factors in the revolutionary movement. Without it, the new socialist society could not produce the new man, the new subject.

The debate within Marxism between economic determinism and dialectical humanism was vehement in France in the years after World War II, and in the 1960's and early 1970's it was symbolized by the controversy between Louis Althuser, who defended a sophisticated form of economic determinism, and Roger Garaudy, who attacked this position, presented Marxist thought as a humanism and tried to create room for the subject.[7] It is hard to believe that the French bishops writing their declaration in 1976 were unaware that the question of economic determinism was at the heart of the inner-Marxist debate in their own country.

2. Related to this is the question of the human person. While it is true that Marx himself and Marxism after him often spoke of the individual as "the ensemble of social relations" and often remained quite indifferent to questions of subjectivity, this is not the only trend within Marxism. When in the 1920's the as yet unknown early writings of Marx were discovered, the humanistic inspiration of the young Marx became suddenly quite clear.[8] In these manuscripts, Marx is primarily concerned with the human subject, more especially with man's alienation from himself, from nature and the human community.

Marx speaks here of alienation—with all German idealists—because he has a normative image of man and holds that capitalist production estranges people from their true substance. The cultural Marxism of Western political thinkers—for instance the Frankfurt School and such well known authors as Erich

Fromm and Herbert Marcuse—has taken seriously Marx's early manuscripts, re-established Marx's intellectual affinity with Hegel, and thus greatly emphasized subjectivity and the role of personal freedom in the revolutionary movement. For these thinkers the very center of Marxism is the quest of the new subject.[9]

After 1956, the turn to the subject took place even among many politically involved Marxist theoreticians. After Stalin's death, the 1956 Congress of the Third International revealed the enormous crimes of the great tyrant and introduced, possibly quite unwittingly, pluralism into the communist camp. Many political thinkers of Eastern Europe and the Western Communist parties were ready to admit the neglect of the person in the Marxist tradition, and associated with it the dearth of reflection on such things as friendship, love, marriage, death, and so forth.[10] These thinkers rejected the view that man is simply the ensemble of his social relations. More than that, they defended civil liberties, the right of dissent, and pluralism within the socialist commitment. To what extent these debates among the people and their intellectual leaders have influenced policies of the various communist parties must be studied separately for each case. It would seem that the political movement called Euro-Communism wants to awaken in Marxism the Western tradition of personal freedom. The second question posed by the French bishops, then, fits very well into the inner-Marxist conversation.

3. What about the third question dealing with totalitarianism? Here too we join a discussion alive within the Marxist camp. After Stalin's death and the recognition of his crimes, Marxist thinkers have felt free to subject life in the Soviet Union to a critical analysis. Has the abolition of private property removed alienation from Russia? The answer is no.[11] While there are no longer any classes in the economic sense, government and party bureaucracy wielding power over production and consumption have taken the place of the ruling class with inevitably alienating effects upon the people. People remain largely deprived, unable to enjoy the fruits of their labor and participate in the collective decisions that affect their future. Since Marx's original vision of socialism included the extension of co-responsibility to the ordinary people, the authoritarianism of the Communist countries has been criticized by

committed Marxist theoreticians. These critics have had a very hard time in Eastern Europe. In Western communist parties we find political thinkers who want to bring to life within Marxism the Western tradition of political freedom, protect the democratic heritage, and understand the needed revolution as the extension of democracy to economic life. Euro-Communism in particular has rejected "the dictatorship of the proletariat," i.e., has committed itself to the democratic tradition, even though what this means precisely may still be an object of controversy in the various parties. The question raised by the French bishops, dealing with pluralism, dissent and participation in society, joins a discussion that is already going on in the Marxist world.

4. What about the final and most important question of the French bishops, the one already raised by Leo XIII over eighty years ago? Is the denial of God a constitutive element of Marxism? Or is it possible within Marxism to acknowledge a divine mystery present in human life? This question is not part of an inner-Marxist conversation. Marxists are committed secularists. Even if there are a few Marxist philosophers (Ernst Bloch, for instance) who appreciate in religion, especially in biblical religion, the utopian dream of an alternative society, they do not for a moment think that this religion could be based on a divine reality. Even the Marxist thinkers who speak of transcendence only refer to the overcoming of inherited categories and institutions. While they may yearn for a society beyond the realm of necessity introducing people to the realm of freedom, they do not acknowledge that this yearning is produced by a God who addresses them. Marxists are committed to secularism—as much as the positivists who presently dominate Western intellectual life. Religion corresponds to any early phase of human history, they hold; it is eventually bound to disappear.

There is, however, a related discussion within the Marxist camp. Marxists are divided in their view whether it is possible, for the sake of the common project, to tolerate and even respect the religion of others.[12] The orthodox position sees in religion only a counter-revolutionary ideology. Yet a growing number of Marxists, especially in Euro-Communism, hold not only that religion may be tolerated but that a certain kind of religion, a socially progressive Christian faith, may even inspire people to involve

themselves in the socialist project and render possible the cooperation between communists and Catholics which is needed, in these
countries, for the success of revolution.

We conclude that of the four questions the French bishops
posed, three are part of the ongoing conversation among French
Marxists. The bishops do not mention this: they create the impression that their questions reveal that Christians differ from Marxists
in their understanding of history, of man and of society, while in
fact some of the Christian objections correspond to critical observations made by Marxists themselves.

A Theology of History

Since the issue of God is of central importance, the French
bishops propose a theory of history, man and society, at least in
outline, from a Christian theological point of view. They do this in
an original way, basing themselves on modern Catholic theology
and on sections of Vatican II, and propose a theological understanding of the world that integrates insights available in the Marxist
tradition and the Marxist critique of religion. Several times the
declaration mentions that aspects of Marxist thought have become
part of contemporary culture and that thinkers, including Christian
theologians, no longer refrain from making use of these in their
own work. The declaration mentions in particular Marx's discovery that labor, i.e., the organization of production, has an impact
on consciousness and the making of human history. This means
that consciousness does not float freely above the material conditions of human life; consciousness always remains, however free
and creative it may be, grounded in particular socio-economic
conditions and hence reflects man's concrete historial situation.

The bishops focus the theological section of their declaration
on the Christian notion of "total salvation." The salvation promised us in the Gospel does not simply deal with man's soul, his
personal being or his heavenly existence after death; it has to do
with man's historical situation; it promises redemption from all the
enemies of life, and this includes the oppressive conditions of his
history. The declaration refers to the important paragraph in the

statement *Justice in the World* of the Third Synod of Bishops held at Rome in 1971, which speaks of "social sin," clearly states that the Gospel promises to save us from sin, including "social sin," and asserts that therefore the Christian understanding of redemption includes "the liberation from all the oppressive conditions of human life." Divine grace has a socio-political dimension. The coming transformation includes the remaking of social structures. The French bishops speak beautifully of "cette passion du salut total de l'homme," even though in a surprisingly apologetical tone they add that this "passion" has always been alive in the Church. They define sin as "un refus de l'histoire telle que Dieu nous apelle à vivre." Sacred history and profane history are not two distinct realities; on the contrary, the whole of human history is the locus of the divine call. Man is created by God and moved by the Spirit as the actor of history. The divine action empowers man to become the active, responsible subject of history, to create the conditions of his own existence and thus to become the artisan of his own humanity. The true destiny of man, still largely hidden from us, is revealed in the paschal mystery of Jesus Christ.

Marxism thinks of man as generating himself. Men and women produce the tools and the organizations they need to survive, to be nourished, to be sheltered, and by doing so create their own consciousness. Christians need not deny this material basis of human spirit. At the same time, Christians who recognize this material grounding of consciousness, the pastoral says, should realize that this does not fully account for the orientation of man's spirit. For men and women will always ask questions beyond the immediate meaning of things; they search for a life that makes ultimate sense. There is an openness is human life which nothing finite can satisfy. Mankind is involved in a religious quest, to which Marxists and other secularists are insensitive. At this point the pastoral could have mentioned the messianic hope implicit in Marxism, which seems to reveal a certain sensitivity to the ultimate, and which distinguishes Marxism from the positivistic secularism so strong in our own culture. For the hard-nosed, value-free scientific thinkers that staff our university departments, Marxism is not secular enough, for it holds that history has a destiny and that the day will come when men and women will move from the realm of necessity to the realm of freedom. The French bishops lament modern man's lack of openness to the infinite hidden in the finite; they regard this insensitivity as a damage done to human nature, a damage for which the individual may not be responsible but which is the product of contemporary culture.

The French declaration speaks of God in a non-dualistic way. We notice here the impact of the Marxist-Christian dialogue on Catholic theology. God is never spoken of as inhabiting a realm distinct from the world, God is not conceived of as at right angles to the flow of history; divine grace does not lift men and women out of their concrete situation to a higher plane and dispense them from their historical responsibility; on the contrary, divine grace is operative in history and empowers people to assume responsibility for themselves and define their own future, personally and collectively. While Marxists see the forward movement of history defined by the logic of contradictions and consequent class struggle, Christians see the forward movement of history defined by the presence of God in human life, summoning and enabling people to reach out beyond present conditions and wrestle against the forms of oppression present in their history. In the words of the French declaration, God as liberator is "the center and the end of history"; God is the forward movement of history overcoming injustices as well as its ultimate horizon of reconciliation. The movement of history toward freedom and equality is thus not exclusively defined by the material evolution based on economic forces and their contradictions: history is at the same time a spiritual project nourished by an energy which is divine.

We notice that French bishops propose a Christian theology that avoids what in Marxist language is called "idealism." God does not refer to a realm over and above history. God is in fact the center and the end of history. More than that, Christian ideals are not received from above and then inserted into the flow of history by pious effort, but since God is present in man's struggle to become fully human, these ideals are rooted in man's historical experiences and, with the help of the Christian message, are derived from man's yearnings and his as yet unrealized possibilities. As the grounding, the forward movement and the horizon of history, God does not stand in the way of interpreting history as man's self-creation. The declaration insists that sacred history does not float above man's concrete relations with nature and society; the divine action manifests itself in the creation of a new consciousness, one that recognizes man's grounding in the material conditions and perceives in them not only the oppressive and dehumanizing elements but also new and untried possibilities for the remaking of society and the following of the divine call toward total humanization. Man's religious vocation fully embraces his secular vocation to assume responsibility for his history. The "materialism" which sees man as organizing his labor and in doing so creating his own consciousness is, therefore, not at odds with the Christian vision as long as the materialistic perspective is completed by the recognition that in this process of acting and thinking a transcendent divine mystery is at work, calling and empowering men and women toward the horizon of freedom and reconciliation.

The declaration concludes with certain practical counsels. Because Marxists have not replied, and may not be able to reply, to the four questions to the satisfaction of Christians, Christians know themselves to be committed to a worldview that is different from, and irreconcilable with, Marxism. They may engage in dialogue with Marxists if they frankly confess this difference. They may cooperate with Marxist organizations on clearly defined issues as long as this does not imply a surrender to the Marxist worldview. Belonging to the French Communist Party, the bishops think, is therefore highly problematic. Why? Because it implies the total approval of a Marxist movement that does not satisfy the Christian requirements. The activist Christians who belong to the French Communist Party, however, have replied to the bishops and defended the view that their political commitment can be reconciled with Christian faith.

NOTES

1. "Le marxisme, l'homme et la foi chrétienne," Déclaration du Conseil permanent de l'Episcopat français, *Documentation Catholique,* July 17, 1977, no. 1724, pp. 684-690.

2. "A Society To Be Transformed," The 1977 Pastoral Statement on Social Justice by the Canadian Catholic Bishops.

3. Pius XI, *Quadragesimo anno*, n. 117.

4. The journals of the "Marxist Christians" in France are *Cité Nouvelle, Lettre,* and *Cité Nouvelle-Midi*

5. John XXIII, *Pacem in terris*, n. 159; Paul VI, Letter to Cardinal Roy, n. 51.

6. Leo XIII, *Rerum novarum*, n. 2.

7. George Lichtheim, *Marxism in Modern France*, New York, 1966.

8. Cf. *Karl Marx: Early Writings*, ed. T. Bottomore, New York, 1964.

9. Cf. Martin Jay, *The Dialectical Imagination*, Boston, 1973.

10. The body of neo-Marxist or revisionist Marxist literature is considerable. Famous are two Polish authors, L. Kolakowski, *Der Mensch ohne Alternative*, Munich, 1964, and A. Schaff, *Marxismus und das menschliche Individuum,* Vienna, 1965; an author from East Germany, R. Havemann, *Dialektik ohne Dogma*, Reinbeck, 1964; and several Czech authors such as M. Machovec, M. Prucha, K. Kosik, R. Kalivoda, and V. Gardavski.

11. A. Carlo, "The Socio-Economic Nature of the USSR," *Telos*, Fall 1974, pp. 2-86.

12. For a study of this topic, see M. Spieker, *Neomarxismus and Christentum*, Munich, 1976, pp. 185-220.

Multiculturalism and Ethnicity

In recent years, Canadians have often insisted that they form a multicultural society. In fact, we are witnessing at this time a government-sponsored revival of ethnicity. Canada is the home of groups of people coming from different ethnic and racial backgrounds, and to speak of "multiculturalism" means that government and citizens want them to retain and develop their cultural heritage. Multiculturalism means that prejudice against minorities is not Canadian; it means that Canadians rejoice that their country is made up of such a variety of peoples and that they regard this diversity not as a handicap but a resource and an asset.

Multiculturalism or the survival of ethnicity, according to many sociological studies,[1] fulfills an important function in advanced industrial society. The mobility of modern life easily tears the bonds that create community, and thus vast numbers of people in the metropolitan areas find themselves alone and isolated. Their place of work (if they have a job) does not provide them with warm human relations. In such a society of forced loneliness, ethnic identity and loyalty offer people a strong human bond and the possibility of community. Ethnic cohesion enables people to escape the individualistic ethos and the purely pragmatic values mediated by modern society. In their own heritage they find resources to lead a more fully human life.

Let me add that from a theological viewpoint the human attitude expressed in multiculturalism is a cause for rejoicing. Since God has created humanity made up of different peoples and different traditions, it is intolerable that the dominant group in a country should despise the less successful groups and make some people feel badly about their ethnic or racial background. To expose children to a climate in which they are made ashamed of their own heritage is a grave social sin. We are called upon to affirm ourselves and respect ourselves for what we are. Since people have not chosen the family into which they were born, believers accept their race, their ethnicity and their cultural heritage as coming from God's hand. Christians receive themselves from God in an act of faith. To say that Canada is a multicultural society means that the country's social organization and all citizens should help minority peoples to say "yes" to themselves and rejoice in their heritage.

We realize of course that in Canada there is also a good deal of pressure against multiculturalism. This can be operative on an unconscious level, even and especially among children. The very institutions in which we live, political, economic and educational, make normative the dominant culture in the schools and tend to make children who come from different ethnic or racial backgrounds feel inferior. There is a great deal of suffering in the schools. Children want to live up to an identical norm; to achieve this they sometimes desire to change their name; they are annoyed with their parents for being different and speaking broken English; sometimes they come to despise their own past. To speak of multiculturalism in this context means that we want all children learning in school and playing on the streets to rejoice in their diverse cultural backgrounds. Canada is to be Joseph's coat of many colors.

Multiculturalism, then, is a good thing. After this general affirmation, however, it is necessary to look upon the contemporary stress on multiculturalism in Canada in a critical manner. Why is multiculturalism promoted at this time by the leaders of public opinion and by the federal and, in some instances, provincial governments? What is the historical reality of this multiculturalism? A few critical remarks are in order.

Relativizing Quebec

In the first place we must ask ourselves whether we have not emphasized multiculturalism in recent years to relativize the claims of Quebeckers to constitute a people. French Canadians have always looked upon Canada as the union of two civilizations, French and English, a *dual* country as it were, where two great nations unite to build a single political entity. English Canadians (and English-speaking Canadians of whatever ethnic origin except French), on the other hand, tend to look upon Canada basically as an English-speaking nation, a dominion within the Empire and later within the Commonwealth, heir to a great linguistic, cultural and political tradition derived from Great Britain, in which remains ample room for many ethnic communities, minorities all, including French Canadians. I suppose for people living in Toronto or the Western provinces, it is almost inevitable to overlook the dual nature of Canada.

What are the reasons for this? For one, we think of Canada as made up of ten provinces, and thus Quebec appears simply as one among ten. Second, since English is the dominant language on this continent, French appears to us as a minority language, useful in the home, the schools and special clubs, but not as a public language in North America. And third, it is the multicultural nature of English Canada that often prevents Canadians from perceiving the dual structure of Canada. At one time English Canada, especially Ontario and the Maritimes, were culturally homogeneous; apart from a French minority, these provinces were cohesively British North American. But over the last half century, especially since World War II, these provinces have become the home of many people who have come from Europe and other continents and who now call Canada their own country. English Canadians have come to recognize that their homogeneous culture has given way to multiculturalism, and in this context they easily rank French Canadians as one of the minorities. As they expect the members of the ethnic groups to address them in English, so they easily feel that the French should use this language in the public realm.

Alas, the French and the English-speaking peoples of Canada have quite different perceptions of the Canadian reality. The French never thought of themselves as a minority; they understood Confederation as the union—the "unequal" union as later critics have pointed out—of two majorities. There can be little doubt, it seems to me, that Quebeckers are a people in the sense defined by the United Nations, a people bound by a common history, a common language, a common culture, and possessing their own political economic and cultural institutions. After the electoral victory of the Parti Quebecois on November 15, 1976, it seems likely that Quebeckers will want to acquire political sovereignty—unless it be possible to change the Canadian constitution and make it a guarantee of the dual character of Canada, where the anglophone and the francophone communities face one another and cooperate as equals.

For many English-speaking Canadians, this shift of perspective is new and difficult to accept. They find it impossible to think of Canada as anything but English-speaking country with several minorities. In this context, the present emphasis on multiculturalism can easily become a way of relativizing the claims of Quebec, reenforcing the plural, instead of the dual vision of Canada.

It seems to me that in the U.S.A. the recent ethnic revival, or "multiculturalism," can also be used to relativize the accusation made by the blacks against the white man. Their forceful insistence that they have been oppressed and excluded from the mainstream of society and that black is beautiful and in fact powerful has made other minorities in America speak out with a clear voice that they too have been oppressed. While it is true that the immigrants from the European continent, even though belonging to the white race, have been deprived of their heritage and suffered discrimination affecting their social and economic existence, it is quite misleading, it seems to me, to stress the similarity of their situation with that of the blacks who were brought to America against their will by the slave trade or even with Mexican Americans who were forcibly joined by political annexation. The new stress on ethnicity in this context easily becomes a way of relativizing the claims of the blacks that racial discrimination is the central vice of the American republic. "You think you have trouble," people say to the blacks; "we got troubles too."

False Contrast with America

Secondly, a good case can be made that the recent emphasis on multiculturalism is a way of defining the Canadian identity as distinct from the American. We like to look upon the U.S.A. as "a melting pot" while we have become a beautiful "mosaic." The U.S.A., we like to think, has forced the immigrant people to assimilate to the dominant culture and robbed them of their own heritage, while Canadians, we flatter ourselves, appreciated the diverse cultures of the immigrants and allowed them to keep and develop their heritage.

Is this really true? It can rightly be argued that the U.S.A. has a strongly defined sense of nationhood, a national self-image joined—as some sociologists like to put it—by "a civil religion." Americans see themselves as a people with a mission and a destiny, of which the flag has become the sacred symbol. Immigrant children brought up in the schools learn to salute the flag and absorb the common philosophy. There are then, in the U.S.A. strong cultural factors that promote assimilation.

Canada does not have a developed sense of nationhood. There are regional loyalties in Canada: Maritimers know who they are; Quebeckers have a self-image; Westerners often have a strong sense of identity. In Ontario, prior to World War II, the population was largely homogeneous of British heritage (English, Scottish and Irish) and constituted a community almost as cohesive as Quebec; but since then the influx of immigrants has been so enormous that Ontario no longer has a clear image of itself and often wonders whether it is not becoming Americanized. When it comes to the question of Canada as a nation, Canadians endlessly discuss whether they have an identity of their own or whether we are defenseless against American cultural influence (let alone economic dependency) coming to them from across the friendly border. Immigrants coming to Canada (probably with cousins in Chicago and Los Angeles) are not exposed to strong cultural pressures to assimilate. We do not communicate to them a clearly defined national identity. In this sense, Canada is not a melting pot.

At the same time, while the cultural pressure toward assimilation is weak, there are strong social and economic pressures. The dominant group in Canada, the decision-makers in finance, industry and commerce, is almost exclusively of British origin. Recent sociological studies have shown that the elite structure of Canada has undergone very little change.[2] The upward mobility that has affected so many Canadians in all ethnic groups since the fifties (and that may have come to a stop at this time) has not modified the make-up of the power elite. They retain their hegemony without challenge. It follows that the rising classes model themselves after the elite.

Moreover, the very nature of the economic system, the struggle for survival and the effort to move upward on the social scale demand assimilation of the immigrants. Here, it seems to me, there is very little difference between Canada and the U.S.A. If the spirit of the economic system catches you, if you want to do well and better, then you become a competitive North American who is able to retain very little of his ethnic heritage, unless he comes from a class of European society that already absorbed the competitive spirit. Because the American national identity is so clearly defined and firmly established it is possible for Americans, responding to the new stress on ethnicity, to be more generous in the recognition of multiculturalism than Canadians. For instance, the school system in San Francisco educates pupils in a variety of languages and promotes several subcultures on a scale unparalleled in Toronto or Vancouver. A recent sociological study on ethnic groups in Toronto has shown that despite the developed sense of community and lively ethnic activities, the pull toward assimilation remains as strong as ever.[3] The young want to be like the rest of Canadians (English-speaking Canadians): they follow the same models, they imitate the same styles; they feel increasingly uneasy with the symbols and values in which their parents were brought up. They may not know what a Canadian identity is, but they certainly know who they are as North Americans. Are we really a Canadian mosaic over against the American melting pot?

And what is a mosaic? It is a pattern made of colored stones of different size set in a concrete surface. Mosaics do not move. One must raise the question whether some people promote the idea of a Canadian mosaic so that the various ethnic groups remain content among themselves, preoccupied with their own subculture, leaving the mainstream of society and the important positions in it to the men who have always occupied them? Successful Canadians may well want to think of Canada as a basically

English-speaking land, with a culture largely determined by commercialism and industrialization (and hence culturally resembling lands with similar economic institutions), a busy, sober, hard-working country decorated with picturesque minorities, faithful to their little customs, supplying the successful with color, good restaurants and Old World memories.

We conclude that the promotion of multiculturalism on the part of the government and the leaders of public opinion is not without ideological overtones. It can be used to relativize the French demands for a *dual* Canada by an English insistence on a *plural* nation and, secondly, to define a much-needed self-image of Canada, making it different from, and superior to, the United States.

Let me repeat that if by multiculturalism is meant the generosity and respect extended by society to its subcultures of whatever ethnic or racial origin, we must support it wholeheartedly. At the same time, since in Canada the term has become important in a political context, it deserves a more careful analysis. The search for clarification may raise some unpopular issues, but this is the risk we must take.

Multisubculturalism

We note first of all that multiculturalism is a misnomer. It seems to me that there are only two public cultures in Canada, English and French. The ethnic groups, derived from continental European or from other continents, do not form fully constituted public cultures: they are *sub*cultures. They gladly fit themselves into the political, judicial, economic and educational institutions of the dominant culture, and it is only at certain interstices of the dominant culture, in matters having to do with family life, voluntary organizations, church membership and customs such as music, dance and food, that they are able to affirm their heritage. Culturally they become Canadians, English-Canadians in most instances, even though they form subcultures defined by their cherished values, customs and social styles. In public life, in the field of work and civic organization they speak English and act like Canadians. When Canadians of ethnic origin, even if they have come to this country fairly recently, return to the old country for a visit, they quickly realize how much they have changed, how North American they have become, and how their ethnic identity is restricted to the non-public, familial aspects of culture.

It seems to me, therefore, that it is wholly misleading to call Canada a bilingual and multicultural society as our government likes to do. It is more realistic to admit that Canada consists of two unilingual communities, anglophone and francophone, each the bearer of a public culture, and that this bicultural Canada has many important subcultures. There are of course the native peoples, marginalized and oppressed over the centuries, who hold an altogether special position and cannot be compared with any other group in Canada! The ethnic groups, even when they retain a lively heritage, identify themselves with one or other of the public cultures, usually the English. Since English is the universal language in North America, and since the successful people speak English even in Quebec, it is almost inevitable that the ethnic communities, even when they live in Montreal, identify themselves with English-Canadian culture. They sometimes even react vis-á-vis French Canada with an insensitivity and lack of understanding as if their ancestors had fought with the British on the Plains of Abraham. It seems to me incorrect, therefore, when in the present conflict between English Canada and Quebec, ethnic Canadians, i.e., Canadians who are neither of British nor of French origin, claim that they form a third block besides the two conflicting parties. They do not; they are identified with English Canada even if they constitute vital subcultures within it. Since many immigrants have come to Canada fairly recently and are not yet fully marked by the events of Canadian history, they often have even less understanding of the dual nature of Canada than do the population with a longer memory.

In this context it is appropriate to mention that the tragedy of the present conflict between French and English Canada is that the two are not symmetrical parts: they represent very different social and cultural formations. Quebec is altogether unique on the North American continent: it constitutes a homogeneous community, made up of the descendants of the French stettlers who came to the shores of the St. Lawrence three centuries ago and were largely cut off from subsequent immigration. After the Conquest no more settlers arrived from France; and, living under the conditions of British domination, Quebec struggled for survival and did not attract many of the newcomers who arrived in Canada. Quebec is, therefore, an unusually cohesive society with a strong sense of its history and a common conviction that its destiny, for long under the shadow of foreign hegemony, has not yet been fully defined.

English Canada at one time was also a land of ethnic and cultural homogeneity, but even in those days immigration from Britain continued and English Canada was again and again the land of newcomers. Like other settler countries originally created by Britain, Canada became eventually a modern, competitive, ethnically heterogeneous society, characterized (until recently) by great upward mobility that repeatedly made room, at specific periods, for new immigrants. English Canada became a highly commercial culture, marked by considerable individualism, where people have a weak perception of community but a strong sense of personal responsibility.

Sociologists distinguish between "community" and "association"[4] where "community" is defined by a *strong* social bond between people created by a common history and common values and "association" by a *weak* social bond of a purely legal or contractual kind, leaving people free to fend for themselves, promote their own career and adopt the worldview of their personal choice. Following this distinction it is possible to say that Quebec largely resembles "community", while English Canada, along with the other English-speaking societies outside of Europe, resembles more what sociologists call "association." What Quebec has been wrestling against is not simply the dominance of the English language or the power of the Anglo boss; it also struggles against the arrival of the modern, individualistic, cosmopolitan society that dissolves "community" and makes each person stand alone in the struggle for economic existence.

In this assymetrical situation, we find Quebeckers at this time excited, full of enthusiasm, producing poetry, music and song and discussing, on every level of society, the history and the present destiny of their society. There is in Quebec a popular involvement which English Canada can in no way match. We are not thrilled. We as members of "association" prefer our country to leave us alone. We want our politicians to create the kind of peace that allows us to pursue our own interests and concerns. I still hope, however, that the spirit of compromise that has marked Canadian history shall prevail and that Canada will redefine Confederation as a union between two partners equal in principle.

Fragmented Language and Culture

A second ambiguity of the contemporary stress on multiculturalism is a matter I find somewhat painful to discuss. One has to admit, I think, that the great majority of immigrants from Europe and other parts of the world have come because political or, more often economic factors made it impossible for them to remain in their countries and that for these reasons the language and culture they brought with them often bear the marks of the oppression to which they were exposed in their homelands. Since poor people have been excluded from education and active participation in the formative political and cultural processes, they only too often become the bearers of an underdeveloped language and a fragmented culture. Even when the language of an ethnic group is adequate for family life and the discussion of day-to-day pedestrian issues, it usually does not suffice for a conversation about ideas and the vitally important issues of public and political life. The language of ethnic communities is so easily bastardized because the words of public relevance are inserted in English.

A few ethnic groups may find themselves in a different situation: for example, the Ukrainians who came to Canada since World War II. They arrived with education, middle class culture and a possession of their heritage that produced a subculture or extraordinary viability. One must hope that they and others in similar situations will thrive in the Canadian plural society.

Still, we have to be honest. In many instances the children of immigrants who have the good fortune of studying their inherited language and becoming acquainted with the riches of their culture discover, sometimes with great pain, that the world their parents inherited was broken and incomplete, due to the oppression inflicted on them in the old country. An unthinking recommendation of multiculturalism can easily lock ethnic communities into the highly limited cultural framework created for their class in the society from which they came. It would be ideal if the Canadian provinces could make available to ethnic communities an education that allowed them to acquire in a less deprived and more complete manner the heritage they brought to this country. The stress on multiculturalism usually does not go that far. Sometimes it simply means public support for ethnic dances and cabbage rolls.

For the majority of the immigrants and their children, cultural advancement and political education become more readily available through the institutions of the dominant culture. It has sometimes been the sad fate of ethnic groups that, having lost contact with the old country, they have ceased to develop with their original culture, and, standing apart from Canadian cultural institutions, they fail to develop with their adopted country. It is possible for immigrants and their children to become attached to an immobile past, to become strangers to *two* worlds, the culture of their origin and the new Canadian society, unable to articulate their dreams and aspirations in terms shared by anyone else. Visitors from contemporary Poland, for instance, find the old Polish communities in Canada quaint and curious: this is true of other European visitors as well.

Obviously, for the middle class who can afford prolonged education, the situation is quite different. They are able to develop with Canadian society and play an active part in it, and at the same time keep up with what is happening in the old country, read the latest novels, follow the political evolution, and identify themselves with the culture of their origin in a meaningful and dynamic way. Such a double heritage is a source of great richness. But one has the impression that this is possible only to an elite: it is the result of fortunate circumstances.

In this context one should admit that the new emphasis on multiculturalism, just as the new ethnic consciousness in the U.S.A., sometimes leads individuals to be attached to an ethnic identity that has no content at all. People call themselves Slovac or Italian, and claim that this identification means something to them, but they do not know a word of their beautiful language, they are ignorant of the history of their ancestors and have no appreciation of their authentic cultural heritage.

Peter Gzowski, the great-great-grandson of Sir Casimir, in his speech at the annual meeting of St. Stanislaus Polish Credit Union in Toronto had this to say to his Polish-Canadian listeners?[5] "I speak, read or write not a single word of Polish. Neither my father nor his father nor my father's grandfather spoke Polish, and I have heard it said that when my grandfather's grandfather, Sir Casimir, went backstage in Massey Hall in 1895 to greet Paderewski, he had so forgotten his mother language that he wept at the inability to speak it to his own compatriot." Yet Peter Gzowski claims that something Polish remains in him. "Why do I feel pleasure when Peter Stemkowski plays well for the Maple Leafs or when Irene Mayeska receives good reviews for a role she has just performed?" A few vague sentiments are all that is left of a great culture and heroic history. And yet Peter Gzowski thinks that this special sentiment gives him something—"a sense of identity as an individual within my community." But can such a contentless identity survive very long in a wide section of the population? Such "multiculturalism" may fade away quite rapidly. And if one has ever loved a culture well, does it not hurt a little to see it survive truncated to non-recognition? What must be highly recommended is the present effort of many ethnic groups in this country to educate their members in the history of their culture and if possible teach them their inherited language.

The Solidarity of Labor

We finally raise the question whether the new stress on multiculturalism promotes or impedes the movement for greater social justice. Social change takes place when the people who are disadvantaged or exploited band together, propose a more just vision of society and begin to exert political pressure. If the unemployed in this country were organized and if all the poor people got together to make their claims heard, many things would have to change in our economy. Is it not possible that ethnic loyalty, promoted by the present stress on multiculturalism, could actually divide the lower section of the population into groups that have nothing to do with one another? Ethnic identity weakens class consciousness. Instead of voting for a candidate who stands for greater social justice, ethnic groups may be tempted to vote for a candidate simply because he is one of theirs, even if the party to which he belongs does not promise to help them in their actual predicament. It is not unreasonable to argue that the new multiculturalism may be of benefit to the actual bearers of power in this country since it divides the workers, employed and unemployed, who—if they were together—would be able to demand the reconstruction of society. Sociological research has shown that in some parts of Canada, workers with a strong ethnic commitment vote for the Liberal Party while the more assimilated ethnic workers vote for the New Democratic Party (the Canadian equivalent of the British Labour Party).[6] It would seem then that multiculturalism has something to do with politics.

Ethnic loyalty must be subordinated to social justice. In this context it must be mentioned that ethnic traditions often assign an inferior position to women and that the stress on ethnic identity can be used by a community to keep their women in subjugation.

Conclusion

What conclusions do we draw from these reflections? We rejoice that Canada wants to extend respect and generosity to all minorities and their cultural heritage. We oppose prejudice, personal and institutional; and we hope that the new stress on multiculturalism will create a more friendly and open climate in our cities. At the same time we do not want to use multiculturalism as an argument to put Quebeckers in their place and pretend that we are better than the Americans. Some caution is necessary that multiculturalism does not lock people into their little corners or nourish them with illusions. I have concluded, moreover, that the ethnics on the whole are English-speaking Canadians, that however profound their ethnic commitment, they have identified themselves with English Canada. (There are a few exceptions, for example, the recent immigrants from former French colonies, Vietnam and Haiti, who form subcultures in Quebec.)

Ethnics are anglophones, even if they have an accent! For this reason, it seems to me, they should have opportunities to enter more deeply into the English-Canadian tradition, by which I mean, above all, the political and literary culture derived from Britain and developed in Canada. Ethnic communities while cultivating their own heritage should also pursue a more conscious participation in English-Canadian society. The stress on the many subcultures must be accompanied by a parallel stress on assimilation. British political culture has appeared so attractive to many French Canadians that despite their colonial experience, they cherish the parliamentary tradition and the values and ideals associated with it as their British inheritance. Ethnic Canadians should have the opportunity to become thoroughly at home in the English language and English forms of self-articulation, for the creative contribution they will make in the future will fit into, and thereby significantly change, English-Canadian culture.

Ethnic groups find it difficult enough to preserve their own proper language so that they are not likely to produce their own literary works, at least not for long. The enormous talent present in the ethnic communities of Canada will eventually express itself in English. To argue against assimilation in an unqualified way is to recommend that ethnic Canadians remain in the margin of society. Only through assimilation will ethnic groups significantly modify Canadian public culture.

But above all it seems to me that the present stress on multiculturalism must be subordinated to the demands of social justice. In several recent ecclesiastical documents, the Canadian bishops severely criticize the present economic order; they ask for a new economic system that closes the gap between the rich and the poor and leads to a more just distribution of income. The bishops ask the Catholics of Canada to engage themselves politically on behalf of social justice and to identify themselves, above all, with the interests of the poor, the marginal, the disadvantaged. The present movement toward sovereignty in Quebec must also be subordinated to the norms of justice. For what good would independence do to Quebec workers, employed and unemployed, if their government ruled in favor of the wealthy? There is a danger, it seems to me, that preoccupation with multiculturalism could make some people indifferent to matters of economic injustice. The struggle for ethnic survival could easily make Canadians principally concerned with their own small communities, while justice demands that they see themselves as part of a dual Canada and indeed as part of a world system. There are hazards, then, that an uncritical attachment to multiculturalism and the neglect of assimilation would make some ethnic groups inward looking and indifferent to the social and economic problems that trouble the whole of Canadian society. It seems to me that we need the active involvement of all Canadians, British or French, or of whatever ethnic or racial origin, in order to make this country a more just society and play a more responsible role in a troubled and largely hungry world.

NOTES

1. Cf. Andrew Greeley, *Why Can't They Be Like Us?*, New York, 1971.

2. Wallace Clement, *The Canadian Corporate Elite*, Toronto, 1975.

3. Morton Weinfeld, Ph.D. Thesis, "Determinants of Ethnic Identification of Slavs, Jews and Italians in Toronto", Harvard University, 1977.

4. Cf. Robert Nisbet, *The Sociological Tradition*.

5. Morton Weinfeld, *op. cit.*, pp. 397-98.

6. T. Peterson, "Ethnic and Class Politics in Manitoba", *Canadian Provincial Parties* (ed. M. Robin), Toronto, 1972, p. 69.

Nationalism and Social Justice

The Christian churches are social agents in society that make a significant contribution to the mood, the spirit and the values that animate the people. While the churches have lost the powerful influence they had in the past, they still are voices in Canada that claim some attention. It is interesting, therefore, in these days of uncertainty, to examine the position of the churches on the plural structure of Canadian society. In this essay I shall pay special attention to the Catholic Church. This Church is in a peculiar situation. It embodies the French-English duality typical of Canada. The Canadian Episcopal Conference, the highest Church authority in Canada, had until recently a majority of French bishops; today the number of English-speaking bishops is slightly higher. Besides, many of the recent immigrant groups are Catholics, among them Poles, Ukranians, Italians, Portuguese, and Hungarians. These constitute communities speaking their own language within the English-speaking Catholic Church. It is of special interest, therefore, to examine what this Church has to say about the plural Canadian society.

We find two distinct messages in the Church's recent pronouncements, one dealing with the French-English axis of Canadian society, the other with the stringent demands of social justice. These messages are not easily brought together. At least, the official Church documents do not try to reconcile them. I suppose it is up to Canadians to see whether and how these two messages can be brought together in a single policy.

The Centennial Statement

In 1967, the centennial year, Canada's hundredth anniversary, the Protestant Churches and the Anglican Church published

218

brief statements in which they thanked God for the first hundred years of confederation. The Catholic Church was unable to compose such a statement. The French Canadian bishops felt that giving thanks to God for confederation would sound to their people like interfering in party politics. Are we so sure that God is on the side of confederation? The Canadian bishops were obliged to prepare a very thoughtful document on Canada, a letter addressed to the Catholic people, which examined the problems and possibilities of the country and came to conclusions that were startling to English-speaking Canadians. According to this letter, the defining axis of the Canadian reality as well as the locus of its chief malady is "the co-existence in Canada of two great linguistic and cultural groups which, by a rather curious state of things, stand as two majorities, each a challenge to the other." The Catholic Church on the national level operates out of this duality as no other church and very few institutions in Canada do. The Canadian Episcopal Conference is truly bilingual: each member of the Conference speaks in his own language and no translation is necessary.

The duality that defines the Canadian reality is source of the gravest problems. Why? Because of "the deep discontent felt by a growing number of French Canadians at the difficulties which their community must face in its attempts at growth, and the uneasiness which the claims of the French-speaking group arouse in other parts of Canada." It is beyond dispute, the document continues, that the French-speaking people of Quebec have the right to existence. The Canadian bishops explain that the French Canadian people are not an ethnic minority in Canada: they constitute "a linguistic and cultural group with roots three centuries old in the soil of Canada, the soil which has served as the 'cradle of their life, labour, sorrow and dreams.' . . . They are vividly aware that they make up a community enjoying a unity, individuality and spirit of their own, all of which yield them an unshakable right to their own existence and development." The French Canadians may be a minority as against the whole of Canada, but in Quebec they constitute not only a majority but a compact, cohesive body. That is why, the letter continues, Quebec so easily sees itself as a nation: "No peace can come to Canada without honest recognition of the social fact which is the French Canadian people and effective recognition of the rights of this people." The most serious problem in Canada is, therefore, "that of finding a remedy for the tensions engendered by the co-existence in Canada of two great linguistic and cultural groups which, by a rather curious state of things, stand as two majorities, each a challenge to the other."

On what principles do the Canadian bishops make these claims for the people of Quebec? They appeal to social justice, understood in terms of the distribution of wealth and power. Social justice, they say, is often defined as equality of opportunity, and they are willing to accept this definition derived from liberalism if they are allowed to interpret it in a new way. "It is a feature of the twentieth century," the bishops state, "that the drive for justice is no longer carried on by persons only, but also by peoples, regions and ethnic communities." If Canada represents a duality, a union of two civilizations, then justice demands that both of these enjoy equal opportunity for self-development.

The episcopal letter is also concerned with justice for the many minorities in Canada, beginning with the native peoples, but they subordinate these considerations to the basic duality of the Canadian reality, for unless this duality is embodied in just institutions, there will be no peace in Canada. We find these strong words in the episcopal document: "Injustice is a hateful thing which fosters hate. In its own fashion, it is a form of violence and an endless source of revolt. To hope to found peace on injustice is an illusion."

While the Catholic bishops see the French-English duality as the central axis of the Canadian reality, this vision is not shared in many, if not most parts of English-speaking Canada. Where I live, in Toronto, people do not think of Canada as a duality, a union of two civilizations. What are the reasons for this? *First*, anglophone Canadians tend to think of Canada as made up of ten provinces, and hence Quebec is seen as one of these ten. French Canadians are a minority. *Second*, since English is the dominant language of the continent, French appears to English-speakers as a subordinate language, useful perhaps in the home or voluntary organizations, but not as a public language in North America. In Toronto, children of French Canadian families feel as embarrassed about their private language as do the children of the recent immigrants about theirs: to be part of society means to speak English. To ask people for directions in French is more natural in Zürich or Amsterdam than in Toronto. Our schools teach the French of France. There is no sense of the Canadian duality. *Third*, the duality of Canada is made less visible by what we call, rightly or wrongly, multi-culturalism. At one time English Canada, especially Ontario and the Maritimes, were culturally homogeneous. Apart from a French minority, these provinces were cohesively British North American. English Canadians knew who they were; they had no identity crises in those days. But since World War II, the homogeneous parts of English Canada have taken on a new aspect. While the traditional elite has kept its position intact, the country has become the home of many different people, from Europe and from other continents, who rightfully regard Canada as their country but who are wholly unprepared, by their history and their daily experience, to recognize in Canada an essential duality. They experience themselves as minorities situated in British North American society and have no difficulty whatever in accepting English as the only public language. They desire in many instances to protect their own traditions as a respected subculture, but they never doubt for a moment that the country's official culture is Canadian, by which they mean English Canadian. Since people in English Canada are surrounded by the justified claims of these minorities, they tend to place the claims of French Canadians more and more into this new context.

Finally, the duality inscribed into Canadian society has little visibility in English-speaking Canada because it is difficult for English-speaking Canadians to believe that French Canadian society is really different. Since our culture is largely determined by common North American institutions, and since we share with the United States the same tastes, the same aspirations, and the same style of life, we find it increasingly difficult to imagine that a people living on this continent can really be different. Since

English-speaking Canadians constitute a contractual society, pluralistic, heterogeneous, individualistic, held together by law and common economic interests, it is difficult for them to recognize that in their own country exists a homogeneous people, united by strong social ties—common values, common religion, a common history of struggle.

These are some of the reasons why the duality which defines Canadian existence and is the locus of its most serious threat is not strongly perceived by the vast number of English-speaking Canadians. Unless this duality can be brought out more clearly and expressed in legal institutions that provide equal opportunity for both civilizations, Canada has no future.

What strategies can be devised to protect and promote the French-English duality? There have been essentially *two* such projects. One is promoted by Prime Minister Trudeau: it is an attempt to make Canada a bi-lingual country. By this he means that Canadian citizens, whether English or French-speaking, can address themselves to public institutions in any part of Canada in their own language. I find this project theoretically inadequate and practically unworkable. It is theoretically inadequate because it understands equality of opportunity, in keeping with the liberal tradition, only in individualistic terms. This sort of bi-lingualism does not deal at all with the rights of communities—in this case the French-speaking community. The project, moreover, is unworkable because Canada is for the most part a uni-lingual country. Toronto and Vancouver are as uni-lingual as San Francisco. There are subcultures that cherish their own languages—and San Francisco is more willing to promote these languages in its school system than are the Canadian cities—but the only public language, the only language spoken by the educated and successful class, is English.

Why do English-speaking people find it so difficult to learn other languages? Because acquiring other languages is easy only if there are urgent institutional and economic reasons for learning them. Dutch children brought up in tiny Holland recognize from earliest youth that without foreign languages the wide world will remain closed to them. The Dutch take the learning of languages in their stride. In English Canada there is no urgent institutional reason for learning French. Good will may suffice for a few gifted people, but for ordinary people, even when placed in positions of public office, much greater pressure than their own good will is required. To suppose that Canada can become a bi-lingual country, in the minimal sense recommended by the government, is derived from a local Ottawa experience, but it ignores the character of English-Canadian culture.

What is the other strategy for protecting and promoting the duality of Canadian existence, without which Canada cannot survive? It is the political effort to give this duality constitutional reality. In the 1960's some political leaders spoke of "special status" for Quebec. Since the French presence has been successfully crowded out of Western Canada and downplayed in Ontario — we all remember the brutal manner in which the school questions were solved in Manitoba, Saskatchewan and Ontario — all provinces, with the exception of New Brunswick, are basically uni-lingual. English is the only public language, even if French should be sponsored as a non-public, ethnic heritage. The only way in which the Canadian duality can be constitutionally expressed is by making Canada more clearly a union of two civilizations. Is a special status for Quebec adequate for this task? Some political thinkers suggest that it is possible to grant sufficient power to Quebec, as one among ten provinces, so that it can protect its culture, express its social aspirations and define itself in greater freedom. Other political thinkers have suggested that this duality can only be expressed in a Canadian commonwealth in which two partners, English Canada and Quebec, are associated on equal footing. This position is defended by an increasing number of social scientists in English Canada.

Let me add that once Canada's essential duality finds constitutional expression, then it should be possible to put more emphasis on the development of the many cultural minorities in Canada. In particular, if the political status of French Canadian culture is guaranteed by law, it should be possible for the Quebec government to promote the development of the English minority in Quebec without fearing that its singular sociological position,

its connection with the rest of English Canada and the entire
North American culture, would weaken the solidarity of the less
well-connected French Canadians.

The 1976 Labour Day Statement

We now turn to a second message contained in the official
teaching of the Canadian Catholic Church. While Church documents have always been concerned with social justice, since the
third synod of bishops held in Rome in 1971, ecclesiastical teaching has undergone a significant shift to the left. At this synod, the
bishops introduced the notion of "social sin" and argued that the
salvation which Jesus Christ offers to the world includes the deliverance from social sin and hence implies "the liberation from
all the oppressive conditions of human existence." The synod
declared that "action on behalf of justice and participation in the
transformation of society" must, in the present age, be regarded
as "a constitutive element" of the Christian life. The Gospel contains a social message. To be a Christian means to be actively
engaged in the struggle for justice.

After the Roman synod, the Canadian Catholic Church
sought the ecumenical cooperation with the other Christian
churches in Canada and jointly with them created several inter-
church committees, whose task it was to make a critical study of
the economic and social issues important in Canadian society and
to offer policy recommendations to the churches' governing
bodies. On the basis of these studies, the Canadian churches have
taken positions on public policy, submitted briefs to the government and government committees, and influenced their members
as to what precisely social justice means in Canada.

Early in 1976, the leaders of the major Canadian churches
presented the brief "Justice Demands Action" to the prime minister and the federal cabinet. It began with this declaration: "We
stand in the biblical tradition of the prophets where to know God
is to seek justice for the poor and oppressed." The brief then turns
to the dangerous inequality of wealth and power in Canada: "The

present economic order is characterized by the maldistribution of wealth and the control of resources by a small minority." In Canada and in the third world, powerful corporations plan the use of natural resources without the participation of the people who are most directly affected by this. "The human consequences of the present economic order," the brief continues, "are dependency, loss of human dignity, poverty and even starvation."

This theme is amplified in the 1976 Labour Day Statement of the Catholic bishops. Here the Catholic people are reminded that "something is wrong with the present social and economic system," that it "results in the very uneven distribution of wealth and the control of resources by a small minority," and that affected by these ills are not only the peoples of the third world but also people in Canada. In the various regions and communities of Canada there are signs that people desire the end of the present waste, want, and exploitation and wish to find a new economic approach that makes better use of human and material resources. What are the practical steps recommended for Catholics by the Labour Day Statement? Catholics are asked to understand the Gospel as a message of social justice, to modify their life-style if they are wealthy, to listen to the victims of injustice in their own communities, to speak out against the injustices in the country, to participate in actions to change the causes of these injustices, and to provide assistance to the poor and the oppressed groups. These recommendations are startling indeed.

In the Catholic Church a significant shift of social philosophy has taken place, the meaning of which we are only beginning to assess. Catholic social teaching in the past was formulated largely around what political scientists call "myths of origin." Here experiences of the past, alive in memory, become the guides for social policy. Associated with the origins of society are intense experiences that retain their power in people's minds and become principles of social action. Sometimes this return to origins had to do with blood and soil, with kinship, with ethnic identity, with nationhood; at other times—this is true especially in the Catholic tradition—it had to do with the birth of European civilization as a feudal order, that is, as divided into social hierarchies united by a common spirit of faith, hope, and love. Catholic social thought derived its critical power from this ancient ideal. Even Pius XI's repudiation of monopoly capitalism was based on the myth of origin; it was feudal harmony that stood in judgment on contemporary capitalism that organizes production for the sake of profit and hence increasingly widens the gap between the rich and the poor. Even the centennial letter written by the Canadian bishops in 1967 still invoked the myth of origin, in this case the Canadian duality. What has taken place in Catholic teaching since then is the shift to what political scientists call "myths of destiny." Here the vision of the future society provides norms of action. The picture of what society ought to be like becomes the guide for the making of policy in the present. In a remarkable paragraph, Pope Paul VI, in his letter *Octogesima adveniens*, defends the political fruitfulness of "the utopian imagination." Following the analysis of the Marxist thinker Ernst Bloch, the Pope shows that imaginary visions of what society should and could be act as critiques of the present order, reveal the as yet uncovered possibilities in the present, and direct the social dynamism in a new direction. The most recent Catholic social teaching, then, no longer operates out of the memory of feudal society, but actually argues out of a concept of a cooperative society defined (as feudalism was not) in terms of equality.

Let me note in passing that the Canadian bishops have followed their own advice and involved themselves in several public issues. They have spelled out what, in their view, are the requirements of social justice in connection with world food policy, Canadian immigration, and the development of the northern territories. They have been accompanied in these involvements by the leaders of the other Christian churches of Canada. What the Canadian bishops have failed to do, however, is to communicate the new social teaching to the Catholic people. The collective statements were not promoted by the bishops in their dioceses.

This shift to the left on the part of the Canadian churches has been the object of public criticism in recent months. The successful members of the business community and more especially the directors of the large corporations—who, for reasons I do not have to analyze here, belong mainly to the Anglican Church and the United Church of Canada—have appealed to church leaders to desist from this new involvement. While church documents have always been concerned with social justice, the shift of the social justice perspective to the center of Christian proclamation is unparralleled in Christian history and represents a significant development of doctrine.

The Unresolved Question

The emergence of social justice as the principal moral issue puts a question mark behind nationalism and the movements of national liberation. In its teaching, we recall, the Catholic Church has always been suspicious of nationalism, whatever may have been its practice in some situations. As late as 1967, Pope Paul, in the encyclical *Populorum progressio*, declared that "nationalism isolates people from their true good." The Pope indicated, however, that this harsh judgment does not imply a critique of the peoples who seek independence from colonial conditions nor of those who with pride defend their cultural traditions against assimilation or conquest by a more successful society. But even here, nationalism must be subordinated to social justice.

How can the message of social justice be reconciled with the first message of the bishops on the need to protect and secure by law the dual structure of Canadian society? The only way to this, it seems to me, is to subordinate this duality to the demands of social justice. More important than the protection of the Canadian duality is the deliverance of Canadians from exploitation and oppression.

We notice immediately that movements of national self-affirmation are of different kinds. There is a nationalism of the right, often promoted by the traditional elite, that wants to shut off people from outside influence and new ideas and thus protect the inherited values, including the social (and ecclesiastical) hierarchy. Such a nationalism is inward-looking and isolationist. If ordinary people, the workers in particular, can be persuaded that national identity is the supreme value, they may be willing to support their national leaders even if they do not promise social change and a more just distribution of power and income. Then there is bourgeois nationalism, a movement inspired by the rising middle class to gather the people in a common struggle against the remnants of feudalism or the legacy of colonial oppression. The successful middle class, excluded from the highest positions in industry and commerce by the heirs of the colonial ruling class, yearns to occupy these highest positions and increase their wealth and power. In this movement, the middle class needs the loyalty of the workers. As long as the national struggle lasts, the national leaders promise the workers a more important place in the new society. Finally there is socialist nationalism, a national movement in which the workers play the central role. The workers hope that by helping their people to achieve unity and independence, they will be in a better position to introduce radical social change and significantly reduce the gap between the rich and the poor. In Quebec we find these three forms of nationalism.

If social justice is the principal perspective, then the first two forms of nationalism , sponsored by the old elite and promoted by the new class of businessmen and technocrats, have very little to offer. The success of such nationalism does not promote a more just distribution of income and power in the country. It only prevents people from seeing the social and economic mechanisms that cause their exclusion from the public wealth. It is only the nationalism of ordinary people involved in production and services (including, of course, the unemployed) that can be a stepping stone to greater social justice.

It is difficult for me to judge to what extent the Parti Quebecois is identified with the interests of the French Canadian business community, or to what extent it aspires to a social democracy that favors greater economic equality. It seems to me that nationalism can be very dangerous for lower income groups and the poor, for the shift of power that takes place through a nationalist movement places the position of responsibility into the hands of the local bourgeoisie who tend to see society as their own exclusive project. It is even possible to encourage nationalism as a passion among workers to make them misread the cause of their insecurity and dependence. One may even wonder whether workers in Quebec who speak only French and are unable to use English as a working language will become more dependent on, and subservient to, their French employer, since for them the range of job opportunities will be restricted to Quebec. It seems to me, therefore, that from a socialist perspective it is not easy to say whether it is better for workers and the lower classes in general to pursue the goal of an independent Quebec, or whether it is of greater advantage for them to strengthen their solidarity with the low income groups in the whole of Canada and together struggle for a more just society.

Social justice, moreover, demands that the nation state (in our case, the bi-national state) increasingly understand itself in a wider political context and acquire bonds of solidarity with other countries. Within a single nation it is taken for granted that an underdeveloped region receives support from the more developed parts; since today the entire world has become economically interconnected and bound by the same interests and fears, it is becoming inevitable that the underdeveloped regions of the earth receive support from the developed nations. For the sake of the survival and well-being of all and to avoid chaotic conditions of life from which even the wealthiest regions will not be saved, the nations will have to transcend their narrow self-interest and think of themselves as constituting wider, trans-national unities. Moveover, since monopoly capitalism has led to the creation of giant corporations that exceed the boundaries of any one nation, there is no government left that can control them at this time. In Canada, as in many countries of the third world, we do not own the major part of our industrial developments and hence are unable to determine the economic policy of our own country. The concern with the central duality of Canada and the possible separation of Quebec may be quite unrealistic when in fact Quebec and English Canada, united or apart, have lost the power to regulate their economic life. The only way to control these giant corporations will be through joint action of many national governments. What is needed is greater solidarity among the nations. From this point of view, nationalism is passé.

I now come to the troubled conclusion of this chapter. How can the two central problems of Canada be solved simultaneously? We must protect the Canadian duality that is threatened at this time by English Canadians who defend the political status quo and by Quebec separatists who want nothing to do with the rest of the country. And—more important still—we must create a more just society defined by a more equitable distribution of wealth and greater participation of people in the political and economic institutions of which they are part. I am a member of a Toronto-based group, called Committee for a New Constitution, which is concerned with the preservation of the Canadian duality, in a way acceptable to Quebec and English Canada, in view of gaining greater economic independence for the entire country. The committee holds the view that the present national crisis may become the occasion for Canadians, French and English-speaking, to restructure their political and economic institutions to promote a qualitatively better society.

Science and Commitment: Historical Truth According to Ernst Troeltsch

It is often supposed that only Marxist thinkers and scholars on the left deny the value-neutrality of the social sciences and suppose that political commitment inevitably affects the manner in which research is undertaken and conclusions are brought forth. As a matter of fact, the link between science and commitment is also defended by liberal scholars, especially if they have a religious background. Christians spontaneously feel that love affects the way in which one perceives reality. Unless you love, you do not know God, the apostle wrote, and the reader suspects that this applies also to the knowledge of people and their history. Knowledge, then, is dependent on the social location and the mind-set of the knower. Philosophers refer to this as the historicity of truth.

In this essay I wish to analyze how one great Christian thinker, Ernst Troeltsch, a theologian and a sociologist, defended the historicity of truth in the social sciences and in this context made observations of great interest for contemporary theology.

The historicity of truth was at stake in a famous debate, carried on in Germany in the early decades of this century, on the difference between the natural and the human sciences.[1] A widespread philosophical trend, if not the dominant one, in line with the Enlightenment tradition, advocated the application of scientific method, worked out on the model of physics, to the study of the human world and thus sought to assimilate as much as possible the human sciences to the natural sciences. Against this trend, various historians, social scientists and philosophers of science stressed the radical difference between the human and the natural sciences and asserted the historicity of truth in the former.[2]

This controversy is not as well known in English as it deserves. The historicity of truth in history and the social sciences has mainly been studied in English under the rubric of relativism. The historicist thinkers were usually understood as making all truth about the human world relative, as regarding scholarship vulnerable to the climate of the age and the mood of a particular group, and thus as undermining the foundation of the human sciences. Best known in English, and possibly the principal book used at universities for studying the debate on historicism in the early decades of this century, is Maurice Mandelbaum's *The Problem of Historical Knowledge*.[3] In this book, Professor Mandelbaum studied scholars he regarded as relativists, such as Dilthey and Mannheim, and scholars who sought to overcome relativism, such as Rickert, Simmel, Troeltsch and Scheler, yet who, according to the author, attributed such an active role to the knowing subject in the act of knowledge that they were unable to overcome relativism and establish the objectivity of historical truth in the human sciences.

Mandelbaum's study seems unsatisfactory. He does not adequately present the thought of the scholars studied. It is ironic—and yet highly significant—that a philosopher of history who sets out to defend the objectivity of truth comes to present unrecognizable pictures of the positions held by scholars belonging to a cultural tradition different from his own. At the same time, Mandelbaum deserves great credit for sensing, over a generation ago, that this controversy over the historicity of truth, carried on mainly, though not exclusively in German, deserves the careful attention of historians and social scientists in the present situation.

Ernst Troeltsch produced a considerable body of literature dealing with history, social sciences and questions of methodology. In this essay I shall concentrate almost exclusively on Troeltsch's massive study entitled *Der Historismus und seine Probleme*,[4] published in 1922, a few months before his death, in which he had collected in a single volume studies on the historicity of truth, written over a period of ten years. While it was Troeltsch's intention to write a second volume, comparable in size and thoroughness to the first, dealing with the resolution of the problems posed by historicism, his life was not long enough for this. Invited to lecture in England in the spring of 1923, he prepared several lectures that were to anticipate some of the ideas for his second volume. When, after his death, these lectures were published as a slim volume,[5] it turned out that they contained nothing concerning the resolution of historicism that was not said more carefully and more clearly in his first volume.

The Historical Object

To understand Troeltsch's view of historical truth, we must examine how he understands the social reality studied by the human sciences and the observer's relationship to this social reality. If we do not begin with this basic question, we will inevitably misinterpret Troeltsch's position. It is useful, for our purpose, to analyze why Mandelbaum, in the important book mentioned above, failed to understand Troeltsch's principal point. Mandelbaum was interested almost exclusively in the refutation of relativism. He understood the historicist authors studied by him, including Troeltsch, to say that all research in history and sociology is influenced by the personal and social situation of the researcher, by his personal bias and cultural prejudices, and that even if he tries hard to overcome these, he will never achieve perfect objectivity. Research and conclusion in the human sciences inevitably bear the mark of the scholar's historical standpoint. But if this is all that the historicist authors wanted to say, then their view is hardly worth reporting. Most scholars studying the human world realize only too well the possibility of unconscious bias in themselves, and while they try hard to overcome this, they are usually quite aware that despite their efforts, this sort of self-purification can never be fully achieved. When they defend, nonetheless, the objective and value-free character of the human sciences, they propose this as an ideal to be striven after even if it may never be fully realized.

According to Mandelbaum's analysis, the historicists denied the objective and value-free nature of the human sciences simply because the scholar's historical standpoint inevitably introduces distortions in his perception and his reasoning. What Mandelbaum fails to consider is that the historicist authors, including Troeltsch, had quite a different understanding of the social reality studied by the human sciences and of the scientist's relationship to it. Mandelbaum is insensitive to this problem. He presupposes, in line with the principal tradition in scientific thought, that a researcher is a rational subject, equipped with powers of perception and knowledge, facing the social reality not of his own making, and studying it as an object of his mind. Mandelbaum reads the historicist authors as if they understood the relation of subject and object in the human sciences, in the same way. Yet it is precisely this subject-object model which was rejected by Troeltsch and the tradition he represented.

In his entire work Troeltsch tries to show that man may not be looked upon as an empty, isolated, intelligent substance facing society and its history. This simple subject-object model may be useful in the natural sciences: in the human sciences it is wholly inadequate. "From the brittle, isolated, empty ego consciousness, however mitigated by theories of the non-substantiality or the unknowability of this ego, it is quite impossible, by whatever psychological theory of stimulus and response, to arrive at an understanding of human individuality."[6] Human individuality here refers to man inasmuch as he is both a personal unity and an embodiment of a wider reality in which he participates. Yet human individuality also characterizes the object of the human sciences, namely people and their interaction. Both the observer and the observed participate in a wider reality that enters into their self-definition and creates a relationship between them. The great problem of the historian and social scientist is, therefore, how he can know other people and their actions. He is in some way interwoven with the social reality he studies so that the subject-object model is here not applicable. Since for Troeltsch the key to the problem is human individuality, the model for the knowledge of others is self-knowledge.[7]

Let it be said immediately that Troeltsch rejected the neo-Kantian solution of the problem of historical knowledge, as it was, in his day, proposed by Rickert and Simmel. For these thinkers, categories of the human mind, distinct from those applied in the knowledge of nature, order and constitute the human world in terms of individual uniqueness and inseparable unities. These categories, therefore, produce historical knowledge. While these neo-Kantians overcame the reductionism of the dominant positivist trend and defended the radical distinction between the human and the natural sciences, they did this at the cost of neglecting the historical reality, the real world of men, the dynamic reality which is history. While Troeltsch in his early years had sympathy for Rickert's understanding of history and the social sciences, as an historian he could not for long remain content with a theory that made the creative force in history the human mind of the observer and thus failed to acknowledge the original, basic, and overriding reality, namely history itself, which even brings forth the observer.[8] Central for Troeltsch became, therefore, the peculiar character of what he called "the historical object," i.e. the human world studied by the historian and social scientist.

Troeltsch devoted a large section of his book on historicism to the analysis of the historical object. The main characteristic is the uniqueness and individuality of this object. This individuality is axiomatic for Troeltsch. The objects of historical knowledge are unities, or, as he likes to call them, "totalities," wholes, whether they be individual persons or larger groupings, in which these persons are embedded, such as families, clans, classes, nations or cultural spheres. These historical objects are never reducible to the sum of their component parts; they are, instead, wholes, alive by continuity of meaning and value, which precede their individual elements at least in the sense that they assign significance to these elements. The primary reality is life itself, passing itself on in a many-leveled process and constituting itself in individualities that orient and organize the elements that go into their making. Life never simply repeats itself; it is unique, original, inexhaustible.

The meaning-continuity, which creates the totality, responds to new historical conditions and thereby modifies itself creatively, Troeltsch sometimes calls "the spirit." While it is through the spirit that life becomes conscious, grows and expands, the spirit is not, for Troeltsch, an independent metaphysical entity. Meaning-continuity is spirit in the sense that it is alive with unpredictable vitality, generating new responses and creating new values. It is spirit, moreover, in the sense that this meaning is immanent in the totalities, woven into their total reality and never identical with man's consciousness or his rational awareness of his own plans and purposes. The meaning and values that constitute the vital unities making up the historical object are tied so deeply into the structure of life that man's response to them and thus the process of his becoming are not rationally analyzable in chains of cause and effect. If it is to be grasped at all, this must be by a different sort of analysis altogether. To understand the historical object we must lay hold of its spirit.

What arguments did Troeltsch offer in support of this view of history? He presented long and detailed analyses of the various attempts, made by philosophers of history, to account for the historical object and found them all wanting, all except one—the approach he himself follows. The theoretical account of the nature of the historical object must, for Troeltsch, correspond to the actual experience of the historian, coming to grips with and understanding the life of another person or the history of another period. In the last analysis, the unique and total nature of the historical object cannot be demonstrated. It can only be affirmed by a man who lays hold of his own life in a creative way, by a man who refuses to regard his own life as made up of parts, each of which follows a determined law of science, but who asserts in an act of faith the unity and uniqueness of his life and, in fidelity to this, responds to the challenges of history. Again self-knowledge is the source of man's knowledge of other people and their history. But as self-knowledge is not an aloof inquiry into one's life, but a commitment, a gesture of trust, an act of self-making, so is the recognition of the historical object as individualities and totalities ultimately a personal choice based on the experience of the spirit.

One might argue against Troeltsch that meaning-continuity, if it exists, ought to be demonstrable. One should be able to reconstruct and render an account of the unitive meaning present in the historical object. Troeltsch would reply to this by recalling that this meaning is immanent in the manifestations of life and hence can never be made fully conscious. Since the unitive meaning remains largely unconscious to the human world created by it, it can be grasped only by an act that is not purely cognitive but lays hold of life and intensifies consciousness. The great problem which follows from this, "the unresolvable antinomy"[9] as Troeltsch called it, is how to understand the relationship of the individual person to the wider totalities to which he belongs. How is the spirit of the person related to the spirit of the community?

Many scholars educated in the Anglo-American tradition with its individualistic, empiricist trend read Troeltsch and other German thinkers using similar language as if they were poets offering a high-minded, idealistic description of human life, without adequate recognition of the biological and other material factors of man's personal and social existence. Mandelbaum read Troeltsch in this way. To talk about the spirit of people and their communities suggests to them metaphysical vagaries and theological pretensions supposedly contained in German idealism. Even H. Stuart Hughes, who has analyzed European social thought in his well-known *Consciousness and Society*,[10] often falls into this trap. In a passage, which students of Max Weber must find amusing, Hughes tries to explain what the great German sociologist meant by *verstehen*: Weber's method of *verstehen* is a "vestigial remnant of Weber's idealistic past. . . . Crudely put, *verstehen* can be characterized as the German formula for giving philosophical standing and dignity to a source of knowledge that in the Latin world was either called intuition or simply accepted as something inexplicable."[11] Yet for Max Weber, as is well known, *verstehen* was something much more hard-headed. Since human action is never simply behavior but includes meaning, the sociologist must understand the meaning which people assign to what they do. Without this sort of *verstehen*, no sociological analysis is possible.

As a student of sociology with some sympathy for the German intellectual tradition, I have not read the work of Troeltsch as though he were a romantic. I do not regard him as an idealist fleeing from empirical research to unverifiable intuitions and metaphysical speculations. It is true, as we shall see later, that

Troeltsch believed that a profound analysis of how we can know other people ultimately leads to metaphysics or theology, but the whole trend of his philosophical work as well as his historical and sociological analyses went in the opposite direction: namely to remain as close as possible to the empirical study of historical objects, to exclude standards and concepts not drawn from the historical object itself, to deny categorically universally valid norms, and to refuse to separate the ideal factors from the material ones in the creation of culture and society. In his major work, examined in this essay, Troeltsch regarded the metaphysical or theological question as marginal and, to the disappointment of some philosophical readers, only sketched his views. For this reason, then, we must understand Troeltsch's account of the historical object as an attempt to analyze how persons or other social unities are related to the wider social and cultural frameworks to which they belong. Troeltsch is interested in the mutual relation between person and society. I read his major work, then, as an exercise in sociology.

Troeltsch clearly recognized that society precedes the individual, that through language, symbols, values, concepts, practices and institutions to which men are exposed from childhood on, they come to be like historical subjects, that the social reality on various levels is not something outside of men but has become in some way constitutive of who men are as persons. Even the categories in which a man experiences himself and expresses and assimilates his most private encounters with the world are in some sense societal. Emile Durkheim, far removed from the tradition of German idealism, regarded society as partly intrinsic to man. At the same time, the individual person is never wholly determined by the primary or any subsequent socialization. There does remain in man an originality; otherwise one could not account for history at all. There are some insights, some responses, some actions proper to the person, which affect his personal life in a new and unexpected way and hence inevitably modify some level of the wider society to which he belongs. Yet even this newness, produced through personal originality, is not injected into the social reality as though coming from some independent realm of values; the newness itself is socially grounded, proceeds from man's embeddedness in his culture, and carries forward a trend or inclination present in the society to which he belongs. Again, the Durkheimian expression *humo duplex* comes to mind. Affirming this twofold character of man does not suggest that man's societal and individual dimensions can be neatly separated, but rather that they inseparably cohere and qualify one another, that man is at one and the same time an instance of his societal world and a uniquely original individual.

Troeltsch's analysis of the historical object showed that man's relationship to the social reality facing him can never be reduced to an subject-object model. The historian or sociologist who looks at other people and their social interrelation is never the empty subject, endowed with intelligence, attempting to understand a reality wholly extrinsic to him. Such an objectivity would be an illusion. For the intelligence, or whatever other name one may use to designate the knowing mind, is itself constituted through social participation. Both the knowing subject and the social reality to be known have come to be in historical processes that are closely related to one another; and if it is a question of understanding a contemporary feature of one's own society, the knowing subject and the historical object may indeed have been created by the same historical process. To come to the knowledge of other people and their institutions, then, is a complex and subtle intellectual quest by which we find ourselves in these others and, in turn, find them in ourselves. Troeltsch does not use this famous formula drawn from Dilthey;[12] he does not seem to have been aware how closely he followed Dilthey's analysis of historical knowledge. Yet for him the intellectual effort of the historian was to discover his own roots in the historical object studied by him and, conversely, the presence of this historical object in his own personal self-understanding.

It is true that for Troeltsch the knowledge of others, be they persons or social unities, was ultimately possible because of metaphysical or theological reasons. We can pass from self-knowledge to the knowledge of others only because the meaning immanent in their totalities is not wholly foreign to us; it exists potentially in us, and hence points to a common ground of life, present as hidden source in all people, making conversation and mutual understanding possible. However, this divine ground is not a universal norm or value. Troeltsch's theological metaphysics in no way made him less empirically oriented, less reliant on research and science, less open to learn from the wholly unprotected encounter with the historical and social reality.

The Three Phases

Troeltsch analyzed the knowledge of the historical object by pointing to two distinct phases which, in turn, give rise to a third and final phase. *The first phase* is the effort of the scholar to understand the social reality he studies, be it past or present, extended or contained, through categories and norms taken entirely from the totalities under examination. Troeltsch vehemently rejected the positivist trend and the common sense impulse to measure other human realities in concepts drawn from one's own world of experience. The scholar must make an enormous effort to abstract from the categories and norms proper to his culture and his personal life, to lay hold of the historical object as a totality alive with a meaning-continuity of its own, and to understand it in terms brought forth by its own proper life. Troeltsch called this "the immanent critique."[13]

In this first phase Troeltsch displayed the passion of the scientist to shed subjectivity, to make the utmost effort to be objective, to forget himself, his values and preferences, and use all the available methods of research to acquaint himself with the historical object. Here the scholar must be open to the unexpected, the inconvenient, the inexplicable. Here he must use the rigor of scientific methods. His aim is to understand historical totalities in terms produced, not by himself, but by them. He knows that he can be objective in regard to the life and action of others only if he is willing to interpret them in terms generated by the actors themselves.

According to Troeltsch, the historian and sociologist may not take for granted any transcultural norm or category. The study of history has convinced him that there are no universal concepts, applicable across the ages and cultural spheres. The diversity, richness and multiplicity of history transcend all expectations. Instead of beginning with the concept of a common human nature, or a natural law of any kind, the scholar must immerse himself in the historical object of his study and discover in it the measures, in terms of which it is to be understood. This effort is the famous *einfühlen*, advocated by many German historians, which to English readers, raised in a more positivistic climate, often sounds romantic, sentimental, or at best poetic. What this *einfühlen*, however, refers to, especially in Troeltsch, is the adoption of a rigorous method for understanding an historical individuality in terms of its own immanent meaning structure.

Troeltsch rejected every kind of universalism. The assertion that there is a principle operative in all cultures and societies, thanks to which we can understand them and account for their development, was in his eyes a wholly unproven and nonscientific claim, without empirical evidence to support it. Each historical object demands a new effort of the scholar to understand it. Troeltsch repudiated the various universal systems of world interpretation, whether they were the Church doctrine of the universality of Jesus, or the Enlightenment doctrine of a universal human nature and the uniformity of reason, or the Hegelian interpretation of history as a logical unfolding, or the Marxist view of history as a necessary dialectics of economic classes. While Troeltsch was influenced by Marxism in the course of his study of historicism, he rejected it with all other kinds of "holistic historicism." Each new object of research, each historical totality must be studied with total detachment, with *verstehen,* with *einfühlen*, with scientific rigor, through which the scholar tries to grasp the meaning structure implicit in people's lives and constitutive of their culture and institutions. Marxists, Troeltsch thought, were no longer free to make an immanent critique; they had already determined, before studying the historical object, the terms in which they should understand its dynamics.

This first phase of historical knowledge remains unavoidably incomplete. The scholar is so deeply tied into his own categories that his immanent critique of another historical object remains partial. The effort to separate himself from his personal and cultural presuppositions, however, necessarily leads to a return to self-examination. The unity of mental life is such that we cannot understand and evaluate other people and their action without bringing them into relation to our own understanding of the world. Thus we come to *the second phase* of historical knowledge, which consists of analyzing and reconstructing, under the impact of the newly gained knowledge, our present situation and, inseparably from this, our vision of the future.

According to Troeltsch, man always has some sort of knowledge of himself and the wider social context in which he stands. This knowledge, however vague it may be, is associated with an ideal or desire for the future. The "is" and the "ought" are so closely connected in human experience that only in wholly exhausted cultures and depressed personalities do we find attempts to perceive reality without any critical impulse and without desire of what should be. For Troeltsch, the knowledge of the present is almost without exception oriented toward its transformation through action. Where this connection between "is" and "ought" is severed, the transmission of life becomes problematic. The picture of the present we make for ourselves not only implies a vision of the future but is already a preparation for the action that creates this future. The basic analogy, here as elsewhere, is man's knowledge of himself which is always based on some sort of vision of what he should be or might be, and which is already an act creative of this future. Troeltsch extended self-knowledge to include a person's awareness of the wider social, cultural and political framework to which he belongs. We experience ourselves as beings in a world, moving toward the future. Any systematic analysis of where we stand includes a view of where we are going and is, in itself, a first step of moving ourselves toward this goal.

A scholar's view of the present, it may be presumed, has been rationally tested and thus become largely conscious. It is with this view of the present that the first phase of historical knowledge is being confronted. Since we ourselves are individualities, alive by immanent meaning, we cannot but relate these two sets of categories and values and make the new historical knowledge act as critique on our view of the present. The knowledge derived from phase one will raise question marks behind certain aspects of our own cultural ideal and the categories in which we understand ourselves. Challenged by the knowledge of another culture or another personal life, we discover the problematic nature of some of our own assumptions, we see through aspects of life that had remained disguised, we discern hidden connections and interrelations and come to deeper self-knowledge. We may find that this confrontation makes us see more clearly where we are going and demands that we modify our personal and social ideal. This creation of a new cultural ideal is phase two of historical knowledge.

Phase one and phase two generate *a third and final phase* where the immanent critique of the historical object and the cultural ideal linked to the view of the present combine in the creation of a single perspective, in which the historical object is truly and validly known by the historian or sociologist. This new perspective is gained by a dialectical process in which phase one and phase two affect one another. Phase one, as we said, leads to a rethinking of the cultural ideal, and this, in turn, enables the scholar to become more aware of his own presuppositions, separate himself more successfully from them, and thus come to a deeper understanding of the historical object in categories immanent to it. This will again pose new problems for the scholar's self-understanding and his vision of the future; it will make him see a little more clearly what goes on at present and thus modify his ideal of the future to be created. These two phases operating on one another create the third perspective in which the scholar eventually discovers the present in the object he studies and the object in his present situation; in other words he discovers the historical development that has taken place, from the historical object studied by him to his present cultural synthesis.

To look upon an historical object wholly as outside of oneself and one's world is not to know it at all. Aloofness of this kind distorts and misjudges history. Since this object and the observer are participants in the same history, since the observer has come to be by reacting in some way to this object, and since the object can be fully understood only as its influence on contemporary and subsequent totalities is taken into account, true historical knowledge includes the interrelation between object and observer. By a single glance the historian must see the development that relates him to the object he studies; by a single glance the sociologist must see the dynamic interconnection between the social reality studied by him and the social world to which he belongs. This is historical truth.

Historical Development

Historical development was, for Troeltsch, another central notion, studied by him with the same care he expended on the historical object. He carefully examined the various attempts of philosophers to deal with development in history and found most of them wanting. Thus he totally rejected the scientific approach of the positivists who sought to reconstruct, according to the model of the physical sciences, a cause-and-effect chain in history as the explanation of the changes taking place in it. This approach violated the nature of the historical object. In physical objects— at least according to the mechanistic physics still dominant in Troeltsch's day—every complex motion may be reduced to tiny, measurable steps of necessary changes going on in the component elements. The objects studied by the human sciences, on the other hand, are totalities; they are not reducible to the sum of their elements. They develop through a continuity of meaning that is not constituted by the combination of the component parts but, on the contrary, assigns to these parts their value and significance. Thus historical development creates its own time, distinct from mechanical time, its unique tradition, its own originality. Troeltsch, as we mentioned above, laid great stress on this moment of originality and creativity in history.

At the same time the German scholar was not an idealist. The continuity of meaning is not derived from a spiritual realm distinct from history. Historical development expresses itself in processes that may and must be studied in terms of biological, psychological, economic and other material causalities, as long as these studies are understood as checking and verifying the historical work proper, concerned with the overriding meaning-continuity, and are not used in an attempt to construct a total picture and render a full account of the historical development. Troeltsch insisted on the need for sociological research in the study of history. Even though he was a theologian, he was adamantly opposed to any dualistic understanding of man and his history. History was not alive by some separated or separable spirit, operating according to a law of its own. The spirit of a totality was generated by history itself. Historical development was for Troeltsch a process created by various trends actually existing in society, including various material factors, whose confluence and interaction were not determined by any mechanistic or other material necessity; on the contrary, while this process was always conditioned by the material factors, it was open to redefinitions and reorientations, at least at certain crucial times, drawn from the possibilities present in the flow and creativity of life itself. Troeltsch thought of himself as being altogether empirically oriented, except that for him the empirical reality studied by the historian was not made up of small physical elements moving according to definable laws, not of elements to which a soul had been attached, not of parts moved by some sort of world soul, but by distinct but interrelated totalities, each of which could only be understood in categories they themselves had generated in their own self-definitions. The ideal factors of history were generated by history's own flow and creativity.

As Troeltsch rejected the positivist reduction of history, so he objected to an evolutionary understanding of history. For him the claim that there exists a universal principle of development was wholly unproven. World history has never been studied. All that scholars have done is to study the civilizations closest to them. We do not even know whether we have enough information to study the history of mankind. But to project principles, operative in the parts of history familiar to us, on the entire human world is arbitrary. Troeltsch also criticized the neo-Kantian attempt to account for historical development. By locating the ordering of the historical world in the human mind, the neo-Kantians lost the sensitivity for the objects of the human sciences and their development. As the final argument against Rickert and Simmel, Troeltsch insisted that the account these thinkers rendered of the creation of historical knowledge did not describe the labor, the care, and the involvement of the historian who tries to get close to his object and discover in it the continuity of meaning that accounts for its actual development.

The reduction of history to the natural sciences and thus the dissolution of the historical object into a casually-connected chain of events, Troeltsch called "bad historicism."[14] The thinkers who held this view, he believed, had lost the true sense of history. Their scientific passion for measurement, precision, and necessity destroyed the values that keep history going and constitute the various totalities of which it is made. While Troeltsch also rejected as unscientific a universalist understanding of history, be it dialectical or biological, he regarded the dominant positivist trend as his principal opponent. Bad historicism has a destructive effect on culture. It leads to unrestricted relativism and produces a cynical attitude among the learned. It created an attitude of unconcern and detachment in regard to man's historical experience and his human problems. It may easily lead to a certain academic frivolity where scholars pick the topic of their research arbitrarily and report on the conditions of human life by removing themselves from their human responses. Finally bad historicism leads to a paralysis of personal life and political action. Science without commitment was, for Troeltsch, a threat to the scientific enterprise and an undermining of cultural and social creativity.

But there is not only bad historicism. Troeltsch tried to defend "good historicism" which recognizes values in history, operative in shaping it, that are themselves derived from history, not from a source beyond it. He opposed the dissolution of values by the positivists, he refuted the transcendental approach of the neo-Kantians, he had sympathy for, but ultimately rejected, the holistic historicism of Hegelian or Marxist dialectics. Where, then, do these values come from? They are generated by life itself. As life passes itself forward it creates totalities, and these in turn achieve a certain self-awareness. Man is able to discern the values he lives by. While these values may be different in different totalities and possibly have no relation to one another unless this relation is created by history itself, they are nonetheless values, focal points of life, significant moments through which life is expanded and intensified and achieves greater self-awareness. "The only possible resolution of [bad] historicism is in accord with the insight, more widely recognized today, that all knowledge of the finite has a practical conditionedness and intentionality, that it is never simply knowledge in itself, but at once a selection and construction of the finite in the service of the unfolding and deepening of the spirit."[15]

Even though Troeltsch is so close to *Lebensphilosophie* in his descriptions of the generative powers of life and history, he did not look upon Wilhelm Dilthey as his master. He devoted many pages of his vast study of historicism to an analysis of Dilthey's thought. He objected principally to Dilthey's psychological and positivistic orientation. Troeltsch realized that Dilthey had modified his approach later in life, but he thought that this change of position was due to the influence of Husserl's phenomenology which tried to move from a psychologically oriented description of experience to the essence of things. Troeltsch firmly held that reflection must ultimately move toward metaphysics. He was unable to detect in Dilthey the thinker who analyzed man's relationship to the human world, past and present, in terms very similar to his own. He did not see that Dilthey regarded historical knowledge as a careful reading of the social reality according to hermeneutical principles he had adapted from Schleiermacher's theological hermeneutics. Troeltsch rejected *Lebensphilosophie* as a system of thought based on psychological analysis and hence ultimately relativistic. He mentioned specifically that Dilthey at the end of his life became aware of the chaos and the dissolution of values.[16]

Perhaps it was Troeltsch's sociological orientation in the study of history that made him insensitive to Dilthey's thought and unaware of Dilthey's influence on him. Dilthey was indeed a great psychologist: he made biography, in fact autobiography, the principal way into the study of history. In personal life, especially in one's own, a man is best able to discover what words and actions really mean. It is out of this knowledge that the historian must approach a wider field of study. Troeltsch was also concerned with self-knowledge, but this always meant for him a greater realization of how the self is tied into the wider sociological context. For Troeltsch, the human sciences must look upon a man as an instance of wider totalities. He complained that so many biographies were written from a psychological point of view, without the recognition that a man's life becomes understandable only as he is seen as part of a wider societal context.[17]

Both Dilthey and Troeltsch were aware of the values and norms generated by life itself as it constituted the historical totalities and became conscious of itself. Even if Dilthey rejected all metaphysics and adopted a moderately positivistic stance, he was just as much as Troeltsch an heir of a powerful spiritual current, a Hegelian-Protestant feeling of life, a deep faith or conviction that what happens in the lives of people and their cultures has meaning, that history gives birth to great values, and that the creativity of people in this history, interacting with one another and relying on their own originality, moves this history in ever new and unexpected ways. Dilthey was unwilling to move from this general feeling, so widely spread in the German Protestantism from which he came, to metaphysical or theological considerations. He was indeed a relativist, but one who marveled at the variety and richness of values. The denial of ultimate meaning did not lead him to cynicism and despair. Troeltsch, too, denied that there was an ultimate meaning in life and even refused to admit that history itself was one and undivided, but he thought that the philosopher had to move from experience and reflection to metaphysical considerations. If a thinker pushes to the limit the question of the knowledge of others and the creativity of peoples and their cultures, he comes to acknowledge a ground of life effecting a bond between people, stirring them up to transform life and reach out for greater self-awareness. For Troeltsch this ground of life was divine, and hence he was able to affirm that despite the diverse and even conflicting values in various cultures, despite the absence of any transcultural category or standard, there is no unrestricted relativity, no total breakdown of meaning, no chaos of values, no justification of cynicism. This divine ground, we note, was not some sort of absolute value or ultimate norm. Troeltsch denied the existence of absolutes and ultimates. This divine ground gave expression to the Hegelian-Christian *Lebensgefühl* that present in life is a wholly inaccessible mystery, beyond conceptualization or objectification, which is the source of life's up-ward movement and the richness of its manifestations. This is the "good historicism" which Troeltsch opposed to the bad histori-cism that leads to cynicism and inaction.

Historical development—to return to our topic—was the discernment proper to the third phase of Troeltsch's analysis of historical knowledge. In this phase the past leads to a better un-derstanding of the present, and in turn the present to a better understanding of the past. Troeltsch calls this "a circle."[18] This circle—he does not call it "hermeneutical"—generates historical knowledge. Troeltsch describes the circle many times. Since life is connected to life, any historical moment is related to the areas of life surrounding it, influences them and reveals in them its meaning and power. The widening of the area of historical inter-connectedness eventually leads to the inclusion of the social world of the observer. The observer, then, cannot come to an understanding of his own situation without reflecting on the trends of the past that have created it and cannot understand the past without taking into account his present experience. This cir-cle is not a vicious one; it is the creative circle that constitutes historical truth and makes man an historical agent.

Commitment to Vision

For Troeltsch the direction of this circular interpretation is guided by the scholar's commitment to a future ideal. Man's his-torical situation is such that he must lay hold of the present, with its various trends and possibilities, produced without his doing in past historical developments, in order to mediate this present into a not yet wholly determined future. For Troeltsch, then, the study of history and the social sciences is an historical act. It is never a purely contemplative activity by which men meditate on an object outside of themselves or even within themselves. It makes a con-tribution to the creation of history. Since the vision of the future is inevitably tied to the hermeneutical circle by which the thinker comes to the understanding of the social reality, his scientific activity itself creates an action-oriented consciousness.

The sources of this activist understanding of science are not Marxist. While Troeltsch was influenced by Marx, had considerable sympathy for Marx's analysis of social change, and defended Marx against many unjust accusations, he could never accept class struggle as a universal principle of social life. Troeltsch thought not so much in economic as in cultural and humanistic terms. The ideal of the future that directed social science and human action was a synthesis of past developments, present possibilities, and the vision of a deeper humanity generated by these. Troeltsch shared this general trend with *Lebensphilosophie*. But while Dilthey thought that man's choice of one among several world views was ultimately arbitrary, Troeltsch held—as we shall see—that the ideal of the future could be argued about and in some sense demonstrated. Nonetheless it is from *Lebensphilosophie* that Troeltsch derived his conviction regarding the link between science and commitment.

The biblical roots of this conviction are obvious. According to a central theme in the Bible, knowledge and love are inseparably connected. Without love the truth does not become available. He who does not love looks upon reality in the wrong perspective and becomes inevitably a liar. It is only as man is related to reality in love that its meaning is disclosed to him.

Troeltsch is closer to *Lebensphilosophie* than he realizes. With Dilthey he held that the standpoint of the observer inevitably entered into his perception of reality, his scientific methodology, and his understanding of society past and present. There is no neutral ground on which a scholar might stand, for he has been constituted an historical subject by participating in various cultural and symbolic worlds. Men are never simply individuals; they are, rather, instances of wider totalities. Society in some sense inheres in them. Their historical standpoint, therefore, is not simply the source of distortions affecting the perception of the social reality but also and especially the ground for laying hold of this same social reality. While this standpoint, we hasten to add, has to do with the particular social situation in which a person finds himself, it also has to do with certain judgments he makes in regard to history and society. By fitting himself consciously into his past and present he adopts a critical, evaluative stance in regard to his world. While a man is born into a situation and through his education participates in various worlds of interest and meaning, the standpoint he adopts is to some extent his own choice. The standpoint includes man's commitment to an ideal for the future.

Troeltsch mentioned two particular judgments that enter into the standpoint of the historian and social scientist. Examining the social reality, past or present, the scholar must decide what are the boundary lines of the various totalities that constitute it. What social expressions are held together by the same meaning-continuity? The judgment regarding the boundary lines of totalities is crucial in the study of history, for historical development takes place, not through the interaction of disparate parts, but through the interaction of these parts within a totality, which, through this process, carries life forward and becomes the bearer of the new. How do we determine these totalities? Troeltsch showed that the division of history into periods (antiquity, middle ages, modern times) is a significant judgment that has built into it a set of values, an interpretation of the present, and a vision for the future. The delineation of historical totalities, in other words, is always based on a commitment.

We might apply this principle to the sociologist who studies marginal groups in contemporary society. He will have to decide whether he wants to look upon these groups simply as marginal and thus understand them in terms of the wider society, in whose margin they exist, or whether they constitute totalities, groups alive by vital continuity of meaning, making them capable of original responses, of growth and development. Is a particular religious group a fringe phenomenon or does it have its own, authentic life? Is the youth movement simply a by-product of industrial society or is it a totality to be understood through concepts derived from its own self-understanding? Are homosexuals marginal figures to be understood in terms created by the wider society to which they belong, or are they in some sense a totality demanding an interpretation of their life in terms generated by themselves? These judgments regarding the boundary lines of the totalities making up the social reality partially determine the standpoint of the social thinker, are related to value options made by him, and inevitably affect his research and his conclusions.

A second judgment of the scholar to which Troeltsch attached great importance was whether he was living in peaceful or in revolutionary times.[19] This judgment, too, affects the standpoint of the historian and social scientist and inevitably modifies his understanding of the social reality, past and present. We live in a peaceful age, Troeltsch held, when we expect the future to be a simple prolongation of the best elements of the past; we understand our age as revolutionary when we anticipate that the future will be created by a radical transformation of the inherited categories, a transformation derived, to be sure, from the historical experience itself and generated by the vitality of this history, but emerging in radical discontinuity with the very trends a more peaceful age would regard as the best and most stable ones. Troeltsch regarded himself as a revolutionary, not indeed in a Marxist sense, but in a sense in which many German intellectuals, sensitive to the idealistic tradition, longed for and anticipated the overcoming of bourgeois science, economics and individualism. Despite the First World War, the defeat and the hopeless political situation of Germany, Troeltsch felt himself situated at the edge of a cultural age, expecting the birth of something new. He believed that the historicity of truth and the role of commitment in the human sciences were shaking the foundations of the established order.

With the *Lebensphilosophie* Troeltsch regarded as crucial not only the standpoint of the observer in historical knowledge but also the future-orientation of human experience. The very structure of experience makes it a passage from the past through the present to the future. It is through man's experience that life is forever pushing on and reaching out. As we mentioned above, it is here, in man's encounter with life, that the values emerge according to which he creates his future. Man's critical reason and his power to choose are operative in the assimilation and orientation of his experience. There is no separated spiritual or rational world from which men can draw their standards. They must be in touch, rather, with the creative thrust and the possibility of expansion within their history.

Is it possible, we must ask, to specify any norms for the

creation of the cultural ideal? Are the options free and hence ultimately arbitrary, or is it possible to argue rationally and come to an agreement about the measures by which men choose their future? Dilthey held that there were several world views a man might adopt and there was ultimately no reason why one should be preferred to another. In this sense he was a moderate relativist. Troeltsch tried to overcome this relativism by deriving valid and verifiable measures for the creation of the future from the experience of history itself. These measures, however, were no abiding laws, no universal truths. In each age man must make himself sensitive to and opt for those elements of his past and those possibilities of the present that lead to an intensification of consciousness, an unfolding of human potential, and the fulfillment of life.[20] The norms operative in man's commitment and understanding are produced by a vital, not a logical necessity, but they can be argued about and defended by studying the past and demonstrated by analyzing the present. According to Troeltsch, this is in fact the task of the human sciences.

Intensification, unfolding and fulfillment of life are terms familiar in the humanistic tradition of German idealism. To some readers they sound vague, to the others possibly romantic. Yet they may also be interpreted as hard-headed terms describing the process of humanization taking place as men overcome the alienation that makes them strangers and enemies of one another. Then these terms have a political as well as a therapeutic meaning. Troeltsch himself never succeeded in producing a convincing ideal of the future and spelling out the norms for its realization. At the end of his large volume, he tried to present a cultural synthesis, but he never made it quite clear what concrete political or even cultural options flowed from it. He spoke of the rebirth of Europe, the rebirth of the great currents of wisdom, classical antiquity and Christian tradition, under the impact of German idealism.

Despite the obvious weakness of Troeltsch's attempt to come to grips with the problems of Germany after World War I, his analysis of the human sciences retained its significance. According to him, there is no objective, value-free, supra-temporal history or social science. Truth is historical in the twofold sense that it depends on the historical position of the observer as well as on the values or vision of life to which he is committed.

NOTES

1. My interest in this debate was created by Professor Trent Schroyer's lectures given in the spring of 1970 at the New School for Social Research, New York City.

2. The scholars proposing the historicism has no necessary connection with the "historicism" denounced in K. Popper's well-known *The Poverty of Historicism*. We shall see that Ernst Troeltsch, who regarded himself as an historicist, rejected any appeal to a universal interpretation of history or a common destiny of mankind.

3. Maurice Mandelbaum, *The Problem of Historical Knowledge* (New York, 1939).

4. The work was first published as Vol. III of Troeltsch's *Gesammelte Schriften* (Tübingen, 1922). The same edition was photostatically reproduced and republished at Aalen 1961. In the following I shall refer to *Der Historismus und seine Probleme* as H.P.

5. The lectures were simultaneously published in German, under the title *Der Historismus und seine Ueberwindung*, Berlin, 1924, and in English, under the title chosen by the editor Baron von Huegel, *Christian Thought, Its History and Application* (London, 1923; republished by Meridian Books, New York 1957).

6. *H.P.*, p. 209.

7. The problem of the knowledge of others (*Fremdverständnis*) and its rootedness in self-knowledge is a recurrent theme in Troeltsch's work, a theme that ultimately leads him to metaphysics. Cf. *H.P.*, pp. 71, 170, 679-84.

8. For Troeltsch's changing relationship to Rickert's philosophy of science, see W. Bodenstein, *Neige des Historismus* (Guetersloh, 1959), pp. 147-52.

9. *H.P.*, p. 44.

10. H. Stuart Hughes, *Consciousness and Society*, (New York, 1958).

11. *Op. cit.*, p. 310.

12. "Understanding is the rediscovery of the I in the thou," in W. Dilthey, *Pattern and Meaning in History* (Selections from Vol. VII of Dilthey's *Gesammelte Schriften*) (New York, 1961), p. 67.

13. *H.P.*, p. 119.

14. *H.P.*, pp. 67-68.

15. H.P., p. 113.